Rikke Kristine Nielsen, Frans Bévort, Thomas Duus Henriksen,
Danielle Bjerre Lyndgaard

Navigating Leadership Paradox

De Gruyter Transformative Thinking and Practice of Leadership and Its Development

Edited by
Bernd Vogel

Volume 3

Rikke Kristine Nielsen, Frans Bévort,
Thomas Duus Henriksen, Anne-Mette Hjalager,
Danielle Bjerre Lyndgaard

Navigating Leadership Paradox

Engaging Paradoxical Thinking in Practice

DE GRUYTER

ISBN 978-3-11-078885-3
e-ISBN (PDF) 978-3-11-078887-7
e-ISBN (EPUB) 978-3-11-078892-1
ISSN 2701-4002

Library of Congress Control Number: 2023932790

Bibliographic information published by the Deutsche Nationalbibliothek
The Deutsche Nationalbibliothek lists this publication in the Deutsche Nationalbibliografie;
detailed bibliographic data are available on the internet at http://dnb.dnb.de.

© 2023 Walter de Gruyter GmbH, Berlin/Boston
Cover image: wacomka/iStock/Getty Images Plus
Typesetting: Integra Software Services Pvt. Ltd.
Printing and binding: CPI books GmbH, Leck

www.degruyter.com

Advance Praise for *Navigating Leadership Paradox*

"*Navigating Leadership Paradox* provides an evidence-based approach to managing dilemmas that stump traditional decision makers. Our global/local, VUCA and multiplex world creates organizational challenges where no obvious solutions exist. This author team provides a clear framework and process to make this complexity manageable iteratively over time, helping managers expand their comfort zones and capacity for both reflection and action."
—**Denise M. Rousseau**, H.J. Heinz II University Professor of Organizational Behavior and Public Policy, Carnegie Mellon University

"I think this book is really needed. This is an area that has continuously gained more attention in the past years with the increased complexity of today's world. I can picture myself using it as a textbook in my Bachelor, Master and Executive level classes. In my mind, managers are those who are eager to learn and develop this area most. I can see them buying the book autonomously or within the context of a leadership course. I personally would assign the book and recommend it."
—**Dr Camille Pradies**, EDHEC Business School, France

"More than ever managers need to master and embrace the complexity of a new era ripe with leadership paradox. Managing through the pandemic in a world that has become even more digital and uncertain has accelerated the need for managers to be able to balance a range of both personal and organizational leadership paradoxes. Spanning from strategic insights and decisions to execution in a (global) world, where not much seems to be as it used to, this book provides managers with relevant, 'easy-to-use' inspiration and tools that helps you navigate the high level of leadership complexity and grasp the new reality."
—**Kinga Szabo Christensen**, Deputy Director General, The Danish Confederation of Industry

"This is a wonderfully thoughtful, imaginative, evocative, and helpful book. It focuses on paradox in practice, and shows the opportunities paradoxes create for navigation by leaders and other managers, not only recognizing and accepting tensions, but also acting on them meaningfully. Further, the action can take place in managerial groups, and based on action learning approaches; it does not have to be taken alone. Anyone who encounters paradoxes and tensions in their daily (work) lives can benefit from this book."
—**Jean M. Bartunek, Professor, Robert A.** and **Evelyn J. Ferris Chair**, Department of Management and Organization, Boston College

https://doi.org/10.1515/9783110788877-202

"Paradox in organizations is one of the main reasons why we need leadership and leaders. These are the situations where we need to be capable of navigating and relating to the consequences of our decisions. Therefore, it is important to train paradox leadership – for all of us to become better managers. The insights and tools of this book will help you navigate leadership paradox in practice."

—**Rikke Molter**, COO, Knudsen Extrusion

"Anyone with leadership responsibilities will benefit hugely from this book. Developing a paradox mindset is possibly one of the most important leadership abilities for effectively navigating the complexity of today's business activities. This book provides a much needed compass for developing the capacity to work through the tensions and contradictory demands that consistently bedevil all organisations, large and small. Real examples of leadership paradoxes will be easily recognisable. Importantly they provide rich food for thought, when charting your own course in practice. An extensive toolbox mapped to each stage of the navigation process will strengthen your ability to lead organisations that thrive in the face of a volatile and uncertain future."

—**Jane McKenzie**, Professor of Management Knowledge and Learning, Henley Business School

"The ideal of paradoxical thinking – the ability to reconcile apparently polar positions – and the accompanying challenge of putting this ideal into practice captures the essence of this intriguing volume. The authors immerse the reader in the challenges posed by organizational life in an increasingly volatile, uncertain world. Getting away from rather static either-or thinking, the idea of and/also positioning is crucial given the persistence of these challenges over time, where short-term, trade-off thinking is literally incapable of producing desired, sustainable outcomes. Rather than necessarily viewing all of this as a series of stresses literally cascading on top of each other, the volume underscores that understanding the power of paradox can be energizing, providing a conceptual road map of how to make sense of the myriad tensions that surround us. This highly readable volume provides deep insight into the processes of navigating paradox – the ability to understand (mindset) and create meaning (action/ meta-skill set) – with a host of highly usable tools and techniques to guide the reader through this messy process."

—**Anthony F. Buono**, Professor Emeritus, Bentley University

"*Navigating Leadership Paradox* is a very timely addition to this book series. Global crises have exposed many tensions that were bubbling under the surface and put those in charge under great pressure. Trade-offs can create even bigger challenges when you are dealing with complex problems in a changing world. The authors bring paradox to life with 10 common examples that are easy to relate to. Then they offer a process and a suite of tools to help managers grapple with the paradoxical problems facing them in their own world. It's a mindset and skillset that is sorely needed, if we are going to step up and engage with the pressing global challenges we are facing."

—**Dr Sharon Varney**, leadership and change consultant, author of Leadership in Complexity and Change: *For a world in constant motion*

We collectively dedicate this book to navigators of paradox, their co-navigators, helpers and educators in practice and research. May you never loose faith in your capacity for taking action and responsibility for leadership and organizational paradox.

Rikke Kristine Nielsen, Frans Bévort, Thomas Duus Henriksen, Anne-Mette Hjalager, Danielle Lyndgaard

Acknowledgments

This book is the result of the joint efforts of a transdisciplinary author collective representing both academia and practice. Yet, it is also a collective endeavor reaching far beyond the group of authors who have relied on the engagement and support of several other stakeholders and conversation partners that we wish to credit.

First and foremost, we wish to thank the courageous managers from private and public companies as well as civil society organizations who have participated and co-created our research on leadership paradox. Researching leadership paradox in practice is only possible if organizations and managers are willing to welcome researchers into their challenges and dreams. We are deeply grateful for their engagement – they are all role models in a world where we need just-in-time, relevant research more than ever!

From the research project *Leadership GPS for New Times – From Comfort Zone to Competitiveness* funded by the Industry Foundation we wish to credit the 11 participating companies: VELUX, DEIF A/S, Arne Pedersen A/S, Aasted ApS, Titan Wind Energy (Europe) A/S, KMC amba Grundfos, Knudsen Extrusion ApS, Lindpro A/S, Spæncom A/S, and Trelleborg Sealing Solutions AB. We also wish to highlight the contributions of researchers and consultants participating in this project in addition to the author collective: Mette Mogensen, supervisor, Work Environment in Denmark, External Lecturer, Copenhagen Business School and Roskilde University; Henrik Holt Larsen, Professor Emeritus, Copenhagen Business School; Signe Vikkelsø, Professor, Copenhagen Business School; Per Geisler, senior advisor, Danish Confederation of Industry; and Jørgen Andersen, vice president HRM, ambu A/S.

From the research project *Long Lasting Leadership in Turbulent Times – Paradoxical Leadership in Practice* funded by Royal Danish Defence College in collaboration with Aalborg University we wish to credit Head of Section Michael Pingel Hansen as well as managers, project managers, and employees with the Acquisition and Logistics Organisation, The Danish Ministry of Defence.

From the research project *A Taste for Sustainable Fish* supported by the Velux Foundations we wish to highlight the contributions of the Copenhagen Hospitality College (CHC), Project Manager Michelle Werther along with managers, faculty, and students at CHC in addition to Associate Professors Alice Juel Jacobsen and Mikkel Fugl Eskjær, Aalborg University.

We also wish to thank the many other companies and organizations who have participated in our workshops and seminars on paradoxical leadership over the last decade giving us the opportunity to sharpen our thinking and insights into paradoxical practice even further – particularly the Danish Confederation of Industry, NOCA – Network of Corporate Academies, Local Government Denmark, the municipalities of Billund and Fredensborg, the association of Danish HR Professionals, and not least Djøf trade union whose affiliated publisher, Djøf Publishers, published our first book (in Danish) on paradoxical leadership that was the springboard for developing this

https://doi.org/10.1515/9783110788877-203

book (Nielsen, Mogensen, Bévort, Henriksen, Hjalager and Lyndgaard, 2019). Also, we wish to thank Jakob Larsen of Djøf Publishers for laying out the first version of some of the central illustrations used in this book.

In preparing this manuscript we have also relied on the insights and help from the De Gruyter team, including editor Steven Hardman, commissioning editor Faye Leerink, content editor Jaya Dalal, Project Manager Anne Stroka, Books Marketing Manager Heather Goss and freelance marketer Natalie Wills as well as De Gruyter Transformative Thinking and Practice of Leadership and Its Development series editor Bernd Vogel. We are excited to be part of this series and encourage readers to explore other volumes of this series.

Finally, we wish to thank our external peer reviewers, Associate Professors Josh Keller and Camille Pradies, for their constructive comments both in evaluating our initial book proposal as well as the final manuscript. Their constructive comments and insights have been much appreciated.

The gift of feedback is invaluable to paradox navigation in both research and practice, and we feel fortunate that the scholarly paradox community is as vibrant and curiosity driven as the managerial paradox navigators that we work with in practice.

Foreword

> Paradoxical thinking is about being able to reconcile seemingly incompatible, or even mutually
> exclusive, ways of acting, i.e., cultivating the ability to 'have your cake and eat it too . . .'
> – *Navigating Leadership Paradox: Engaging Paradoxical Thinking in Practice* (2023, p. 4).

If that is not a reason to start working with this book, I do not know what is!

When I learnt about the possibility of this book to be included in our series . . .

. . . I had just one thought: "Here again! Exactly what we hoped for."

Let me start with the not so obvious: *Navigating Leadership Paradox: Engaging Paradoxical Thinking in Practice* allows you to be a *leading activist* and not a *leading bystander* in dealing with paradoxical challenges at work and in society. And that is key, when making a difference in the little time that is left for leading towards a desirable world for all.

And then the obvious: This *is* a contemporary, ambitious, and innovative book. Be assured that after reading it you will have a "broadened imagination and understanding of what transformative leadership and leadership development involves" and when you start to make this book work and sweat for you, you will go away with "a widened and actionable repertoire of tangible and generative insights, activities and practices of leadership and its development". The authors also invite us to view insights and practices lived and built in other international contexts than the UK and the US. Are there differences or not? Not so much my point. Just good to hear more global voices and have broader representation, given that most business and societal leadership challenges are global and intercultural.

More so, *Navigating Leadership Paradox* has a focus on equipping managers to deal with and navigate paradox. This is *not* another musing *about* paradox. This book makes your thinking space spin *and* enables you to get your hands dirty in paradox work.

The book is also complementary to the earlier books in the series: Sharon Varney's on leadership *in* complexity and change and Aidan McQuade's on ethical leadership which deals with individuals staying on course in situations full of contradictions.

Navigating Leadership Paradox is your book if you have noticed these situations in your teams, organizations, or collaborations across boundaries where aspects of your remit are contradictory or opposing considerations. They do not nicely reconcile, and you still aspire with your group to pursue both or more of those contradictory ambitions over time. By the way, you then also figured that some parts of our leadership reality just do not follow our typical illusion of and hope for consistency, alignment, and clarity – leadership is about dealing with messiness and ongoing tensions.

https://doi.org/10.1515/9783110788877-204

A book that is just waiting to be worked with!

In whatever way you chose to work with *Navigating Leadership Paradox*, this book can nourish your appetite for understanding or feed your urge to immediately apply the practical guidance for navigating paradoxes in your leadership life spheres.

The book demystifies paradox without claiming it is easy for managers. See the "10 paradoxical tensions in leadership" – what a treat. When I read and explored the tensions, I found myself immediately in the midst of those areas we address in our work at the Henley Centre for Leadership or with clients. The "five phases of paradox navigation" are a rich journey to go through in your team or with your collaborators.

Finally, the book ends with a real trick. Let's face it, introducing leading with paradox to your organization and to your colleagues, while very appealing, also means quite a shift in how to work and how your organization functions. The last sections of the book, for example, the "five thresholds in facilitating paradox work", function as quasi meta-skills to translate the language, logic, tools, and instruments of dealing with leadership paradox into a sustained practice in your organization. That will assist you as a reader even further in bringing the book's ideas to life and to becoming a *leadership activist*.

Rikke, Frans, Thomas, Anne-Mette, and Danielle, thank you so much for presenting this book to us.

Bernd Vogel
Henley-on-Thames, UK
March 2023

Contents

Part III: **Paradox navigation 2.0 – working through paradox with stakeholders**

Part I: **Paradoxes in leadership: What? Why? Who?**

Chapter 1
A paradox perspective on modern leadership challenges

> As complexity, change and ambiguity intensify in organizations, so does the value of a paradox lens and both/and approaches to theory and practice.
>
> (Schad et al., 2016, p. 5)

The point of departure of this handbook in paradox leadership is that one of the most significant management challenges in modern companies and organizations is dealing with unavoidable, complex paradoxes in organization and management. Paradoxes are "[c]ontradictory yet interrelated elements – elements that seem logical in isolation but absurd and irrational when appearing simultaneously" (Lewis, 2000, p. 760), and they "persist over time" (Smith and Lewis, 2011, p. 382). It is also our point of departure that research insights about organizational paradoxes present a frame of inquiry that matches the complexity and ambiguity of contemporary organizational life (Smith and Lewis, 2011; Schad et al., 2016; Smith, Lewis et al., 2017a). Accordingly, academic knowledge pools can support leaders' decision-making and sense-making in organizations.

Paradox leadership is not about deciding once and for all or prioritizing tough trade-offs, but about navigating between opposing considerations. You must seek balance, as a person, a manager, an employee, and a company. In much the same way as there is not only one particularly important direction on a compass, this book is about finding your way in leadership based on a recognition that the world is multidimensional, multipolar, and multipurpose. It is necessary to find your own way in a multifaceted and dynamic world. Increasingly, classic management challenges assume the characteristics of paradoxes rather than problems or dilemmas. It might seem like a moot point or aloof theoretical dispute over the words "dilemma" or "paradox". After all, a difficult challenge is problematic, no matter what we call it. Nevertheless, there is significant difference in how these different challenges are handled or coped with in an efficient manner (Lüscher and Lewis, 2008). When possibilities compete with one another, each with advantages and disadvantages, the decision maker is faced with a dilemma. A paradox is "when the possibilities are contradictory and related in such a way that a choice between them is only a temporary solution, after which the tension will reappear" (Smith and Lewis, 2011, p. 387).

In other words, paradoxes are leadership challenges that persist over time. They both contain the other and are interdependent like yin and yang. Take, for example, the well-known managerial terms "exploitation" and "exploration". In organizations it is necessary to develop new products and services to be able to survive in the long run (exploration). However, if new developments are not implemented in operation, or if the organization is so preoccupied with development that operations (exploitation) are neglected it will be

https://doi.org/10.1515/9783110788877-001

threat to survival (March, 1991). Paradoxical thinking is about being able to reconcile seemingly incompatible, or even mutually exclusive, ways of acting, that is, cultivating the ability to "have your cake *and* eat it too" or "ride two horses *at the same time*". The point about paradoxes is not necessarily to try to find a compromise or a golden mean between two points or otherwise attempt to identify a new common third way, meant to make the causes of the problem go away or dissolve (Smith, Lewis et al., 2017b). This is one of the aspects that distinguishes paradox thinking and leadership from classical managerial thinking and from the way many managers are used to making decisions.

Seeing modern management from a paradox perspective invites the manager to make sense of a contemporary management challenge as something that is not appropriate (or possible) to opt out of (Cameron et al., 2014) or resolve. For instance, it is often neither possible nor desirable to choose exploitation or exploration, local adaptation or global alignment. It is a question of mixing ratios, of accepting grey zones and taking turns rather than sticking to once-and-forever identified trade-offs. In effect, it is also not necessarily helpful to work with mindsets or vocabularies such as "the organization must be more 'glocal'" (rhetorically resolving the tension between local and global) or "leaders must embrace 'coopetition'" (conceptually uniting "collaboration" and "competition"). Managers in internationally operating companies must adapt to local circumstances while simultaneously finding common ground on global, uniform standards. Similarly, managers co-creating value with a diverse group of stakeholders in their ecosystem, including collaborating with competitors (coopetition), are likely to have functions or situations where collaboration remains in the background, and others where collaboration is central, and some that are a mix. It is not a question of either–or decision-making, but rather both–and. While innovative language use combining different poles of paradox may signal a particular ideal, the reality of implementing such an ideal is messier than a catchphrase leads you to assume. At the same time, both–and does not imply the existence of a particular equilibrium, or a "best practice" both–and mixing ratio between competing demands. Equilibrium is conquered, lost, and continuously rediscovered, aiming for "workable certainty" rather than certainty (Lüscher and Lewis, 2008; Lüscher, Lewis and Ingram, 2006).

No need to overcomplicate

At this point, you may be wondering if it is necessary to (over)complicate things like this. After all, there is nothing new in the fact that management contains competing demands. Just think of the evergreen tension between trust and control or between a desire for everyone to follow an established "best practice" across the entire organization combined with the simultaneous need for local adaptation to special circumstances applicable in different functions of a company. On the other hand, contemporary leadership often contains challenges that are paradoxical in nature and where it makes sense to dwell on complexity and inspect the nature of the challenge in more detail. The special attention given to paradoxes in organizational life in recent years is partly because growth conditions for paradoxes are favorable (Smith and Lewis, 2011):

- High pace of change reduces the possibility of appreciating the bigger picture and finding stable, lasting "solutions" to the paradoxes.
- Complexity and ambiguity create interconnections and relationships across internal and external boundaries and borders that will have to be addressed together, because solving one challenge may have (negative) consequences for another.
- Resource scarcity forces several "impossible" choice situations.

Paradoxes become particularly visible and salient when basic organizational structures and processes are changing, when there is incomplete information, where the situation is complex and ambiguous, and when there is a shortage of resources. Such circumstances may be a consequence of strategic choices or external constraints – either way, they are everyday working conditions for many managers. Therefore, managers can benefit from making sense of the leadership role in a more nuanced manner, which is emphasized by the number and scale of organizational changes. Frequently companies find that several changes take place at the same time; one comes into effect before another is completed, and one change initiative is often in direct conflict with other existing initiatives. Thus, leaders do not just have to navigate and direct movement in the organization from one stage to the next, changes take place simultaneously, point in different directions, and the organization does not necessarily have time to settle into a new (temporary) state of equilibrium before the next change occurs.

The pervasiveness of VUCA – volatility, uncertainty, complexity, and ambiguity – and global crises

The notion of paradox might appear unattractive since it fails to offer resolution to difficult problems. Managers tend to prefer pragmatic solutions to complexity-oriented approaches (Lüscher and Lewis, 2008). However, a paradox lens offers a way through chaos, where standard management tools such as, for example, SWOT (Strengths, Weaknesses, Opportunities, Threats) matrices or contingency models may fail (Smith, Erez et al., 2017). Paradox has been described as a "counterintuitive concept that makes it difficult to comprehend using rational logic but when [it is] made apparent and explained [to us], we resonate with it at an experiential level" (Quinn and Nujella, 2017, p. vii). A recent example of the surfacing of "invisible currents of paradox" (Quinn and Nujella, 2017, p. vii) is the COVID-19 pandemic preparing the ground for explaining and intuitively understanding the concept of paradox. The coronavirus crisis has exposed managers (and employees) to VUCA conditions of volatility, uncertainty, complexity, and ambiguity (Bennett and Lemoine, 2014) in the extreme, and the challenges have mounted up regardless of country, industry, hierarchical level, sector, and so forth. For instance, the concept of interconnectedness, central to definitions of paradox (Smith and Lewis, 2011), has been illustrated generously by the COVID-19 pandemic. It was presumably not the metaphorical wings of the butterfly known from chaos theory, but perhaps the actual moving wings of a bat causing a train of events leading to the global coronavirus pandemic demonstrating the global interconnectedness of business, pleasure, and politics. Managers have experienced not only the interconnectedness of all countries in a very concrete sense, but also the interconnectedness of nature (for example, bats and viruses) and humans, and we have experienced how physical health and financial health are intertwined in a myriad of ways. The COVID-19 experience is a reservoir of collective, practical paradox experience that managers can tap into, learn from, and subsequently use in times of crises, change, and, for that matter, business as usual when thinking about paradox.

Lost and found – where the rainbow ends . . .

Working through paradoxes as a manager is a matter of being able to do "both–and" – to seek the (temporary) *balance* between two outer poles, which are usually perceived as opposites or mutually exclusive. A manager cannot avoid facing paradoxes as a natural part of leadership. Yet, in our experience the ability to cope with paradoxes does not come naturally to most managers. Paradox leadership is not about following a recipe or identifying the "right" position. The word "balance" indicates that there is a special balance *point*, the "right" balance in relation to a particular paradox, but it will be different from leader to leader, from company to company, and from situation to situation. Since we are different, and since companies vary immensely in their approaches to environmental and situational change, balance is something you will constantly be in the process of finding. Balance is not something you *have*; it is an ongoing search to find it. Balancing includes the aiming for a moving target, a bit like looking for the place where the rainbow ends. Finding balance as a leader in relation to the paradox you experience will be a kind of experiment, a continuous step into the unknown. The immanent freedom inherent in the discipline of paradoxical leadership means that there are many pathways to finding balance. On the other hand, the manager is obliged, by taking the first steps, to mobilize the courage to set things in motion (Lüscher, 2017).

Paradox – energizer or stressor?

Embarking on paradox leadership is also about knowing who you are as a person. Not everyone thrives on change and experiments; we do not all have a paradoxical mindset to the same degree (Miron-Spektor, 2018). This applies not only to employees but also to managers. Some are energized by paradoxes, thrive on tensions, welcoming unpredictability and the need for improvisation, while to others, paradoxes are confusing, demotivating, and stressful. As a leader, you cannot write off complexity and opposing demands as irrelevant with reference to your personality. It is, however, always recommended to take stock of the extent to which individual preferences and the availability of personal resources match the effort that must be manifested to succeed in paradox work.

Navigating paradoxes in practice challenges our understanding of what leadership is, what leaders do, and why. Paradoxes *create uncertainty*, while much leadership practice as well as leadership development programs and education (Larsson, Holmberg and Kempster, 2020) aims to minimize uncertainty by solving problems, making final decisions, and establishing a clear strategy (Fairhurst, Oliver and Waldman, 2019). Paradoxes challenge the possibility (and desirability) of setting a clear strategic direction, since paradoxes and the handling of paradoxes require a more balanced, nuanced, and "work-in-progress" kind of decision making. Paradoxical thinking and actions challenge the idea that a significant motivating factor for modern employees and managers is that they can see their work as steps toward a "higher purpose" or vision in the company/organization. A clear "higher purpose" can present difficult conditions in a situation where purpose becomes more diffuse and multidirectional. For that reason, there is a significant communicative challenge in leading paradoxes (see Chapter 11). This leadership challenge demands ability to create meaning and facilitate the creation of meaning for and with others. This version of leadership is perhaps more in line with the muddy picture of reality than we might wish it were (Sveningsson and Larsson, 2006).

Following this book and in the research literature in general, the ability to navigate paradoxes is emphasized as something positive and something preferably to be improved. Being capable of maneuvering in complexity, diversity, and uncertainty is linked to innovation, creativity, increased performance, and competitiveness. We do share this view, as will be clear from this and the following chapters. We have witnessed first-hand how understanding leadership in the context of paradoxes can unleash energy, bring about new ways of understanding challenges, and empower managers to act in chaos. At the same time, we also invite our reader to continuously ask whether it is always beneficial and relevant to focus on challenges as paradoxes. For instance, how much can you as a manager "share" your paradoxes with employees without creating confusion and uncertainty? Is sharing of paradox a de facto shirking of responsibility if paradoxes are left to actors who have little room to maneuver, few resources, or lack the decision-making power to navigate them? This book deals with paradoxical navigation from a leadership perspective, but we encourage readers to consider whether and to what extent this thinking may also be relevant to other stakeholders with whom you collaborate – a point to which we shall return in Part III.

What is your (im)balance point, and where do you want to go?

Working with paradoxes in leadership involves the understanding of leadership in a certain way, but the point is not only to think differently, but also to be able to act differently. A necessary starting point for acting in response to paradox is making paradoxes concrete for yourself and your own situation. If you do not know where you are going, any road will get you there, and so most managers work through their paradoxes for a reason. They approach paradoxical thinking because there is something they want to achieve. Indeed, a first step in working with and through paradoxes is to take stock of your current position. The starting point understood as your current (im-) balance point obviously affects the direction in which you can and wish to move (Nielsen et al., 2020).

As an example, consider a manager who works with the opposing energies and tensions between operational and administration-focused management versus more development-oriented leadership. Over time, the manager have developed tools and practices that are based on detailed knowledge of production processes, control of output, and performance. So, he feels quite on top of the situation and in good control of the "management part" of his job role. It is therefore relatively simple for him to identify and take a starting point at the opposite pole of leadership, that is, the direction in which he needs to move.

When you as a manager first set out to work toward a better balance, you may well find that you must invest rather one-sidedly in moving toward one of the two poles of paradox. In practice, however, a focus on one side of the paradox does not necessarily mean that the other dimension is downgraded or forgotten. Rather, the two can complement each other and are interconnected. For example, managers with a desire to strengthen their employees' and their own self-management competencies, which could be interpreted as a move toward more delegation and trust-based collaboration often do so by strengthening output control and establishing templates and clear rules of engagement with team members, that is classical administrative control levers.

Identifying your starting point, your current (im-)balance is a prerequisite for being able to set a direction. However, it does not determine the specific actions needed. Overall, however, knowing your starting point is indispensable for making a conscious choice. Understanding where you are is a prerequisite for being able to undertake movements, and not least to be able to continuously to recognize where you are going.

Ten paradoxical tensions in leadership

Dealing with paradoxes is a general leadership skill – a craft managers can become more skilled at mastering and managing in line with budgeting, conducting personnel development talks, or meeting management. This competence transcends specific situations or specific circumstances. It is a so-called meta-competence, applicable across time and place assisting the application of other competencies (Nordhaug, 1998). That said, paradox leadership is also about something specific, a particular challenge. When dealing with paradoxes in practice, it is an undertaking in relation to some specific issues. In the same way budgeting in practice is about some specific items, personnel development conversations are about certain employees, and a work group gives rise to certain meeting management challenges, paradox leadership is also concerned something specific: a challenge, situation, or an objective. Throughout this book we will refer to "paradox" and "leadership paradox". When we refer to "paradox" or "leadership paradox" in the singular, we refer to general notion of paradox in the context of leadership as opposed to other understandings of challenges such as problems or dilemmas (also see Chapter 2). When we refer to "paradoxes" or "leadership paradoxes" in the plural, we refer to varieties of paradoxical tensions in leadership that differ in content and/or zoom in on a particular leadership situation, for instance the paradoxical tensions involved in leadership itself, sustainability or talent management (also see Chapter 3).

In this book, we will use the following fields of paradoxical tensions as illustrations throughout the book:
1. Leadership *and* management
2. Leadership: individual leadership *and* collective/distributed leadership
3. Matrix – functional specialization/silo *and* cross-functional, horizontal organization
4. Purpose, passion, *and* performance
5. Employee mobility *and* permanence
6. Hybridity: virtual *and* physical presence
7. Differentiation/localization *and* integration/globalization
8. Innovating outside–in *and* inside–out
9. Digital transformation: human resources *and* non-human resources
10. Sustainability in plural: profit, people, *and* planet

Knowledge of these fields of paradoxical tensions is background knowledge for the more general experiences of navigating paradoxes, as they are presented in the following chapters. At the same time, you might use these as a starting point when choosing a paradox from your own work life that you want to address. The important thing is that you choose a paradox to get started, and it is important that you choose an area of focus that is not just a problem, but contains a paradox, an approach that will be discussed in greater detail in Chapter 2.

It is our experience that these 10 fields of paradoxical tensions resonate with most managers and so they may function as a starting point for personal progress with paradoxes. You can, however, work through any paradox you find relevant. The book's tools and reflections can be used to deal with both these and other paradoxes in leadership. If you choose other paradoxes, we do encourage you to get acquainted with the literature or otherwise investigate the specific tensions involved, for instance the competing demands of homogeneity and heterogeneity of diversity management, or the contradictory pulls involved in seeking work–life balance. We also encourage you to think about paradoxes from other arenas than work and leadership for your inspiration, for instance, the tensions between health and business performance that we have all experienced during the corona crisis, or the conflicting priorities as a worker/colleague and friend/family member that we often talk about as an endeavor to achieve work–life balance. If you work with leadership paradoxes together with others, for instance, colleagues, network relations, or classmates, defining a common starting point in the group can also be an advantage prior to discussing a specific paradox. Taking your point of departure in the paradoxes outlined in this book enables you and your colleagues to gather around a common ground and vocabulary.

Paradoxes – natural phenomenon or creative obstruction?

You may now be asking what choices are available, and whether paradoxes are factual management phenomena, or rather a technique that can be applied to all leadership challenges. Paradoxes can, on the one hand, be regarded as natural organizational happenings that, in line with storms, just appear, and when encountered a response is needed. According to this logic, there is always a certain range of paradoxes inherent in leadership, and they must simply be accepted and experienced as they appear. A different perspective, however, is to perceive paradoxes as creative obstructions that help us to solve complex challenges and further to widen our imagination and consequently our action repertoire. A managerial participant in a research project on paradox captured this approach very aptly, and he described a paradoxical perspective as a set of "glasses" he could wear, but could also take off, as needed.

A recurring point in this book is thus that paradoxes can both be understood as existing phenomena in leadership, which one can find specific ways of addressing, *and* as a particular view based on one's own act of leadership. Accordingly, paradoxical navigation is a way of understanding and creating meaning within the leadership role. Yet, there is still great divergence of opinion in the research literature as to whether one or the other logic is more appropriate or correct (Smith et al., 2017a). Very suitably for a book on organizational paradox theory, we take a "both–and" position: we perceive paradoxes as a perspective and a meta-competence in relation to the leadership role, *and* at the same time we recognize that paradoxes are about specific leadership tasks and challenges.

How do they know?

> As a manager, you are like, 'Oh, no, there's a problem, I have to solve it,' and then you expect there to be a 100% solution. What I have gained from here are some deeper reflections on pros and cons. I have accepted or seen that this is the nature of management.
> (A middle manager participating in the research project "Leadership GPS",
> quoted in Nielsen et al., 2020, p. 73)

This book stands on the shoulder of giants in that we have been inspired by the burgeoning research literature on organizational and leadership paradox that we reference throughout the book – you find references at the end of each chapter as well as in the overall bibliography at the end of the book. We have known managers participating in our workshops at (academic or practitioner) conferences to use research articles as input for reading circles or as a springboard for discussion in network meetings with peers (see Gameplan #3: learning from literature, p. 64–65). Readers of this book wishing to adopt the book for educational or developmental purposes may find inspiration for supplementary readings for learners in this section.

The results, cases, and tools that we present, however, come from research projects on paradox undertaken by one, more, or all the authors:

- *"Leadership GPS for new times – from comfort zone to competitiveness"* (referred to as "Leadership GPS" in later chapters) funded by the Industry Foundation explored leadership paradoxes in an action learning perspective following closely the work of 55 managers representing 11 participating companies. Data include participant observation, stakeholder consultation, interviews, surveys, focus group interviews, and participant logbooks.
- *"Long lasting leadership in turbulent times – paradoxical leadership in practice"* funded by the Royal Danish Defence College is an ongoing project exploring paradox in an organization who have worked with paradoxical leadership for more than a decade. Our data pool includes ethnographic data, participant observations, interviews, and secondary data sources.
- The research project *"A taste for sustainable fish"*, supported by the Velux Foundations, explores the paradoxes of organizational sustainable transformation in a change process at the Copenhagen Hospitality College (CHC). Data include participant observation, interviews, focus groups interviews, and survey.

It is our hope that readers will be inspired to learn more about the research results presented in this book as well as other research projects on leadership conducted by the authors. To this end, we include a separate list of author publications on leadership paradox navigation in practice below so that readers might take a closer look into the machine room of our research efforts. We will introduce and reference these knowledge pools as they appear in the book.

This book gathers and further develops the experiences and tools that we jointly gained and developed throughout these projects. We continue to work with paradoxes in several other organizational contexts, including public organizations and nongovernmental organizations (NGOs). Hence, our examples are harvested from a diversity of sectors and industries, large and small organizations, local and global. The reader of this book will become acquainted with cases and exemplars of managers' work with paradoxes in practice, but all managers and most companies appear anonymously or pseudonymized. This is to ensure that not only the successful managers enthusiastic about paradoxical leadership would share their experiences, but also the more critical voices and the "non-success stories" would come forth.

Managers, leaders – and other change agents

Throughout the book, you will meet a diverse group of paradox navigators. Our focus is on managers because the participants of our research studies (and consulting activities) have predominantly had the job role and title of "manager". Their participation in our research has been focused on dealing with paradox in relation to a leadership role, and so we will refer to them as "managers". As we will discuss in more detail in Chapter 3, some researchers distinguish between leadership and management as two complementary yet different aspects. This distinction is contested, however, and we choose to understand managers as practitioners of leadership, in this book particularly in relation to paradoxes. Consequently, we refer to our research participants as managers, not leaders. We will explore paradox as it surfaces as leadership paradox. Consequently, we refer to the content of that job role in relation to navigation of paradox as paradox leadership.

Leadership practice is diverse and contextual and not even researchers can add theoretical clarity in a jungle of opinions, anecdotes, and contradictory evidence (Poulfelt, 1997) as well as several competing paradigms and perspectives (Rennison, 2014). There is no grand unifying theory of leadership – or as Bennis cautions us: *"we must remember that the subject is vast, amorphous, slippery, and, above all, desperately important"* (Bennis, 2007, p. 2). For the purposes of this book, we have taken our point of departure in an understanding of leadership as actions related to goal setting, problem solving, creation of communicative resources that facilitate discussion of goals and problem solving, and facilitation of collaboration with relevant others (Johnsen, 1984, p. 70). Importantly, this understanding of leadership includes a range of actors – not only persons with a formal leadership title. Leadership behavior is not only restricted to actors with a specific job role but can potentially be enacted by all types of stakeholders in and outside the organization. In a time where leadership is increasingly shared, matrixed, distributed, co-created, or is self-leadership this aspect comes to the fore. Although our data primarily stem from exploration of paradox navigation of formally entitled managers (from a range of functions and hierarchical levels), other groups such as employees or external stakeholders with transformative capacity as change agents are not per definition excluded from our understanding or from finding inspiration in our insights, tools, and cases. Indeed, as we shall see in Part III, managers' paradox navigation is embedded in a broad stakeholder landscape of collaborators that impact one another's room to maneuver.

A guided tour: Reading and using the rest of the book

In this last part of this chapter, we outline how you can concretely use the book's individual chapters to work through paradoxes.

Paradox leadership begins with knowing whether the chosen challenge can be meaningfully characterized as a paradox. In Chapter 2, "On problems, dilemmas, and paradoxes", you can identify whether what you as a leader perceive a challenge is a paradox: Is your challenge the kind of challenge that gives rise to the type of coping and decision making that this book is about? This will enable you to handle this situation differently from how you might otherwise do in your managerial practice, that is, acting out of thoughtful consideration rather than knee-jerk reactive auto-pilot action. Chapter 2 distinguishes between three types of frameworks or "diagnoses" for leadership challenges: problems, dilemmas, and paradoxes. This chapter introduces different management situations and reflection questions that you can use to assess the nature of your challenge and the appropriate courses of action that come with different understandings. Maybe you conclude that you primarily experience problems or dilemmas and can then end here, but it is likely that some of your challenges will have the character of paradoxes.

Chapter 3, "What paradox? Introducing fields of paradoxical tensions in leadership" fleshes out 10 classical and relevant leadership challenges with draft formulations of leadership paradoxes, which you can use to reflect and get inspiration from in your investigations of the paradoxes from your daily life that may need a mileage check and some quality time.

The rest of the book is about dealing with paradoxes in five different phases, below briefly introduced as a central leitmotif and prelude. Those five chapters elaborate on the five phases of paradox leadership.

In Chapters 4–8 of Part II, we zoom in on leadership challenges as paradoxes, that is, leadership challenges that have a degree of complexity that merits closer inspection and attention. Chapter 4, "Phase 1. Choosing and shaping your focus area – paradox choice and qualification" deals with the first phase of paradox leadership. The key activity in this phase is choosing and verifying the leadership paradox you want to work through. Why is this a paradox? How is it a paradox? How does the paradox manifest itself? How and when does the paradox become salient in your daily life? This chapter will help you answer these questions by presenting three concrete tools that can support this work along with some narratives from managers' practices about opportunities, and pitfalls associated with this work. The chapter concludes with five key learning coordinates for your paradox work in Phase 1.

Chapter 5, "Phase 2. Know your paradox – paradox investigation" deals with the second phase of working through a paradox. This phase is about learning about what your chosen paradoxical challenge entails. Is the chosen challenge really a paradox, and have you fully understood your paradox? This chapter introduces new tools to support your efforts in understanding both sides of the case and provides you with a vocabulary to describe both the dark and sunny sides of both poles. It also addresses whether there are other management paradoxes that could complement what you have chosen, or whether you could choose a completely different one. The point here is to turn off the autopilot, dwell on the paradox, and be curious about the paradox before acting. The chapter also concludes with five key learning coordinates for your work on paradoxes in this phase.

The third phase of paradox navigation is presented in Chapter 6, "Phase 3. Charting a course of action – identifying and choosing appropriate actions". When you have invested time and resources into getting to know your paradox well, you have at the same time created a solid base for further action. This is the foundation you will build on in the third phase, where you will identify your options for action. The chapter presents three specific tools for how you can identify individual courses of action while ensuring that you address both sides of the coin; both sides will have some related advantages and disadvantages. It is precisely the nature of paradoxes that pluses and minuses are, to a large extent, mirror images of each other and therefore interact. The chapter also points out that there are probably some action options that you will be more inclined to choose than others, and it helps you recognize other possible paths than the ones you are used to. The chapter concludes with five key learning coordinates for your work on paradoxes in this phase.

In Chapter 7, "Phase 4. Action in practice – grasping and handling your paradox" we move on to the fourth phase of paradox navigation, where we must translate the prioritized action options into specific actions in everyday life. You will learn how the chosen actions are related to the task you want to solve, how the key stakeholders are involved, and which methods you can use. This chapter also serves as inspiration for how to anchor your actions in a joint reflection with your stakeholders. Chapter 7 also provides examples of how paradox management plays out in practice in relation to dealing with some specific challenges. Here you can get an appreciation for what it really means to think of your leadership challenges as paradoxes, that is, where you hold on to the fact that there is a balance that is constantly found, lost, and renegotiated, while at the same time doing something. The chapter concludes with five key learning coordinates for your work on paradoxes in this phase.

The fifth and final phase in paradox navigation is presented in Chapter 8, "Phase 5. Evaluation and follow-up – keeping track of your balancing act". Work associated with paradox leadership in practice must of course be followed up, reflected on, and assessed. In Phase 5, we focus on how you can continuously take stock of progress, while maintaining balance in your paradox leadership. This is important because paradox management is not about *having* the right balance, but about continuously *finding* it. Maintaining balance in paradox leadership also means keeping an eye on both effects and side-effects. The chapter introduces three tools for how this can be done in practice. Finally, you are presented with five key learning coordinates for your work with paradoxes in this phase.

In Chapter 9, "The Paradox Pathway – 25 learning coordinates for paradox leadership in practice" we pull the strings together: the five phases of paradox leadership navigation, the 15 management tools, and a total of 25 takeaways to practice, here called coordinates. If you are an impatient reader or just want the big picture before you dive into the individual phase, you can start by first reading Chapter 9.

Where Part II of the book is primarily aimed at assisting the individual manager in navigating paradox on a more personal level, the last part of the book explores paradox navigation as a "team sport" focusing on collaboration with internal and external stakeholders. Paradoxes exist and are understood in context, and even if coping with a paradox on an individual level is helpful, stakeholders play a large role for the individual's room to maneuver and the available action repertoire. Also, this part of the book is particularly helpful for managers who have already previously worked with paradoxes or for development professionals helping others deal with paradoxes as part of development efforts/educational activities. Chapter 10 is entitled "Paradox Navigation as a team sport: inter- and intra-organizational collaboration on paradox". This chapter deals with paradox coping across different hierarchical levels exploring real-life examples of the ways in which different managerial levels may positively/negatively influence each other's paradox work as well as how subordinates' paradox coping is influenced by managerial paradox navigation. Chapter 11, "Let's talk about paradox! Communicating consistently inconsistent about paradox with stakeholders", deals with fostering paradox resonance and productive interaction with others through leadership communication. Chapter 12, "Facilitating productive interactions with paradox: The role of facilitators, peers, and professional helpers" discusses facilitation of paradox learning and development processes as undertaken by, for instance, a manager with subordinates, as consultant, educator, human resources (HR) professional, or similar. Finally, Chapter 13, "Concluding the never-ending story of paradox navigation", concludes the book by connection and elaborating on the points made throughout the book and putting a temporary stop to the never-ending story of paradox navigation.

We wish you a good read and productive paradox navigation!

References

Bennett, N., and Lemoine, J. (2014). What VUCA really means for you. *Harvard Business Review*, 92(1/2).

Bennis, W. (2007). The challenges of leadership in the modern world: Introduction to the special issue. *American Psychologist*, 62, 2–9.

Cameron, K. S., Quinn, R. E., DeGraff, J., and Thakor, A. V. (2014). *Competing Values Leadership*. Cheltenham, MA: Edward Elgar Publishing.

Fairhurst, G. T., Oliver, N., and Waldman, D. A. (2019, July). Paradox and uncertainty. In *Academy of Management Proceedings* (Vol. 2019, No. 1). Briarcliff Manor, NY 10510: Academy of Management, p. 11398.

Johnsen, E. (1984). Ledelseslærens rødder. *Danish Journal of Management and Business*, 48(1).

Larsson, M., Holmberg, R., and Kempster, S. (2020). "It's the organization that is wrong": Exploring disengagement from organizations through leadership development. *Leadership*, 16(2), 141–162.

Lewis, M. W. (2000). Exploring paradox: Toward a more comprehensive guide. *Academy of Management review*, 25(4), 760–776.

Lewis, M. W., and Dehler, G. E. (2000). Learning through paradox: A pedagogical strategy for exploring contradictions and complexity. *Journal of Management Education*, 24(6), 708–725.

Lüscher, L. (2017). *Lederen mellem tvivl og handlekraft: Paradokser og personligt lederskab*. Copenhagen, DK: Dansk Psykologisk Forlag.

Lüscher, L. S., and Lewis, M. W. (2008). Organizational change and managerial sensemaking: Working through paradox. *Academy of Management Journal*, 51(2), 221–240.

Lüscher, L. S., Lewis, M., and Ingram, A. (2006). The social construction of organizational change paradoxes. *Journal of Organizational Change Management*, 19(4), 491–502.

March, J. G. (1991) Exploration and exploitation in organizational learning. *Organization Science*, 2(1), 71–87.

Miron-Spektor, E., Ingram, A., Keller, J., Smith, W. K., and Lewis, M. W. (2018). Microfoundations of organizational paradox: The problem is how we think about the problem. *Academy of Management Journal*, 61(1), 26–45.

Nielsen, R. K., Mogensen, M., Bévort, F., Henriksen, T. D., Hjalager, A. M., and Lyndgaard, D. B. (2020). *Både& – værktøjer til effektiv paradoksledelse*. Copenhagen, DK: Djøf Publishing.

Nordhaug, O. (1998). Competence specificities in organizations: A classificatory framework. *International Studies of Management and Organization*, 28(1), 8–29.

Poulfelt, F. (1997). Professionel Ledelse? *Danish Journal of Management*, 61, 85–95.

Quinn, R. E. and Nujella, M. (2017). Foreword: Paradox in organizational theory. In W. K. Smith, M. W. Lewis, P. Jarzabkowski, and A. Langley (Eds.), The *Oxford Handbook of Organizational Paradox*, Oxford: Oxford University Press, pp. v–viii.

Rennison, B. W. (2014). Ledelse. In S. Vikkelsøe and P. Kjær, *Klassisk og Moderne Organisationsteori*, Copenhagen, DK: Hans Reitzel, pp. 613–640.

Schad, J., Lewis, M. W., Raisch, S., and Smith, W. K. (2016). Paradox research in management science: Looking back to move forward. *The Academy of Management Annals*, 10(1), 5–64.

Smith, W. & Lewis, M. (2022). *Both/And Thinking: Embracing Creative Tensions to Solve Your Toughest Problems*. Brighton, MA: Harvard Business Review Press.

Smith, W. K., Erez, M., Jarvenpaa, S., Lewis, M. W., and Tracey, P. (2017). Adding complexity to theories of paradox, tensions, and dualities of innovation and change: Introduction to organization studies special issue on paradox, tensions, and dualities of innovation and change. *Organization Studies*, 38 (3–4), 303–317.

Smith, W. K., and Lewis, M. W. (2011). Toward a theory of paradox: A dynamic equilibrium model of organizing. *Academy of Management Review*, 36(2), 381–403.

Smith, W. K., Lewis, M. W., Jarzabkowski, P., and Langley, A. (2017a). Introduction. The paradoxes of paradox. In W. K. Smith, M. W. Lewis, P. Jarzabkowski, and A. Langley (Eds.), *The Oxford Handbook of Organizational Paradox*, Oxford: Oxford University Press, pp. 1–24.

Smith, W. K., Lewis, M. W., Jarzabkowski, P., and Langley, A. (Eds.). (2017b). *The Oxford Handbook of Organizational Paradox*. Oxford: Oxford University Press.

Sveningsson, S., and Larsson, M. (2006). Fantasies of leadership: Identity work. *Leadership*, 2(2), 203–224.

Author publications on leadership paradox related to research projects on paradox navigation in practice

Bévort, F., Henriksen, T. D., Hjalager, A-M., Nielsen, R. K., Holt Larsen, H. and Vikkelsø (2018). *Ledelsesdilemmaer: Strejftog gennem faglitteraturen*. Frederiksberg, DK: Copenhagen Business School.

Henriksen, T. D., Nielsen, R. K., Vikkelsø, S., Bévort, F., and Mogensen, M. (2021). A paradox rarely comes alone a quantitative approach to investigating knotted leadership paradoxes in SMEs. *Scandinavian Journal of Management*, 37(1), 101135.

Henriksen, T. D., Vikkelsø, S., Nielsen, R. K., and Bévort, F. (2021). *From Managers' Practical Problems to Complex Understandings: Three Approaches for Understanding the Development of Management Problems*. Paper accepted for the European Group of Organization Studies 2020 Annual Colloquium, Paradox track.

Jacobsen, A. J., Nielsen, R. K., and Eskjær, M. (2019). *Kortlægning af barrierer og muligheder om bæredygtighed*. Copenhagen, DK: Aalborg University and Copenhagen Hospitality College.

Mogensen, M., Nielsen, R. K., Henriksen, T. D., Bévort, F., and Vikkelsø, S. (2018). *Working with Paradox as Entity and Process – Projecting and Eliciting Paradoxes in Managerial Practice through an Action Learning Programme*. Paper accepted for the European Group of Organization Studies Annual Colloquium, Tallin, Track 06 – Taken by surprise: Expanding our understanding of paradoxes and contradictions in organizational life.

Nielsen, R. K. (2022). *A Sea Of(f) Balance? Facilitating Paradox Navigating between Guardrails and Stumbling Blocks in "Life below Water" Sustainabilities*. Paper accepted for the annual International Organizations Network (ION) conference, February 24 –26, 2022.

Nielsen, R. K., Bartunek, J., Smith, W., Greco, A., Pingel Hansen, M., Bjerre Lyndgaard, D., Omeife, N., Pradies, C., and Keller, J. (2021). *Interacting Productively with Paradox Theory in Practice – Education, Interventions and Dissemination*. Professional Development Workshop accepted for the Academy of Management Annual Meeting.

Nielsen, R. K., Cheal, J., and Pradies, C. (2021). Fostering paradox resonance: Exploring leaders' communication of paradoxes during crisis. *Journal of Management Inquiry*, 30(2), 157–159.

Nielsen, R. K., and Hansen, M. P. (2020). *Exploring the Unintended Consequences of Managerial "Paradox Sharing" with Subordinates and Superiors. The Case of the Royal Danish Defence*. Paper accepted for the European Group of Organization Studies 2020 Conference. Sub-theme 09: [SWG] Organizational Paradox Change for Good? Organizational Paradoxes and Unintended Consequences of Transforming Modern Societies.

Nielsen, R. K., Hjalager, A.-M., Larsen, H. H., Bévort, F., Henriksen, T. D., and Vikkelsø, S. (2018). *Ledelsesdilemmaer – og kunsten at navigere i moderne ledelse*. Copenhagen, DK: Djøf Publishing.

Nielsen, R. K., Mogensen, M., Bévort, F., Henriksen, T. D., Hjalager, A. M., and Lyndgaard, D. B. (2019). *Ledelses-GPS til en ny tid – Håndtering af ledelsesparadokser og dilemmaer i praksis*. Copenhagen Business School, University of Southern Denmark, Aalborg University and Network of Corporate Academies, https://www.industriensfond.dk/Ledelses-GPS-

Nielsen, R. K., Mogensen, M., Bévort, F., Henriksen, T. D., Hjalager, A. M., and Lyndgaard, D. B. (2020). *Både& – værktøjer til effektiv paradoksledelse*. Copenhagen, DK: Djøf Publishing.

Nielsen, R. K., Mogensen, M., and Henriksen, T. D. (2022). *Leveraging Complexity in (Educational) Practice. Exploring the Dynamics of Tame and Wild Paradoxes in an Action Learning Program*. Paper presented at PREP (Paradox Research Education Practice) conference, March 16 –18, 2022.

Pradies, C., Carmine, S., Cheal, J., e Cunha, M. P., Gaim, M., Keegan, A., Miron-Spektor, E., Nielsen, R. K., Pouthier, V., Sharma, G., Sparr, J., Vince, R., and Keller, J. (2021). The lived experience of paradox: How individuals navigate tensions during the pandemic crisis. *Journal of Management Inquiry*, 30(2), 154–167.

Chapter 2
On problems, dilemmas, and paradoxes

> I came with a problem. I left with a paradox. Now what?!?
> (Manager participating in the Leadership GPS research
> project on leadership paradox, first author field notes)

Managers must stand ready to go ahead with problems that employees were unable to solve. Some problems seem to have the magical ability to evade closure. Like a jack-in-a-box they keep on sticking their faces out whenever you thought you were finished with them. Some managers call them "cork problems" as they keep on resurfacing, regardless of how many times you whack them. Others call them "Duracell problems" because these challenges, much like the commercial's "energizer bunny", just keep going and going and going. That kind of leadership problem often contains conflicting issues, and they deprive you of the luxury of choosing either side. They force you to resort to a "both–and" kind of leadership, even though it bristles in every direction. This could appear as managers needing to make decisions concerning both development and operations at the same time. It could be having to rely both on trust in and control of others. And the both–and's could be regarding the combination of free agents and permanent staff. On the basis of current research literature, we refer to such challenges as paradoxes, where it does not make much sense to try to prioritize your way out of the problem. The only viable approach is to go deeper into the challenge, and to navigate competing demands in an ongoing balancing act.

Complex–perplex–paradox?

> When dealing with leadership challenges, you run into one paradox after another. At least it is perceived that way. And then you give up; it is not possible to get any further with what you want. The closer you get to the ideal state, the more resistance arises, or unwanted side-effects overshadow the desired effects of the effort.
> (Johnsen, 2006, p. 245)

It is not our intention to give you more complex challenges by reading this book. It is, however, our intention to offer an alternative, potentially richer understanding of your leadership. The aim is for you as reader and manager to increase your capacity to handle those paradoxes that you are already experiencing by offering a variety of concrete tools for dealing with them. But before we get to the part where you navigate your paradox, it is necessary to be able to identify when a leadership challenge emerges in such a manner where the term "paradox" becomes appropriate. We make a specific point of this because your options for dealing with your challenge depend on how you understand it. Generally, managers tend to focus, often narrowly, on

https://doi.org/10.1515/9783110788877-002

problem stating or problem solving, but sometimes neither stating nor solving are keys to handling the problem. In contrast, we suggest exploring the problem-stating part by digging further into the problem. When shifting emphasis from problem to paradox, you elaborate on your understanding of the problem. Hereby you will enhance your understanding of those actions that will lead you to the results you need.

Our experiences from managers' practical paradox work show:

- Managers benefit from distinguishing problems from dilemmas and paradoxes.
- The more unreasonable, impossible, and complex the challenge, the more advantageous it becomes to view it as a paradox.
- It might appear easy to identify a paradox, as leadership is inherently laden with paradoxes. In practice it is often more difficult than first imagined to select and detangle one paradox from other paradoxes.
- It requires training to view your challenges as paradoxes. Using a lifeline, that is, sparring with colleagues, members of a network, and HR often proves to be advantageous.
- It makes a difference in practice whether you approach a challenge as a problem, a dilemma, or a paradox.
- Problems are solved, dilemmas prioritized, and paradoxes are navigated.
- Most managers tend to be considerably better (and faster) at identifying (and solving) problems than they are at identifying (and solving) dilemmas and paradoxes.
- Managers are professional problem solvers, and it takes quite an effort to harness their "problem-solving itch" if you are dealing with a paradox.
- Managers tend to prefer and are competent in problem solving, but to a lesser extent they appear to be experienced in paradox navigation.
- If you want to manage a paradox, it is necessary to be both willing to try and dare something new, and to be ready to move outside one's own comfort zone.

Being able to distinguish between problems, dilemmas, and paradoxes is necessary to be able to navigate and act accordingly in a complex practice. Subsequently, it becomes important to grasp this distinction and approach them in a competent manner. Certain forms of challenges call for more "problem unboxing" and balanced approaches to achieve lasting results. The trick is to know when a more elaborate approach is required, and when traditional problem solving will do.

Paper, rock, scissors – problem, dilemma, paradox

> The problem isn't the problem; our relationship to the problem is the problem. In other words, we have many of the skills needed to handle what's being thrown at us. But when faced with continual complexity at unprecedented pace, our survival instincts kick in. In a mental panic to regain control, we fight, flee, or freeze: we act before thinking ('we've got to make some kind of decision, now!'), we analyze an issue to the point of paralysis, or we abdicate responsibility by ignoring the problem or shunting it off to a committee or task force.
> (Bourton, Lavoie and Vogel, 2018, fifth section)

Complexity, speed of change, and ambiguity makes it difficult to make sound decisions. As the quote indicates, it is becoming increasingly difficult for managers to make decisions in a suitable manner (rather than by putting your head in the sand, jumping the gun, or getting out-maneuvered by an information overload). Such complexity justifies paradox thinking, as it invites both reflecting and acting. Make no mistake, paradox thinking is no silver bullet. It finds it use where it makes sense, but it should not be applied universally. This implies effectively distinguishing paradoxes from dilemmas and problems. You may see this as merely an academic discussion: "problem", "dilemma", or "paradox" – they all sound messy whatever the words we use. However, it makes a difference when we move on to asking how you as a manager should act upon your challenge.

The point is that we see little need for making life as a manager more difficult than it already is. If your challenge is a problem, then please keep calling it that. But often, the opposite appears to be the case. Managers talking about solving problems when they are in fact dealing with a paradox. In such cases, efforts to deal with the problem often take the form of rearrangements that only scratch the surface but fail to address the underlying tensions. Below the surface, the basic challenge remains intact. In the following sections, we illustrate the difference between problem, dilemma, and paradox, each accompanied with a series of check-questions. These questions aim to help you assess your own management challenge and diagnose whether you are facing a problem, a dilemma, or a paradox (Lüscher and Lewis, 2008; Smith and Lewis, 2011; Smith and Lewis, 2022).

It is important to note that the following checklists are heuristics derived from our interaction and facilitation of managers' work on paradoxes. Research has clear-cut definitions of problem, dilemma, and paradox respectively, that will provide demarcation lines. But as you would expect from research, the definitions are not necessarily in alignment with one another. Our goal here is not to provide yet other definitions of these different types of challenges. As outlined in Chapter 1, we take our point of departure in accepted and widely used research definitions of paradox, and we have based our heuristics on such definitions. Yet, for the purposes of easing transition into paradoxical thinking *and* action, we find that theoretical discussions about the definitions must be accompanied by concerns for actionability. Otherwise, the debate may be educational, but most managers are unable to connect such distinctions to their own practice and problems.

Problem – a substantial, unsettled matter

> 99% of all problems pass spontaneously.
> (Svend-Aage Madsen, chief-psychologist at Rigshospitalet,
> Denmark, personal correspondence, 2020)

> In my experience, sometimes your problems simply come to nothing.
> (Life wisdom shared with first author by anonymous senior citizen)

When you are not experiencing any problems, you may find yourself switching to autopilot and observing as work progresses without conflict or any noteworthy problems. Such occasions tend to be rare in management: A variety of unsettled problems and questions without an answer tend to be directed upward, prompting the manager for a solution to the problem. A problem is an unsettled matter that needs to be addressed, using either analysis or thinking such as an unsolved task in need of solving, an unanswered question in need of an answer, or similar, or as the Google Dictionary puts it (provided by Oxford Languages): "a matter or situation regarded as unwelcome or harmful and needing to be dealt with and overcome" (Problem, n.d.).

As soon as problems arise, we need to stop and consider the situation before we act. In the eyes of many managers, problems exist with the sole purpose of being solved and they make sure to solve each one as expediently as possible to avoid them drawing attention away from the more complex ones. Decide and get on with it. Problems are difficult questions in need of answering, and tasks in need of solving. Just do them and move on.

Reflection questions: Is your challenge a problem?

You are likely to have encountered a problem when:
- on second thought, you can identify appropriate actions, and by implementing those actions can solve the problem on the short and medium run
- your options for solving the problem are not mutually exclusive
- you can find a solution that has little or no side-effects to the problem you are trying to solve, or to other challenges in your management or company
- they lead to acceptable opportunity costs, which implies all sorts of resource consumption related to your effort, considering opting-out on other options, which now are deprived of resources

Dilemma – trade-offs between "a rock and a hard place" and "luxury problems"

> You should not go about being a 'dilemma procrastinator' who postpones the difficult decisions and fails to grab the bull by its horns.
> (Executive Vice President Lillian Mogensen, quoted from first author field notes, May 31, 2018)

While you are probably thinking that there are plenty of dilemmas for managers to take on board, it is often proving more difficult than expected to identify a challenge that qualifies as a dilemma, and not just a problem that makes you uncomfortable to act on. Being conflict-adverse or feeling discomfort thinking of the consequences of acting upon a challenge does, however, not qualify it as a dilemma. A dilemma might cause discomfort and keep you awake at night, but, nevertheless, they are distinct from problems in that they have mutually competing options, each with pros and cons, preventing you from doing both.

For many managers, dilemmas call for prioritization. You will have to go for the option that causes the least side-effects. You might say, "This is an especially difficult kind of problem", as dilemmas require careful consideration and exploration of options before making a choice. The point is that the choice is made from thorough consideration, characterized by being a choice between "a rock and a hard place" or two similarly attractive options, sometimes referred to as "a luxury problem", describing a situation where only positive options are available. Nevertheless, such choices must be made that preclude other available options.

Reflection questions: Is your challenge a dilemma?

You are likely to have encountered a dilemma when your leadership challenge is a situation characterized by the following:
- Your choice makes the challenge go away, which means that when you have made your decision you can proceed down that path while leaving the other option at peace. (You may feel bad about being the person to make that choice, but the challenge is over as you make your choice.)
- Your choices are mutually exclusive, but not mutually dependent or conditioning. This means they are *not* connected in a manner that implies that you "throw the baby out with the bath water" or in some other manner incur opportunity costs from your choice.
- There is a real option for you. This means the consequences/side-effects of choosing one over the other are acceptable (while exactly what is acceptable is a matter of the particular person or organization).
- Your choice is realistic. This means, for instance, that it is not illegal to deselect one of the available alternative options, or that a particular choice will not promptly

be second-guessed or overruled by upper management or other powerful stake-holders due to misalignments with corporate objectives.

Paradox – long-lasting "cork problems"

> [M]anaging paradox is hard and not for the faint of heart. Rather it calls for 'exceptional concep-tual ability to embrace complexity' (Burke, 2012) as one engages to understand and manage ten-sions that are sure to surface in everyday organizational life.
>
> (Jules and Gold, 2014, p. 125)

Some of the challenges you face as a manager are characterized by being paradoxes, not problems, not dilemmas. Examples might be the balancing of operations against de-velopment, standardization against differentiation of services and processes, or the bal-ancing of the need for delivering on both price and quality. These are not either–or considerations but require a both–and approach.

Paradoxes are challenges in which the options are both in conflict with each other and interrelated, implying that a choice between them only offers a temporary solution, whereas the underlying tension will eventually reemerge – just like a cork. The poles of a paradox are as yin and yang; they both contain each other and are mutually dependent.

While a dilemma-based line of thinking invites for prioritization and choices nor-mally associated with the role of a manager, paradox thinking proposes that you, rep-resenting a business and as a manager, should become able to unite conflicting approaches and ideas, perhaps even mutually excluding approaches in your manage-ment. This implies practicing the art of "having your cake and eating it too" while try-ing to place yourself comfortably between two stools without falling to the ground. You need to find you way with choosing A as well as B.

Reflection questions: Is your challenge a paradox?

You are likely to have encountered a paradox when:
- reconsidering your problem, you cannot identify suitable actions to solve it
- identified actions cannot solve the problem on a short or medium range
- your problem-solving bears resemblance to "Sisyphus work", as your stone keeps rolling down the other side whenever you think you nailed a solution to it
- your options consist of conflicting considerations that are mutually connected and condition one another and actions aimed at one alternative also impact the other and vice versa
- it is impossible to find a final solution to your challenge; if you, for instance, choose one over the other, fires break out, forcing you to attend to the neglected side and, soon after, the problem reemerges in a new disguise

– no real choice exists between the identified alternatives, meaning that the consequences/side-effects of having to choose one over the other becomes unacceptable (while exactly what is acceptable is a matter of the particular person or organization)
– the choice is unrealistic, meaning that it would be, for instance, unethical, illegal, or irresponsible to opt out of an option, or that doing so would be overruled from somewhere higher in the organization

The answers to these questions are likely to guide you toward working with a challenge worthy of your quality time and in-depth exploration. The important part here is not to spend too long thinking about it. Build up the courage, pick a challenge, and test it. When you identify a suitable challenge, go through the steps provided in the rest of this book. The worst thing that could happen if it turns out that your paradox is not a paradox is that you will most probably realize this quite quickly in the process. Then you will identify your challenge as either a problem and dilemma and get on with your business. You can then move on to other pressing and recurring challenges that need closer inspection. If you need inspiration to the kind of paradoxes that managers might work with then Chapter 3 presents 10 fields of paradoxical tensions that resonate with many managers.

At this point it is important to note that paradox navigation also involves classical problem solving and dilemma prioritization. Paradox navigation is also about making day-to-day decisions, but in appreciation of the undercurrent of persisting competing demands that run beneath this series of more trivial decisions. For this reason, it is important to uncover and inspect this undercurrent to be able to make sensible decisions over time in full awareness of the full picture. So, first things first – dwell on your paradox.

Working through paradox in five phases

When you have worked your way through the reflection questions, you might already have ruled out some of your challenges, either as problems to be solved, or as dilemmas in need of prioritization. You probably also have a challenge or two that you consider paradoxes, but without getting your grasp on it. Throughout the remainder of this book, we suggest a process choosing, exploring, and acting on your paradox as well as identifying options and concrete actions for navigating paradoxes. This process contains five steps, as illustrated in Figure 2.1.

A chapter is dedicated to each phase in which you are presented concrete tools that guide your work with paradoxes, and supplemented by case illustrations, showing how managers have worked with the phases in their own practices.

It all starts with finding your way into your paradox in Phase 1 – a work that is easier said than done. It should be clear at this point that not all problems are paradoxes, and not all paradoxes energize you, or appear meaningful for you to work

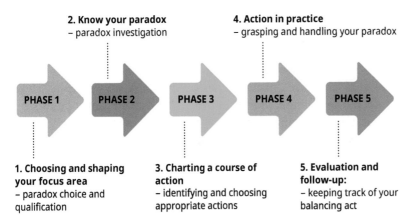

Figure 2.1: Five phases of paradox navigation.

with. The purpose of this phase is for you to identify and choose a paradox to be used as anchorage throughout the following phases.

Phase 2 takes it point of departure in your chosen paradox – dwelling on the nature of the paradox, curiously investigating the stakes and issues involved as well as identifying blind angles. In our experience, we all tend to have a favorite pole of any given paradox, which impedes our understanding of full scale of the paradox, and consequently also some of the options found in more neglected parts.

Phase 3 take its point of departure in a nuanced understanding of your chosen paradox, which makes it possible to consider what practical options this gives rise to. The next questions are then: How can you act on the paradox without simplifying it, for instance by reducing it to a problem, and on the other hand avoid becoming paralyzed? How might you identify suitable options for dealing with the paradox?

Phase 4 uses the identified suitable options as a springboard for implementing them in a practice dominated by competing agendas, existing systems, and tools in your organization as well as employees and management colleagues. This is about how to make plans for acting appropriately on the paradox, but also to envisage how you can involve immediate surroundings in a meaningful manner, how they can contribute to working with the paradox, and perhaps even work with their own paradoxes.

Eventually, in Phase 5 you take stock on how your work with paradox has progressed. Did it result in any significant change regarding what you sought to achieve? Have your actions caused any changes, and might they even have caused something to change that you were unaware of? Paradox leadership is an activity that never ends. There are naturally occurring, inherent contradictions in leadership, and progression causes friction and releases energy, but also builds up positive/negative synergies, making this final phase more of a pitstop than a grand finale.

The Paradox Pathway: 5 phases, 10 paradoxes, 15 tools, 20 cases, and 25 learning coordinates

On your way through the 5 phases, and possibly inspired by the 10 paradoxical tensions in leadership described in Chapter 3, you will be equipped with 15 practical tools that can help you get to work. In addition, you will be accompanied by 20 cases illustrating the successes and failures of real-life managers, as they work through their individually chosen paradoxes. Taken together, this forms a possible pathway or map to deal with paradoxes in thought and action (Figure 2.2).

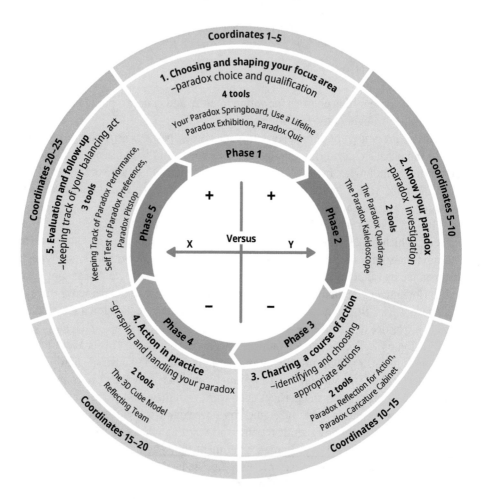

Figure 2.2: The Paradox Pathway – roadmap of paradox navigation.

In the very center of the map is the paradox you have chosen to work on using the tools presented in the five phases, identifying the bright and dark side of both poles of your paradox, here illustrated by a plus and a minus at each end of the double arrow. This is where you insert the paradox that you want to work with. It could be one of the 10 paradoxical tensions described in Chapter 3 or another of your own choice.

The five phases of paradox leadership are illustrated in the circle around the center. All these phases aim at helping you explore and learn more about your choice of paradox, the paradox itself as it occurs to you, your options for acting upon it, how you implement your choices for acting, and finally how you might follow up on your work. By illustrating the phases as a circle, it is illustrated how the work is a continuous, iterative effort. A set of tools are linked to each phase to help you onwards in your paradox navigation. These tools are listed in the next circle. In the illustration's outer ring are the 25 landmarks and indicators to help you navigate through each phase.

Kurt Lewin is often quoted for stating that "nothing is as practical as a good theory" (Greenwood & Levin, 1998, p. 19). However, central to the rest of this book is choosing a practical paradox, that is, your paradox that you will be working with. Concrete tools to help you do it are provided. There might be other books – theoretical or practical – that explain in greater detail the various research breakthroughs on organizational and leadership paradox. But this is your book – it is about navigating *your* leadership paradoxes. This makes it a roadmap of managerial paradox work that requires you to roll up your sleeves, stay committed to curiosity and dedicated to exploring your leadership role in a new way.

Ready for paradox? The three "Cs"

You can walk through our entire Paradox Pathway, or you can hop on and off the bus along the way in the best sightseeing style. No matter for how long you wish to remain on the ride with us, we know from our work with paradox leadership in practice that you will get the greatest benefit out of paradox leadership if you acknowledge "the three Cs":

1) **Change.** There must be something that you want to change, something that you want to do differently. Precisely because paradox leadership is not a "quick fix" you must be committed to changing your view of leadership and the way in which you exercise your leadership.

2) **Curiosity**. You need to be curious and ready to step outside your comfort zone, or at least be interested in mapping your comfort zone and reflecting on what are the current limits for you.

3) **Challenge**. Working with paradoxes makes the most sense if you find a specific, individual challenge. It can become very abstract and vague to simply think and talk about paradoxes on a general level. Sometimes a sterile, abstract debate can be tantamount to a form of procrastination and intellectual diversion strategy keeping paradox at arm's length from personal challenges. Also, opportunities and challenges are most clearly seen when you have a carefully selected, and personally relevant situation to consider, and if you are ready to anchor your thinking in specific actions or processes that you want to incorporate into your daily life.

Modern organizations, managers, and employees do not only have to possess a personality with a readiness for change. In our view, it makes more to sense to become generally "paradox-ready" when continuous change is "both–and". In the following chapters it will become clear that you cannot rapidly and overnight become paradox-ready or follow 10 easy steps to become ready. Consequently, the book contains tools that will assist *you* in analysing *your* paradox and facilitating *your* paradox work, not telling you how you go about dealing with a particular paradoxical situation.

References

Bourton, S., Lavoie, J., and Vogel, T. (2018). Leading with inner agility. *McKinsey Quarterly*, March 29, McKinsey.com, https://www.mckinsey.com/business-functions/organization/our-insights/leading-with-inner-agility, accessed October 16, 2022.

Greenwood, D. J., & Levin, M. (1998). Introduction to action research: Social research for social change. Thousand Oaks, CA: Sage

Johnsen, E. (2006). Paradoksledelse. *Danish Journal of Management & Business*, 69(4), 245–246.

Jules, C., and Good, D. (2014). Introduction to special issue on paradox in context: Advances in theory and practice. *The Journal of Applied Behavioral Science*, 50(2), 123–126.

Lüscher, L. S., and Lewis, M. W. (2008) Organizational change and managerial sensemaking: Working through paradox. *Academy of Management Journal*, 51(2), 221–240.

Problem (n.d.). https://tinyurl.com/bp6bnzpe, Google Dictionary, accessed October 7, 2022.

Smith, W. K., and Lewis, M. W. (2011). Toward a theory of paradox: A dynamic equilibrium model of organizing. *Academy of Management Review*, 36(2), 381–403.

Smith, W. K., and Lewis, M. W. (2022). *Both/And Thinking. Embracing Creative Tensions to Solve Your Toughest Problems*. Boston, MA: Harvard Business Review Press.

Chapter 3
What paradox? Introducing fields of paradoxical tensions in leadership

Comprehending paradox begins with an understanding of contradictions.
(Lewis and Dehler, 2000, p. 711)

[N]aming the paradox is not enough, but a precondition for being able to navigate paradox.
(Lewis and Dehler, 2000, p. 711)

Working through paradox is an endeavor anchored in a specific situation, context, and person. Although we maintain that there are some general phases and landmarks to go through during the process of navigating any paradox (cf. Chapter 2 and Part II), navigating paradox in practice is acting on a specific paradoxical challenge. Accordingly, as indicated by the opening quote, naming your paradox is a precondition for getting the process started. We presume that our readers experience all kinds of paradoxical tensions, and we cannot go into detail about all paradoxes. We must understand that paradoxes in leadership are an inexhaustible source of renewable friction energy. We do, however, want to give some more specific examples of the types of challenges and tensions that managers face when they, in practice, use a paradoxical understanding and action mode. To this end, we will present ten fields of paradoxical tensions in leadership:

1. Leadership *and* management
2. Leadership: Individual leadership *and* collective/distributed leadership
3. Matrix *and* functional organizing – balancing organizational flexibility with specialization
4. Purpose, passion, *and* performance
5. Employee mobility *and* permanence
6. Hybrid collaboration: Virtual *and* physical presence
7. Differentiation/Localization *and* integration/globalization
8. Innovating outside–in *and* inside–out
9. Digital transformation: Human resources *and* technological non-human resources
10. Sustainability in plural: Profit, people, *and* planet

Each of these fields will be introduced in more detail and could be considered an inspirational catalog of paradoxes. Readers may jump straight to the field that they find most relevant, or you can read through them all.

At this point, however, it is important to note that our list of paradoxes is by no means exhaustive or a top 10 of leadership paradoxes. There are many other paradoxes. For instance, Smith and Lewis (2011) chart the archetypical territory of organizational paradox in four categories of paradoxes of organizing, performing, learning,

https://doi.org/10.1515/9783110788877-003

and belonging. Rather, our 10 areas of paradoxical tensions are leadership challenges that can attract managerial attention in a variety of organizations. In our experience, the 10 zones of paradoxical tension can serve as "ice breakers" for thinking and talking about contradictions and paradoxes. We have identified these paradoxes to start the conversation and practical paradox work. Getting on with thinking and acting on paradox can become very intangible and abstract if you do not choose something specific to work with – preferably take a starting point in something that you as a manager recognize from your everyday life. The chosen challenges and paradoxes may arouse the necessary curiosity.

The 10 zones of paradoxical tension introduced in this chapter are more than mere boundary objects (Leigh Star, 2010) or "suitcase-like words" (Minsky, 2007, p. 10) that you can fill up with whatever content you see fit. We do subscribe to the idea that it is possible to identify "evergreen paradoxes" in organizational life and theory. As you shall see in Chapter 4 on the first phase of paradox navigation, we encourage you to seek additional information about the specifics of your paradox. In the Leadership GPS research project on which we base large parts of the argumentation in this book, we conducted a literature review of each of the paradoxical tensions involved. In this process we were particularly mindful to avoid presenting the chosen challenges as problems to be solved, as contradictory elements to be synthesized, or as "old ways" in need of being replaced with "new ways". It also entailed a dedication to viewing paradoxes as inherently different from dilemmas. This literature review was turned into a white book and distributed to all participants. In later research projects touching on other paradoxical tensions, new literature search guided our way and inspired our presentation of the challenges.

The contradictions and interconnections, however, manifest themselves and are experienced quite differently across groups of managers. In our experience, no paradox is set in stone, not all paradoxes are experienced by all managers, and they are experienced differently by different managers. Consequently, when you proceed with the reading of the cases in Part II where managerial colleagues work with the same paradox, you will see that they flesh out the content and the personal challenges involved very differently. In our view, a necessary first step is to identify a challenge to address. From there, paradox navigators will (using the tools in the book) define the paradoxes involved in their leadership role, context, and situation. This process leads to increasing complexity, and sometimes it will generate new and other paradoxes. The important thing is that you have a starting point and a springboard for deciding on a paradox you might wish to work with. We shall now discuss each of our chosen 10 fields of paradoxical tensions in leadership in turn:

#1: Leadership *and* management

This field of paradoxical tension is that of the interconnected yet opposing demands of two aspects of management – an administrative, operations-focused "management" component as well as a developmental and values-based "leadership" component. Is the relationship between managers and followers transactional or transformational, based on commitment or control? And how can both aspects be balanced by the individual manager? Organizations need strong leadership *and* strong management to achieve optimal efficiency. In today's dynamic workplaces we need leaders who can challenge the status quo and inspire and convince the organization's members. We also need managers who can contribute to the development and maintenance of a smoothly functioning workplace.

For the past 50 years, the discussion of leadership has been a tango between the two concepts of leadership and management. The phenomenon of leadership embraces both concepts, although both research and practice show significant differences of opinion regarding the conceptual and practical distance between leadership and management, and how much they overlap (Örtenblad, Hong, and Snell, 2016; Lunenburg, 2013; Kniffin, Detert and Leroy, 2020). The managerial tension consists of finding the right balance point in terms of mobilizing (quantity and type of) leadership and management in a concrete, management-demanding and challenging situation. It requires active navigation for the individual manager to balance mobilization of leadership and management in a concrete challenging situation. This is because resources and the imagination of those managers are limited, and because prioritization of an effort in one aspect of leadership or management often takes resources from the other area. The two focus areas can even be conflicting or incompatible, or they may ultimately (in some researchers' eyes) not be compatible.

The tensions underlying these two different aspects of the managerial role can also be regarded as an underlying tension between "exploitation" versus "exploration", or in other words "operation" versus "development". Should the company utilize what it is good at and nurture its expertise in precisely that area? This strategy may lead to competitive advantages in the short run. Alternatively, should it move outside its comfort zone and develop new skills and products? The assumption here is that it pays off in the long run. Maybe an intelligent market assessment is enough to support a decision to this question. However, there is also an underlying tension about the way management and employees choose to develop their competencies. Within learning theory, the two types of development have been described as "single-loop learning" and "double-loop learning", respectively. The latter tends to be considered superior or better. Nevertheless, it is more appropriate and useful to consider them as two considerations that both must be considered. Hardly any human being or any organization can cope with only one type of development. In practice, there is a need to strengthen the special abilities and competencies through repetition and refining in training rooms or in daily work. On the other hand, one-sided training can block other types of experiences and discovering new sides of oneself. In companies, it can become a tension between, on the one hand, continuing its product portfolio as efficiently as possible based on the hypothesis that it remains marketable for at least two or five years, or on the other hand, experimenting with product development or with completely new production systems.

Ambidextrous organizations are organizations that can strike a good balance between taking risks and innovating, and at the same time are able to prioritize and operate its processes effectively (O'Reilly III and Tushman, 2013; Andriopoulos and Lewis, 2009). A possible response to increasing complexity and the need to unite different foci is thus to build a comprehensive mindset and a repertoire of actions that enables the organization and the individual leader to play multi-handedly and make it legitimate and recognized to switch between different positions. However, it is easier said than done, and the answer must be found in concrete forms of mixing and coexisting decisions. How the good mix is achieved will differ from company to company (D'Souza, Sigdyal and Struckell, 2017). Here, the individual company and manager must navigate and balance development and operation.

#2: Leadership: Individual leadership *and* collective/distributed leadership

Is management, as it is comprising both the operational, administrative "management"-components as well as developmental leadership components someone's responsibility or everyone's responsibility? This field of paradoxical tension is about the fact that management is both a role played by some specific people, namely the leaders, and at the same time something that is deeply dependent on a lot of other people and factors. Although there is still a focus on the importance of the individual leader, management is increasingly seen as a shared responsibility, which is distributed within and integrated into the organization (Pearce, Conger and Locke, 2008). There is a growing focus on "self-management", that is, when the employee is expected to take the lead and take responsibility for himself or herself to a considerable extent (Stewart, Courtright, and Manz, 2011; Manz, 1986). Many leaders are even rooted in a professional community, where working with management as a profession and task is a challenge. There is a delicate balance between, on the one hand, a personal exercise of a role and, on the other, a focus on the contribution of the many people and the leadership that is built into the way in which we organize. Thus, professional management is a balancing act between the many different actors who have a share in the management, even if they do not have a management title.

It is not easy to know what the role the manager should take in the modern organization. Modern self-employed and competent employees can and will lead themselves. Employees are often way more professionally competent for the task they are to perform than their leaders, and they are closer to the customer or citizen than the manager. Organizational systems, procedures, rules, and models set the framework for and control what employees must do. Demands from customers, citizens, or politicians are so well specified that the work is often already in a fixed framework. When that is the case, does it make any sense to focus on the manager as a person and role when developing the company or organization? Too much focus on what managers do can in many cases even be a barrier for the development of the organization.

Despite – or perhaps precisely because of – these developments, there may be a growing need for the manager role, but in new ways. The manager role may include the need to be less direct and heroic, but still leadership is more important than ever. Who sets the framework for and supports the self-directed and competent employees? Who interprets and communicates the overall meaning of the demands placed on the organization and the group? Who is interested in and practices the fine-tuning of the way things are managed and organized in the individual company? It is primarily the manager who can handle these tasks.

The paradoxical tensions become apparent as the need for a manager develops and the focus shifts. Changes in company structures and the general development of society affect the role that the manager can have and most appropriately takes in the management. The manager may have to increasingly work with the management of employees, who to a large extent manage their own work. The manager may to a greater extent be the one who makes sense of a complex reality rather than solving specific professional problems. If management is simply about telling others what they need to do for the organization to perform, then the manager will be the central person and role that all management is about. If only the manager succeeds in doing her or his job, then the management works well. Unfortunately, it is not that simple: We want to develop and improve the organization's management, but at the same time avoid falling into the trap of focusing exclusively on the manager as a person and as a role.

These tensions are relevant for all managers, not least for managers in companies where the technical and professional professionalism is strong. When this is the case, the management role is often relegated into something in the background. It is also relevant for companies that are managed by very strong charismatic management profiles, where the founder during the early development phase undertook many aspects of the management process, first as a manager, and later as a unifying symbol, but where the need for management changes with the development. In short, the challenge is about re-evaluating and developing the content of the "manager's job description" to reflect the needs of the employees and the organization. Simplicity, efficiency, and transparency can be favored when the responsibility for management is placed with one (or few) persons. But these qualities must be balanced against the empowerment, discipline, and flexibility produced by a more complex distributed management system.

Another factor is that the organizational environment to a large extent determines what the managers are empowered to do in their management role. Rosabeth Moss

Kanter says in her article "Power failure in management circuits" (1979, 2017) that a prerequisite for good management is that the individual has been delegated the power that enables him or her to function as a manager and is perceived as a legitimate and interesting partner for employees, colleagues, and customers. In this way, it is critical that the organization provides the manager with a mandate that enables her or him to be a good manager. Without this "power", there is not much even the most competent and otherwise talented manager can do to develop the organization.

In recent years, it is increasingly becoming inappropriate for a manager to decide exactly how tasks should be performed. Self-management is becoming increasingly widespread. It is an additional dimension to this tension that the manager must step out of the limelight, be professionally relevant, and at the same time be skilled in their own primary competence: management. It may well be that the old manager roles are disappearing, but the tensions demonstrate how the reality of modern companies requires much more intelligent efforts from managers to solve the management task at hand.

#3: Matrix *and* functional organizing – balancing organizational flexibility with specialization

Working in a post-modern organization is ripe with tensions, in that they invite you to balance organizational flexibility versus specialization organized in matrix or functional structures (Galbraith, 1971; Lawrence, Kolodny, and Davis, 1977; Bartlett and Ghoshal, 1990). The poles of this paradox can be described in relation to how, and especially by whom, such tensions are managed. In a silo-based organization, employees work with like-minded and skilled colleagues, who are specializing within their areas of operation. Production specialists work closely with other production specialists, and marketing people work with others from marketing. The group enjoys the shelter of a silo guarding them from the numerous tensions that might disturb them on a day-to-day basis. At the opposite pole, members of a matrix organization exist in the flux of tensions, connecting to people, projects, and developments in an autonomous fashion, and doing so without the luxury of departmental confinements. As free agents, matrix members are to navigate paradoxical tensions themselves, constantly having to reflect on how to create meaning in their work life while answering to dual (or multiple) lines of authority, and thus experience paradoxical tensions. Functional managers tend to prefer projects with high-profile, clear output specifications or political significance and such projects tend to attract high-performing individuals with strong track records who appreciate agency and future options. Tensions in abundant amounts emerge when juxtaposing a silo-based versus a matrix form of organization.

Silos feed on categorical differences, and they are consequently everywhere: between departments, between teams, between professions, between day and night shift, between the first and the second office floor, everywhere a distinction can be used for drawing up a line between us and them. Much has been written about the benefits of tearing down silos (for example, de Waal et al., 2019) and the involved difficulties (for example, North and Coors, 2010). Certainly, silos inhibit knowledge sharing and coordination across organizational boundaries. Silos promote group-thinking and a "us against them", based on a lack of insight into what "the others" on the other side of the fence in fact do, think, or want. But silos are also communities of shared expertise and practice professionalism, specialization into tasks, subjects, projects, and specialized deliveries. In this way, they contribute to psychological safety, belonginess, and employee well-being. Silos can be of importance for building and maintaining professionalism, quality, and performance, and can enhance opportunity for agile, self-led teams. As teams build a shared frame of reference and establish common grounds, that is, a group norms and culture, they also, according to Tuckman (2001), start performing.

As organizational and task complexity increases, organizations often respond by mirroring this complexity through the implementation of matrix-based structures. Matrix is a hybrid structure, where projects span functional structures, allowing multidisciplinary teams to combine from different departments into a shared effort. This results in an organizational complexity, in which employees from across the organization work on a shared process. Such a process does not have a designated manager, and a process is comprised of employees, who also have their function or line manager to answer to. Complexity increases as employees become assigned or otherwise get involved with several projects. In that case they must manage their effort according to an array of conditions, which become tensions that pull the employee's time and attention in a multitude of directions. Matrix organizations allow for a more flexible and agile use of their human resources, as employees are allowed to use their expertise across projects, rather than being confined to a functional unit. Additionally, professional expertise can contribute to building services or solutions that better comply with the functional units involved. Hence, rather than embarking on a research and development (R&D) driven development project, marketing might have a cue on what similar products competitors might already have, sales might have an idea of the needs of their customer base, and production on what might be possible to produce. Matrix organizations combine the efficiency of a functional design, with the flexibility and responsiveness of multidivisional forms (Hatch and Cunliffe, 2006), which in practice act as two intermingled structures. Project managers oversee specific tasks relevant to project delivery and completion, whereas functional managers allocate specialists and other resources to projects.

In a concise way, the key tensions of this paradox can be described as, "At what level should organizational complexity be addressed?" A managerial-oriented response would point toward a silo-oriented organization that allows employees to "dig in", while boundary-expanding activities would be handled by a manager. An employee-oriented response would point toward a matrix-oriented organization, which throws its employees into the heat of battle while having to deal with organizational tensions, dual structures, and varying managerial attachments, while autonomously navigating the organizational flux of tensions.

#4: Purpose, passion, *and* performance

A company cannot survive in the long run if it does not "perform", that is, performs on the success criteria that are relevant to it. However, a one-sided look at performance may result in the fact that the employees do not engage themselves. If the lack of commitment manifests itself in dissatisfaction, insecurity, or perceived meaninglessness, it becomes a threat to performance. The task is therefore to find the balance between on the one hand ensuring organizational performance and, on the other, creating a leadership environment with good conditions for employee engagement. In recent years, this paradox has been exacerbated by the fact that companies' performance is no longer simply measured on traditional, quantitative ratios (for example, sales, productivity, bottom line, and market share), but also on the company's social and ethical standing. It is further sharpened by the fact that the employees' commitment (ultimately in the form of passion) is not only linked to the close working conditions, but also – and especially – the company's overall purpose (identity), identity, values, and responsibility. The assumption is therefore that purpose leads to passion, which in turn leads to performance.

Managerial discussion in the nineteenth century was concerned with diverging ideas on how to make businesses thrive. On one side, Frederick W. Taylor emphasized performance through scientific management (Taylor, 2004). On the other stood the unions and their emphasis on employee well-being and working conditions. During the twentieth century, this debate found new forms and arguments, but how to effectively manage engagement is a remaining issue. The two poles of this paradox juxtapose a purpose-oriented versus a performance-management oriented approach to building and maintaining employee engagement. At the first pole lies the performance and measure driven understanding seen in performance management, and it concerns shaping and directing of employee efforts in the right direction and to a proper extent. This involves breaking down complex tasks into measurable sub-tasks. It integrates behavior that allows for quantitative calculation, monitoring, and comparison. At the opposite pole is the purpose-oriented approach to driving employee engagement through commitment to a compelling organizational purpose and by fostering passion for the task. This approach opposes the heartless work situation embodied by Taylorism at the Ford factory assembly lines, and instead aims to bring meaningfulness into the job.

The task of measuring is often handed to HR, tasked with defining the key indicators that provide a valid image of performance according to company strategies. Such measures often address "hard data" in terms of production and sales figures, but increasingly also "soft data" in behavior, well-being, management style, or engagement.

This approach is often cited in the words attributed to Einstein or Cameron (1963, p. 13): "not everything that can be counted counts, and not everything that counts can be counted.", stating the performance indicators often fail in grasping the complexity of tasks, with a consequent shift of employee engagement and efforts elsewhere. Focusing extensively on performance is likely to have a lopsidedness in terms of employee well-being. However, this may be a one-sided relationship, as while low well-being would be expected to lower performance, high well-being does not necessarily lead to better performance.

Building passion is no easy task. We find passionate employees in professional communities who engage in doing a good job and developing their mutual knowledge within the field, and we find engagement among professionals, who engage and identify with the company's or organization's purpose. Through employee branding efforts, the individual employee can become an important part of what the company is trying to achieve, for example, the phoner contributes to freeing unjustly imprisoned individuals. Another, who sweeps the floor, contributes to putting satellites into orbit or cleaning world oceans. It is expected to create an inexhaustible motivation, that can compensate for stressing work–life balance and endless unpaid overtime. Just as engaged professionals are of extreme value to companies, just as difficult can they be to manage as they tend to "overdo it", not following company strategies or complying with standards, but instead focusing on making a solution tailored to their professional understanding. This might result in too detailed, too complex, and too cumbersome designs if the manager fails to engage with the professional argument and guide efforts in a more appropriate direction.

In the tensions between these two poles, it is fair to say that neither passion nor performance measures are likely to produce an employee who is engaged in fulfilling the company's aim and following its strategies. While both sides of the paradox appear sound when viewed individually, juxtaposing them helps to reveal their downsides, indicating how neither are likely to provide the intended engagement, but are both good starting points for exploring its tensions.

#5: Employee mobility *and* permanence

As free agents and loosely affiliated employees become increasingly common in today's labor market the question can be asked how do you manage, not just them, but the tensions created between those employees, who are in for a brief visit, and those who are planning to stay? This paradox highlights people management in a market that both calls for the flexible use of temporal specialists, and for the prolonged and stable build-up of practice and routine.

This paradox addresses the tensions that emerge when using a combined workforce of permanent staff to ensure deliveries and build-up of routine with temps who provide the company with those extra hands and specialist knowledge when needed. Both may be found to be needed for building profitable businesses and effective organizations. To better understand the tensions of engaging free agents, their use is elaborated in terms of incentives, tasks, knowledge, and concept.

Incentives are key to effective leadership, regardless of the employee's contract. Being a free agent is a matter of choice or necessity. If driven by necessity, temporary employment and zero-hour contracts are reluctantly accepted due to lack of better options. To those driven by choice, being a free agent becomes a lifestyle of flexibility and freedom, allowing them to pick and choose relevant, interesting, educational, profitable, or prestigious assignments, either as a full-time profession, or as supplement to more traditional employment. Not all free agents are happy about the assignment they accept, and not all free agents are cheaply available for all assignments. Agents of choice often have more bargaining power, especially when compared to those of necessity. To permanent staff, the role of stable and predictable employment should not be neglected.

Not all tasks are equally suited for free agents. You rarely see free agents working near the reactors of a nuclear power plant, neither do you see them on the production floor in facilities with very stable production flows, for example, financial institutions or dairies. Apart from mission-critical, highly confidential, high-risk and high-stability tasks, free agents are seen taking care of almost everything else. For such tasks, it becomes necessary to build up stable operations by retaining a permanent staff.

Knowledge brought into a company through a free agent is temporal, and managers are expected to make the most of it while it lasts. Using free agents allows companies to bring in specialist knowledge and expertise within areas that are either found to be unavailable or unviable to retain at permanent basis. A different kind of free agent is brought in as extra hands, either to man an outlet, help out during seasonal bustle, or to build a roof. The bargaining power of such agents is greatly determined by the state of markets, but generally significantly lower than that of the specialist.

At this point, it is tempting to conceptually think of a free agent as an employee, who is loosely employed with the company, but the free agent is not necessarily a specific person. As companies increasingly use Internet platforms for posting tasks or problems, those postings are often addressed by a community, who co-jointly offer a solution, either on how to do it, or offers to do the practical work. Designers would make their talents available through platforms, either for co-creative processes, or by offering concrete solutions, often to parts of the posted challenge, just as support workers would make their services available, either directly to a company, or through a temp agency. In this sense, free agents can be thought of as professional networks that can be utilized for companies, either to comply with events in a flexible manner, or as an expansion strategy. Despite often being seen as a stop-gap solution, the use of free agents should reflect a strategic choice, just as hiring an employee would.

An orientation toward the free agent pole of this paradox carries several advantages. Free agents allow access to specialist knowledge, offer high flexibility in terms of recruitment and termination, which allows companies to quickly adapt to market opportunities and emergencies. From an HR perspective, free agents offer employment without benefits, and can be used for having candidates on trial before deciding on more permanent employment. When the use of free agents takes the form of outsourcing, companies can expand their workforce without growing their capacity costs. An orientation toward the other pole and relying on more permanent staff carries with it other advantages. A key advantage is the gradual build-up of trust, routines, standards, and quality, as well as being able to deal with more complex problems as they would be unsuitable for splitting up and define the elements necessary for a free agent to be able to work on them. A permanent staff also allows for the long-term development and monitoring of key competencies. As free agents and permanent staff work under different conditions and enjoy different privileges and benefits, tensions are likely to arise as they call for different kinds of managerial attention. As free agent and permanent staff contribute differently to the company, such tensions should be explored to provide a better understanding, both on how they should be managed, and eventually also on how they might contribute in new and more productive manners.

#6: Hybrid collaboration – physical *and* virtual presence

During the COVID-19 pandemic various lockdowns caused white-collar workers all over the world to be sent home. Working from home became the new normal in a situation that had little normal about it. Organizations rapidly moved their footing online, and thanks to the creativity of employees for making ends meet, work continued from a distance. While managers gradually realized how employees were able to perform while working from home, and employees became accustomed to the flexibility of doing so, light began to appear at the end of the tunnel: What would happen next?

The two poles of this paradox each suggested very different scenarios: Would companies and organizations force their workers back in a Monday to Friday schedule, working nine to five, or would they realize how well employees function without their offices, and ultimately adopt a model of shipping office equipment home to employees, for them to sell off their cooperate domiciles. Neither scenario seemed appealing to employees, who recognized the benefits of not having to commute, being able to flexibly schedule according to private concerns and focus on their tasks. But at the same time, they envisaged the cost of being deprived of face-to-face contact with colleagues and managers, spontaneous conversation and knowledge sharing, and from the commodities of going to the office. Managers were caught between having to pay capacity costs for unused offices on one side and experiencing how the wear and tear of the online solution started to negatively affect knowledge sharing, innovation processes, and also employee retainment and well-being.

While often synonymous with working from home, distance work could be working from anywhere but the office, while being somewhere else than one's manager. This includes the traveling salesperson and construction workers visiting geographically dispersed customers, and project managers stationed overseas. Geography is merely one among several distances to consider. Subsidiaries and developers overseas are often affected by time differences, so is the night shift when compared to management's office hours, and prior, physical meetings, collaboration experience, and trust greatly affects the quality of working at a distance. Lojeski and Reilly (2020) describes the ideas of the conception of virtual distance, and thereby the factors that subtly pushes us apart when working at a distance. Working at a distance runs on trust and well-established common grounds. A key contribution of distance working is the remarkable better use of resources. Rather than doing two visits per day to customers or construction sites, virtual meetings could be done, saving valuable transportation time and efforts. A specialist can become available to distant outlets digitally, allowing for them to operate by maintaining only a minimal crew with generalist skillsets. Time spent commuting to and from the office can be used for something else. Greater flexibility can impact the work–life balance.

To test the manifestation of the paradox, a manager might ask: "Does this act of management require my physical presence, or would sending a mail suffice?" or put to a head in terms of communication, "What can I get away with?" Contemporary communication theory subscribes to Daft and Lengel's (1986) notion of using the richest possible communication media, ranking face-to-face communication as the richest, and Short Message Service (SMS) and similar as poor communication media. A rich communication media is characterized by providing immediate feedback, for example, as confirmatory nodding and facial expressions, whereas poor media provide little context for understanding the message and is easily subject to misunderstanding. Post-modern distance management emphasizes using the barely adequate, rather than richest media. If a mail would do the job, why have an online meeting or show up in person? Choosing the right media requires a high degree of managerial techno skill to ensure that digital media are used in deliberate, intuitive, and effective manners. If not, focus shifts from the intended message to the troublesome use of communication media and away from what we are trying to achieve. But digital media also have their limitations. Due to the slight delay in video conferencing, you cannot time your words, and a confirmative "yes" easily becomes a disturbance in the other end.

Compared to being physically present, this impacts spontaneity as speaking online requires considerable techno skills. Being physically present can be expensive and time consuming, requiring both coordination and a space to be, but has several advantages that cannot be made up for online. Eye contact cannot be achieved online due to the physical placement of the webcam. Being able to look the employee or manager in the eyes and get the feeling of physical presence allows for you to build trust and relations, and a shared frame of reference is immanent in the dialogical nature of face-to-face meetings. Imagine telling a joke to someone (or something romantic to your partner) and they freeze up. One second passes, two seconds pass, and then they react. That would be how your brain experiences being in an online meeting, compared to a physical meeting. A physical meeting allows a much wider bandwidth of impressions to be registered and processed. In comparison, distance management relies on limited communication channels, for example, by only conveying what is shown to the camera.

As the demand for hybrid working arrangement increases, it is not only a question of navigating the tensions involved in virtual collaboration in insolation. Rather, in the hybrid workplace managers need to lead and collaborate in hybrid formats as well as under conditions of hybridity with employees and managers being physically and virtually present at the same time.

#7: Differentiation/localization *and* integration/globalization

A core classical challenge of leadership and organization is concern how to ensure the right differentiation and at the same time an appropriate integration (Lawrence and Lorsch, 1967). In organizations, frequently a decision must be made on how many hands are available for the tasks and at the same time it is necessary to ensure that work is done in an integrated manner. Tensions emerge as soon as two or more people must undertake a task: Should they perform the same task in parallel, or should they divide the task so that one of them solves part of the task and the other undertakes the rest? The first method has the advantage that both people have an overview of and responsibility for the overall task, but also the disadvantage that they may solve the task differently. Conversely, the other way allows each person to refine and streamline the task solution for his or her own part, but it also means that the two of them become dependent on each other's work and may begin to argue about which part of the task is the most important.

This tension is particularly salient in global or multinational companies. On the one hand such organizations need to differentiate their services and processes to meet local production conditions and customer needs in the different markets, but on the other hand they also want to integrate across the organization to save costs as well as to utilize unique competencies and knowledge optimally. Corporations and organizations often experience the liability of foreignness when moving into new markets, and in effect suffer a globalization penalty vis-à-vis local competition in different markets. At the same time, they are forced to consider the potential non-transferability of domestic competitive advantages and business models, when moving into new territory and they may have to adjust to cater to different customer preferences and other local specificities in a variety of markets simultaneously. Further, international and global collaboration is more complex than local collaboration. Consequently, corporations need to be better at collaborating to receive the same effect compared to domestic operations alone. Since culturally and strategically employees and managers at all hierarchical levels have some limits in their understanding of each other, and language barriers may on top of that place a strain on communication and collaboration. Transaction costs rise as corporations move from high-context collaboration with low psychic distance in a domestic setting or between relatively similar groupings, where many things are shared and taken for granted. In such contexts, everything needs not be explicated as it would in a low-context communication setting where little or no common ground can be taken for granted.

A central argument in this respect is how a global mindset entails a broader and more multi-faceted conceptualization of globality and global operations than a traditional cross-cultural understanding. Navigation of the local–global divide involves boundary-crossing and an awareness in a broader sense of the word "global" going beyond geographical borders and national cultural group affiliation. This is in keeping with an interpretation of the word "global" as involving or relating to all the parts or aspects of a situation, being all-embracing, inter-disciplinary, and holistic. For example, according to the *Collins Cobuild English/English Dictionary*, "global" means both "1) Concerning and including the whole world" and "2) Involving or relating to all the parts or aspects of a situation". The second definition of the word, for example, allows for an understanding of "global" as transverse, total, and interdisciplinary. And holistic. Individual and organizational navigation is not only a question of border-crossing and cosmopolitanism, but an ability to successfully handle the duality of local and global, the need for simultaneous diversity and homogeneity. As such, there is an increased need for intercultural sensitivity among a larger number of persons, and this is just one tension involved in operating in globality. Balancing the paradox of the simultaneous pursuit of simplicity, standardization, and cost-efficiency as well as differentiation and sensitivity to local specificities adds to strategic complexity.

The research literature on international management and global leadership suggests that *"[a] company's ability to develop transnational organizational capability and management mentality will be the key factor that separates the winners from the mere survivors in the emerging international environment"* (Bartlett and Ghoshal, 1987, p. 7) and that the content and processes of multinational firms' sensemaking systems can be a distinct competitive advantage or disadvantage. Often it is suggested for organizations to develop an overall global mindset or "glocal" organizational culture. Only recently, researchers have begun to view the local–global tension as a paradox that needs not be synthesized into one common third way, but rather co-existing forces that managers and organizations must balance on an ongoing basis. So, when referring to the local–global tension in exemplars throughout the book we take our point of departure in the fact that the local and the global are interconnected aspects of international/global operations, a persisting tension that poses managers with the challenge of pursuing local and global objectives at the same time.

#8: Innovating outside–in *and* inside–out

Innovation is claimed to be a prerequisite in all types of organizations, private business as well as public institutions and civil society organization. But should organizations try to keep their good ideas to themselves? Should they protect them against digital and physical espionage? Develop them under the highest degree of secrecy? Or should they rather talk widely about the ambitions regarding the development of products and services? Bombard customers, suppliers, even competitors with animated information? Will such an attitude and practice increase the chance and opportunities to acquire unexpected, yet useful feedback, even response that could change the direction of the organization's more fundamental endeavors, its key competences (Hjalager, 2018)?

Interdisciplinary collaboration with, for example, customers, competitors, civil society, and public actors place great demands on companies, not least a balance between being able to reap profits and anticipate the costs of user involvement, but also make oneself vulnerable to new risks. Involvement processes require a conscious strategy and leadership for the manager to make them work. The speed of change in society embraces a critical argument for a more open innovation style as amply demonstrated by the COVID-19 crisis. If an enterprise cannot expect to be able to monopolize its ideas and create surplus economic and other advantages for itself for very long, it might as well be open about its ambitions. Terms like "open innovation", "co-creation", "co-innovation", "crowdsourcing", "user-driven innovation", and so forth are flooding the management discussion. The general advice to managers tends to lean toward the more the better of the open knowledge flows, yet it is a balancing act. A priority is given to the outside–in, and organizations should try to harvest whatever comes from it. More infrequently, the opposite, the closed inside–out, is advocated. But there may be something to protect in the organization, sunk costs to beware of, valuable traditions and brands, that constitute the foundation of an organization, without this immaterial capital being shielded, it would be vulnerable to eager copycats. There is a tension that can be investigated and can deliver insights for the individual organization beyond the managerial buzzwords.

Managers may consider a range of aspects of the paradox. These aspects are critical for the managerial balancing exercise. One of the questions that the enquiries into knowledge flows raise concerns the nature of the information needed. Is the organization drained for inspiration? Is it stuck in its habitual thinking? Maybe the customers and suppliers are also ready on the doorstep to deliver their inputs, but the organization is closing its ears? We know better, we have been in this business for ages? But observed in connection with challenges that may be emerging in society, management should ask what knowledge is nice to have, and what is needed.

A check of the organizational culture is also worthwhile. By virtue of their task, some organizations are very closed, and employees may talk to and get inspiration from one another, but not (openly) from outsiders. In most enterprises, the cultural preconditions are flexible and amendable. But management's signals and expectation could perhaps be more transparent. In some organizations, employees chose not to talk a lot about their job to family and friends; in others the identity of the staff is so much connected to work, so they will be living information hubs – inside–out and outside–in. Managers cannot overnight change knowledge flows that employees are comfortable with. However, generational shifts in organization can be underway, and under the surface, attitudes are changing, perhaps with the managers not being fully aware. Conflicts and tensions may be the immanent response to differences in the way knowledge is handled at all levels of the organizational hierarchy.

The R&D department may be as closed as an oyster, closed with seven locks, impermeable in all ways. The marketing department is, however, showcasing all aspects of its operation. Criticism from customers, lack of likes in social media, are signals immediately reacted on, and successes in attention go viral. This is the most stereotypical understanding of knowledge management internally in a corporation, and they represent the far ends of a scale. But in terms of reflecting on paradoxes, this may be a too limited and constraining understanding of the benefits of open versus closed knowledge flows. The peripheral positions may benefit from being seen in new light.

Generally, departments and activities with very visible and ever-changing outputs have less to lose from openness in knowledge policies. Contrarily, the cumbersome investment in hard-to-access knowledge invites a higher degree of protection. Hence, managers will have to weigh openness versus closedness on a cost and investment scale. These years, the cost aspect is supplemented with a new dimension, as the user-based knowledge, for example via crowdsourcing, can be free or at least cheaper than building and maintaining internal departments. However, other types of costs are invoked in the outside–in side, as also the handling of external inputs, and the creative collaboration with outsiders will demand resources and competences. Does the organization possess relevant profiles for such tasks?

The cost perspective has other aspects. The evaluation of new ideas and creative inputs requires organizational memory. If staff turnover is high, the organizational memory suffers. If the organization also works with talent development programs that move staff rapidly away from functions where they dwelled for some time, there may be a self-inflicted paradox. Talent and career programs have an embedded double impact: Perhaps knowledge will be moved with the career seeker to another place in the organization that can benefit, if addressed in a proper way? Or good knowledge is lost in the transition? This paradox is an integrated, although not well-considered side of corporate life.

Significant core competences in the organization stand against and should be contrasted with an understanding of core rigidities. When considering the basic ideas of knowledge flows, the rigidities at all levels become interesting. Society is moving constantly, but "old" knowledge can be revitalized, as is presently the case in the societal and business fields of recycling, upcycling, and so on. Both material and immeterial assets are potential sources of rigidities. Social agendas can change the relevance and the benefit of those who out of foresight or conservatism let themselves be left behind with some of the traditional resources. Most managers will be aware of both competencies and rigidities, but often they celebrate only the competences.

#9: Digital transformation – human resources *and* technological "non-human resources"

> We used to believe that 'thinking work' was insulated from mechanization. However, what machines
> have wrought on 'doing work' for the last 300 years they will do to 'thinking work' in the next 50.
> (Phan, Wright and Lee, 2017, p. 253)

Digital transformation is an ongoing phenomenon in most organizations. The so-called fourth industrial revolution foresees revolutionary technological changes that will profoundly impact work and competences. These changes stem from digitalization and automation as well as increased use of intelligent machines and give rise to new business models and value-producing opportunities. The emergence and demand for hybrid working arrangements in many companies discussed in field #6 is but one of the technology-supported or induced changes taking place. But technological developments do not just mean new technological solutions. New technological opportunities have the potential to disrupt markets, work processes, relationships, forms of management, and professions. Complexity increases, and paradoxes arise when new solutions bring with them both new possibilities and side-effects, which must be dealt with at the same time.

The interplay between human and non-human resources is essential when companies want to be able to capitalize on new technological possibilities. But the interplay also contains many opposing movements and considerations that call for not only technical know-how, but also management innovation to be able to handle both technology and the derivative effects in a value-creating way. Examples of such fields of tension could be the interaction between (wo-)man and tools, be it collaborative robot technology, chatbots, large language models, and algorithms. The use of intelligent machines for augmentation and/or automation of human tasks must be balanced against each other and new interconnections between supplementary machine-assistance and substitute machine usage emerge (Raisch and Krakowski, 2021).

Also, so-called explainable decision support via artificial intelligence (AI) and machine learning versus "unexplained"/black box artificial intelligence create new tension: Intelligent machines may have "better" answers, but no one understands why. Complexity reduction through the processing of Big Data can lead to complexity amplification and information pollution, where we may become wiser, but at the same time confused on a higher level. Likewise, new ethical challenges appear by virtue of the possibility of monitoring/tracking employees in new ways accompanied by additional need for securing civil rights, (cyber)security, and privacy. Virtual relationships with, for instance, customers and employees are at the same time made more tailored and personal through technology, and at the same time more distanced and mechanical. Competence destruction takes place side by side with competence development, and work must be done to avoid a division into A- and B-teams between the technically intelligent and the less technically gifted. Increasingly, non-standard workers are connected to corporations through online labor platforms performing quasi-management functions, thus disconnecting central management functions from the hiring leader's responsibility: *"Although the workers are officially considered independent contractors, many platform firms are tasked with workers' recruitment, selection, evaluation and retention, even if some of these traditional management functions are performed by automated algorithms"* (Kuhn and Maleki, 2017, p. 183; also see #5, Employee mobility and permanence). "Gadget fascination", pressure to follow "management fashions", and unreflective hyper-adaptation to the media landscape must be assessed against specific needs and consequences for the organization's core services, values, and resources.

New technology involves an opportunity to reorganize work in new ways; algorithmic management is not solely a concern in platform work. Increasingly, other types of work are organized by algorithms and substitutable technology: *"We find that about 30% of the activities in 60% of all occupations could be automated. This means that most workers – from welders to mortgage brokers to CEOs – will work alongside rapidly evolving machines. The nature of these occupations will likely change as a result"* (Manyika and Sneader, 2018, p. 6). Management is among the least automatable activities but there is still a significant number of management tasks that are automatable. For sure, administrative tasks are prone to automation and digitalization and so we must foresee a situation where managers will be driving a job content revolution among their employees that also affects their own work significantly.

Some have speculated if artificial intelligence and digitalization could produce better leaders making better decisions: *"What if leaders knew as much about their organizations as Google knows about them? By deploying appropriate technologies, it is possible today for organizations to capture data on practically every interaction and consolidate every performance metric in an organization"* (Aurik, 2018, tenth paragraph). Thus, improved decision-making and a more all-inclusive overview that also gives voice to unexpected results is potentially a consequence; at the same time management by algorithm poses the problem of understanding and trust. Explaining the decisions made by machine learning algorithms is technically challenging, and so managers may make potentially more evidence-based decisions, but cannot explain how they came about to followers or investors and so on. In a similar vein, ethical considerations are central to working with intelligent machines. One observer commenting on the future of leadership in the wake of technological change:

> *No doubt many people think this is where managerial leadership is headed, for they presume there can be a formal or computable theory of leadership into which its professionals can be trained – a curiously dogmatic approach that seems to deny our socio-historical circumstances, reminding us*

of the Icarus fable. No computing system will be able to anticipate humans' ability to mess up our society and thereby render leadership obsolete. A fully computable society is as dystopian as it is unlikely. (J. C. Spender cited in Örtenblad, 2018, p. 4)

We will not try our luck as futurists, but we will observe that technology-driven organizational change is a paradoxical tension on the rise as new technology brings about a reorchestration of the division of labor between machines and humans, be it employees or managers. Managers and their followers face the task of dealing with all these paradoxes agilely and efficiently – and not least together across professional boundaries and disciplines.

#10: Sustainabilities – profit *and* people *and* planet

Sustainability leadership and transformation encompass multiple dimensions: Per definition organizational sustainability demands the integration of environmental, social, and economic outcomes (Benkert, 2021) sometimes framed in an organizational context as a simultaneous consideration of "people, planet, profit" or the "triple bottom line" pursuing "development that meets the needs of the present without compromising the ability of future generations to meet their own needs (World Commission on Environment and Development, 1987). This has also propelled the "responsible" ESG-agenda in the investment community (Evironment, Social, Governance). As such, leading and managing sustainability is a question of addressing sustainability in plural, *sustainabilities*, in that the individual aspects of sustainability are interconnected in a myriad of ways, where advancement of one dimension of sustainability may create both negative as well as positive synergies to other dimensions (Jay, Soderstrom and Grant, 2017; Gao and Bansal, 2013; Hahn et al., 2018). Sustainability has been described as a paradoxical, wicked problem (Starik and Kanashiro, 2013) characterized by multiple stakeholders, disputed values, complex interconnectedness, foggy problem definition, limited or contested knowledge, and ongoing change (McMillan and Overall, 2016). The consequence is that it makes sense to explore dimensions of sustainability together instead of one-dimensionality to capture interactive effects as well as side-effects.

Grand societal challenges such as environmental sustainability foresee the concerted action of a web of stakeholders (Schad and Smith, 2019). Collective paradox navigation by different stakeholders involved in sustainable transformation also involves a normative dimension in that coping with paradox can be facilitated by educating stakeholders in paradox thinking as well as educating stakeholders about the paradoxes involved in paradoxes of sustainability. Sustainable transformation foresees a break with unsustainable norms, habits, practices, and structures, and so ability and motivation to engage in sustainability paradoxes also involves a change of beliefs and values about sustainability (Boström et al., 2018). The importance of personal values for the absorption of knowledge related to sustainability has been emphasized in a study by van Poeck, Goeminne and Vandenabeele (2016). Driving a value transformation involves the ability of leaders to avail themselves of a diverse set of perspectives to understand different positions and points of view.

Research literature on sustainability development often portray such an endeavor from a counterpoint or conflict perspective, where different development and learning objectives are seen as contrasting, competing approaches. The theoretical fields of learning for sustainable development and sustainability education distinguishes between two different learning foci – and instrumental focus or a focus on inner motivation. The instrumental views conceive of sustainability development as *"a remedial vehicle by which such qualities as increased awareness and understanding, and attitudinal and valuative change leading to action towards environmental protection can be attained"* (Sterling, 2010, p. 513). That is, the objective of developmental activity is predefined and known beforehand, whereby the advancement of certain predefined sustainability goals is seen as the preferred outcome. By contrast, the developmental view takes its point of departure in learners' motivation and the development of learners' ability to make adequate choices facing uncertainty and complexity.

A middle road between the instrumental and the developmental view of sustainability development is a view of change activities as aimed at the advancement of "culture of critical commitment", trying to foster enough engagement to make a behavioral difference, yet at the same facilitating critical-reflexivity so change actors learn and adapt from experience (instead of mindlessly sticking to, for example, plans or rules), keep options open and calibrate to novel situations, contexts, or knowledge (Sterling and Gray-Donald, 2007). The growing literature in paradoxical tension in sustainable human resource development (Hughes, 2019) also points to a middle position in organizational development purposes suggesting the combination of common vision and plan as an umbrella for a) obligatory behaviors, b) encouraged behaviors and c) voluntary behaviors to ensure common ground, yet leaving room to maneuver (Ren and Jackson, 2020).

Leading sustainable transformation is fraught with tensions due to the need for simultaneous consideration for contradictory objectives (economy, social, environment) as well as within-tension conflicts due to knotted paradoxes (combination of different paradoxes) and nestedness of paradoxes across different stakeholders and contexts, that is, conflicting or contrasting views and responsibilities related to the pursuit of paradoxical sustainability goals. Acting is central, but no closure is realistic, as the balancing of competing demands will continue to demand attention and navigation on an ongoing basis (Smith and Lewis, 2011, p. 387). Sustainable transformation involved is developmental leadership efforts aimed at facilitating sustainable behavior, yet the degree to which competency development should be instrumental or critic-reflexive is a balancing act.

Opening Pandora's box of leadership paradoxes

Having read through the 10 fields of paradoxical tensions in leadership, you may have identified two or three fields that you find particularly relevant. Or perhaps you have been inspired to think of other paradoxical challenges in your leadership role that would be interesting for you to explore in more detail? In our experience, most managers find the concept of paradox leadership relatively accessible when it comes to their individual leadership paradoxes. However, when it comes to grasping the connection between organizational paradoxes and individual paradoxes it often gets much more complex and difficult. Regardless of your choice of paradox, we encourage you to work with a paradoxical tension from your everyday life that connects with the wider organizational paradoxes in your workplace. At the outset, you may think of the tightrope of work–life balance, or the difficulty involved in combining a managerial identity with an identity as specialist/professional, for example, "As an engineer, I love large projects; as a business manager I love a portfolio of small projects." But if you fail to connect individualized aspects of your chosen paradox with wider organizational concerns, your efforts are likely to find too little support in your environment when you get to acting on your paradox. In the given examples, you might want to connect your personal challenges of work–life balance with field #6 on hybrid work arrangements (if that is an issue in your organization), or you may connect your challenges of balancing a specialist role with a managerial role to field #3 about horizontal and hierarchical forms of organization (if this is a relevant challenge in your organization). So, you are advised to start with a paradox that resonates with both you and your organization, but to only choose one paradox to work with (at the same time). After having been presented with specific examples of paradox, people often respond by reflecting, "OK, but aren't they intertwined?" And yes, they are – one paradox rarely comes alone. For instance, sustainability encompasses multiple dimensions of environmental, social, and economic considerations – and typically a lot more once you unfold sustainability paradox from an individual manager's perspective. Also, tensions can be nested within tensions and knotted, entangled in bundles of paradoxes (Andriopoulos and Lewis, 2009; Jarzabkowski, Lê and Van de Ven, 2013; Henriksen et al., 2021).

Current advances in paradox theory focus on paradoxes in plural and the ways in which paradoxes intertwine, bundle, and interact with one another (Jarzabkowski et al., 2022). Exploration of nested and knotted paradoxes as multiple, bundled sets of paradoxes that interact negatively or positively has been put forth as one particularly relevant aspect of paradox theory (Putnam, Fairhurst and Banghart, 2016). Researchers have been called upon to focus on the interrelationships of tensions and paradoxes that function as triggers, mitigators, or amplifiers of other paradoxes and that lead to tangled knots (Sheep, Fairhurst and Khazanchi, 2017). Certainly, these are important developments and may also lighten the load when paradox bundling and knotting result in positive synergies. At the same time, they are also developments that increase the complexity of paradox navigation considerably. We advise individual paradox navigators to take it one step at the time, one paradox at the time. Over time – or if you are already an experienced paradox navigator – you may be able to navigate several paradoxes at the same time, but frontloading your process with too much complexity can be counterproductive. The idea is to become energized and inspired to act by going through the five phases of paradox navigation in Part II, not paralyzed by complexity.

References

Andriopoulos, C., and Lewis, M. W. (2009). Exploitation-exploration tensions and organizational ambidexterity: Managing paradoxes of innovation. *Organization Science*, 20(4), 696–717.

Aurik, J. C. (2018). Why automation, not augmentation is needed in leadership, weforum.org, January 19, World Economic Forum, https://www.weforum.org/agenda/2018/01/the-case-for-automating-leadership/

Bartlett, C. A., and Ghoshal, S. (1987). Managing across borders: New strategic requirements. *Sloan Management Review*, 28(4), 7–17.

Bartlett, C. A., and Ghoshal, S. (1990). Matrix management: Not a structure, a frame of mind. *Harvard Business Review*, 68(4), 138–145.

Benkert, J. (2021). Reframing business sustainability decision-making with value-focused thinking. *Journal of Business Ethics*, 174(2), 441–456.

Boström, M., Andersson, E., Berg, M., Gustafsson, K., Gustavsson, E., Hysing, E., . . . and Öhman, J. (2018). Conditions for transformative learning for sustainable development: A theoretical review and approach. *Sustainability*, 10(12), 4479.

Cameron, W. B. (1963). *Informal sociology: A casual introduction to sociological thinking* (Vol. 21), p. 13. New York, NY:Random house.

Daft, R. L., and Lengel, R. H. (1986). Organizational information requirements, media richness and structural design. *Management Science*, 32(5), 554–571.

De Waal, A., Weaver, M., Day, T., and van der Heijden, B. (2019). Silo-busting: Overcoming the greatest threat to organizational performance. *Sustainability*, 11(23), 6860.

D'Souza, D. E., Sigdyal, P., and Struckell, E. (2017). Relative ambidexterity: A measure and a versatile framework. *Academy of Management Perspectives*, 31(2), 124–136.

Galbraith, J. R. (1971). Matrix organization designs. How to combine functional and project forms. *Business Horizons*, 14(1), 29–40.

Gao, J., and Bansal, P. (2013). Instrumental and integrative logics in business sustainability. *Journal of Business Ethics*, 112(2), 241–255.

Hahn, T., Figge, F., Pinkse, J., and Preuss, L. (2018). A paradox perspective on corporate sustainability: Descriptive, instrumental, and normative aspects. *Journal of Business Ethics*, 148(2), 235–248.

Hatch, M. J., and Cunliffe, A. L. (2006). *Modern, Symbolic, and Postmodern Perspectives*. Oxford: Oxford University Press.

Henriksen, T. D., Nielsen, R. K., Vikkelsø, S., Bévort, F., and Mogensen, M. (2021). A paradox rarely comes alone a quantitative approach to investigating knotted leadership paradoxes in SMEs. *Scandinavian Journal of Management*, 37(1), 101135.

Hjalager, A. M. (2018). Indefra-ud kontra udefra-ind. Åbne og lukkede videnflows. In R. K. Nielsen, A. M. Hjalager, H. H. Larsen, F. Bévort, T. D. Henriksen and S. Vikkelsø, *Ledelsesdilemmaer – og kunsten at navigere i moderne ledelse*. Copenhagen, DK: Djøf Publishing, pp. 43–54.

Hughes, C. P. (2019). A paradox perspective on sustainable human resource management. In S. Mariappanadar (Ed.), *Sustainable Human Resource Management. Strategies, Practices and Challenges.* London: Macmillan International Higher Education, chapter 3.

Jarzabkowski, P., Bednarek, R., Chalkias, K., & Cacciatori, E. (2022). Enabling rapid financial response to disasters: Knotting and reknotting multiple paradoxes in interorganizational systems. *Academy of Management Journal*, 65(5), 1477–1506.

Jarzabkowski, P., Lê, J. K., and Van de Ven, A. H. (2013). Responding to competing strategic demands: How organizing, belonging, and performing paradoxes coevolve. *Strategic Organization*, 11(3), 245–280. https://doi.org/10.1177/1476127013481016

Jay, J., Soderstrom, S., and Grant, G. (2017). Navigating the paradox of sustainability. In W. K. Smith, M. W. Lewis, P. Jarzabkowski, and A. Langley (Eds.), *The Oxford Handbook of Organizational Paradox.* Oxford: Oxford University Press, pp. 357–372.

Kanter, R. M. (1979). Power failure in management circuits. *Harvard Business Review*, 57, 65–75.

Kanter, R. M. (2017). Power failure in management circuits. In A. Hooper (Ed.), *Leadership Perspectives.* London, UK: Routledge, pp. 281–290.

Kniffin, K. M., Detert, J. R., and Leroy, H. L. (2020). On leading and managing: Synonyms or separate (and unequal)? *Academy of Management Discoveries*, 6(4), 544–571.

Kuhn, K. M., and Maleki, A. (2017). Micro-entrepreneurs, dependent contractors, and instaserfs: Understanding online labor platform workforces. *Academy of Management Perspectives*, 31(3), 183–200.

Lawrence, P. R., Kolodny, H. F., & Davis, S. M. (1977). The human side of the matrix. *Organizational Dynamics*, 6(1), 43–61.

Lawrence, P. R., and Lorsch, J. W. (1967). Differentiation and integration in complex organizations. *Administrative Science Quarterly*, 12 (1), 1–47.

Leigh Star, S. (2010). This is not a boundary object: Reflections on the origin of a concept. *Science, Technology, and Human Values*, 35(5), 601–617.

Lewis, M. W., and Dehler, G. E. (2000). Learning through paradox: A pedagogical strategy for exploring contradictions and complexity. *Journal of Management Education*, 24(6), 708–725.

Lojeski, K. S., and Reilly, R. R. (2020). *The Power of Virtual Distance: A Guide to Productivity and Happiness in the Age of Remote Work.* Sussex, UK: John Wiley and Sons.

Lunenburg, F. (2013). Leadership versus Management: A key distinction – at least in theory. *Main Issues of Pedagogy and Psychology*, 3(3), 15–18.

Manyika, J., and Sneader, H. (2018). AI, automation, and the future of work: Ten things to solve. www.mckinsey.com, McKinsey Executive Briefing, https://www.mckinsey.com/featured-insights/future-of-work/ai-automation-and-the-future-of-work-ten-things-to-solve-for Last accessed December 22, 2022.

Manz, C. C. (1986). Self-leadership: Toward an expanded theory of self-influence processes in organizations. *Academy of Management Review*, 11(3), 585–600.

McMillan, C., and Overall, J. (2016). Wicked problems: Turning strategic management upside down. *Journal of Business Strategy*, 37(1), 34–43.

Minsky, M. (2007). *The Emotion Machine: Commonsense Thinking, Artificial Intelligence, and the Future of the Human Mind.* New York, NY: Simon and Schuster.

North, M., and Coors, C. (2010). Avoiding death by dotted line. *HFM (Healthcare Financial Management)*, 64 (1), 120–121.

O'Reilly III, C. A., and Tushman, M. L. (2013). Organizational ambidexterity: Past, present, and future. *Academy of Management Perspectives*, 27(4), 324–338.

Örtenblad, A. (2018). *Professionalizing Leadership: Debating Education, Certification and Practice.* Cham, SCH: Springer.

Örtenblad, A., Hong, J. and Snell. R. (2016) Good leadership: A mirage in the desert? *Human Resource Development International*, 19, 349–357.

Pearce, C. L., Conger, J. A., and Locke, E. A. (2008). Shared leadership theory. *The Leadership Quarterly*, 19 (5), 622–628.

Phan, P., Wright, M., and Lee, S. H. (2017). Of robots, artificial intelligence, and work. *Academy of Management Perspectives*, 31(4), 253–255.

Putnam, L. L., Fairhurst, G. T., & Banghart, S. (2016). Contradictions, dialectics, and paradoxes in organizations: A constitutive approach. *Academy of Management Annals*, 10(1), 65–171.

Raisch, S., and Krakowski, S. (2021). Artificial intelligence and management: The automation–augmentation paradox. *Academy of Management Review*, 46(1), 192–210.

Ren, S., and Jackson, S. E. (2020). HRM institutional entrepreneurship for sustainable business organizations. *Human Resource Management Review*, 30(3), 100691.

Schad, J., and Smith, W. K. (2019). Addressing grand challenges' paradoxes: Leadership skills to manage inconsistencies. *Journal of Leadership Studies*, 12(4), 55–59. https://doi.org/10.1002/jls.21609

Sheep, M. L., Fairhurst, G. T., & Khazanchi, S. (2017). Knots in the discourse of innovation: Investigating multiple tensions in a reacquired spin-off. *Organization Studies*, *38*(3–4), 463–488.

Smith, W. K., and Lewis, M. W. (2011). Toward a theory of paradox: A dynamic equilibrium model of organizing. *Academy of Management Review*, 36(2), 381–403.

Starik, M., and Kanashiro, P. (2013). Toward a theory of sustainability management: Uncovering and integrating the nearly obvious. *Organization and Environment*, 26(1), 7–30.

Sterling, S. (2010). *Sustainability Education: Perspectives and Practice across Higher Education*. London, UK: Taylor and Francis.

Sterling, S., and Gray-Donald, J. (2007). Special issue on sustainability and education: Towards a culture of critical commitment. *International Journal of Innovation and Sustainable Development*, 2(3–4), 241–248.

Stewart, G. L., Courtright, S. H., and Manz, C. C. (2011). Self-leadership: A multilevel review. *Journal of Management*, 37(1), 185–222.

Taylor, F. W. (2004). *Scientific management*. London, UK: Routledge.

Tuckman, B. W. (2001). Developmental sequence in small groups. *Group Facilitation*, 3, Spring (2001), 66.

Van Poeck, K., Goeminne, G., and Vandenabeele, J. (2016). Revisiting the democratic paradox of environmental and sustainability education: Sustainability issues as matters of concern. *Environmental Education Research*, 22(6), 806–826.

World Commission on Environment and Development (1987). *Report of the World Commission on Environment and Development: Our Common Future*. United Nations through Oxford: Oxford University Press.

Part II: **Navigating leadership paradox in practice**

This part of the book takes you through the five phases of paradox navigation introduced in Chapter 2 (Figure II.1).

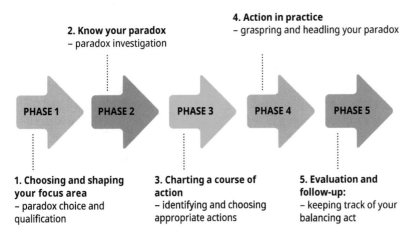

Figure II.1: The five phases of paradox navigation.

The five phases as well as the tools and cases presented in the following five chapters are based on our analysis of data gathered in connection with an action-learning program (Revans, 1998) and associated research project. Impatient readers may go straight to the first phase of paradox navigation in Chapter 4; readers interested in a look into the research machine room of this research project may get further information in the following:

The research project was motivated by a call for research projects exploring "new principles of leadership" made by the Danish Industry Foundation (Danish Industry Foundation, 2017). In particular, the foundation was interested in facilitating development of knowledge that could assist managers and corporations coping with increased complexity and navigating strategically in a constantly changing context. The more specific nature of the challenges to be addressed was outlined in two Delphi-technique (Dalkey and Helmer, 1963) inspired "future workshops" conducted by the Foundation engaging large groups of managers in discussing and defining the most pressing challenges to be addressed (Danish Industry Foundation, 2016; Centre for Future Studies, 2016). Among these challenges, coping with complexity in leadership featured centrally, and our initial research proposal entitled "The Leadership GPS" set out to explore 10 such paradoxical leadership challenges (cf. our expanded and revised presentation in Chapter 3).

The research project had three phases. In Phase 1, the researcher team conducted a literature review of the 10 leadership challenges identified in the proposal phase and collected these in a white book communicated to professionals (Bévort et al., 2018; Nielsen et al., 2018). The scope and center of gravity of the research project,

https://doi.org/10.1515/9783110788877-004

however, was a six-month action learning program, where researchers and participating companies explored complex leadership challenges in practice, the balances they require, and how they can be handled. The research project included close collaboration between 55 managers from 11 local and global (private) corporations (ranging from 200 employees to 20,000 employees), a consortium of 12 university researchers (authors included), and representatives from professional associations with a special focus on management innovation, HR, and leadership development in organizations and corporations. A self-assigned and practice-based project, which addressed a specific leadership challenge and paradox deemed important to both the individual manager and the organization, served as the main axis and focal point of the intervention.

As part of the process, participating managers were brought together with other managers from their own as well as from other participating companies. Throughout the program, the self-assigned project was probed and challenged in smaller groups, as well as through large-group exchanges and reflections between managers, consultants, and researchers. A full overview of the activities involved in the action-learning phase is presented in Figure II.2.

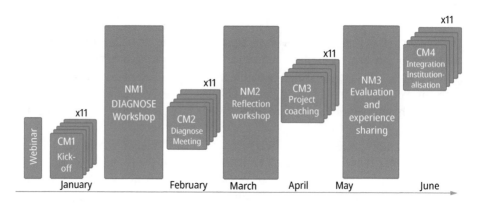

Figure II.2: Overview of the intervention design.

The third phase of the project commenced after the completion of the action-learning intervention, where the research team developed a white book and later research monograph presenting highlights from their data analyses including company cases and practical tools derived from the intervention project (Nielsen et al., 2019, 2020).

While everyone participated in the webinar and network meetings, the company meetings were held in parallel, and exclusive to the participants of that company. The forum of the smaller company-based groups and the large workshops gathering the 55 managers thus acted as crucial arenas for individual and collective reflections. Following an action learning approach, the design supported an iterative process between active experimentation, reflective processes, and the provision of theoretical/generalized knowledge (Revans, 1982). Participating managers worked on many different challenges: tackling the tension between passion and performance in management, the cross-pressure between inside–out development processes and outside–in innovation, or the balance between local and global considerations in internationally working companies. In total, the program offered 27 hours of facilitated activities to the participating managers. All interventions were tape/video recorded; recordings were transcribed following the completion of the research project. In addition, two rounds of survey data were collected on the progress of participants' work. Managers and companies are pseudonymized in this book, but all cases represent one or more managers from the participating companies. The analysis of these data forms the backbone of the qualitative analysis that resulted in the formulation of the five phases. When no other reference is made in the following five chapters, the basis of our argumentation is these data.

It is important to note that the initiation of the paradox action-learning program took place by invitation by the researcher team. Consequently, participation in the program was not tied to a specific organizational development process. Most participants had never previously worked with complexity management, tensions, or paradoxes in leadership; indeed, many had not participated in formal leadership training. After the completion of the research project, we have had the opportunity to use the tools from the research project in many other settings, resulting in refinement, calibration, and explication, the results of which are presented in the next five chapters. We are delighted to say that we have seen the tools come to good use in many companies and although professional help is always recommendable, we have experienced how individuals and groups have been able to use these tools on their own.

References

Bévort, F., Henriksen, T. D., Hjalager, A-M., Nielsen, R. K., Holt Larsen, H. and Vikkelsø, S. (2018). *Ledelsesdilemmaer: Strejftog gennem faglitteraturen*. Frederiksberg, DK: Copenhagen Business School.
Centre for Future Studies (2016). *Trendanalyse*. Copenhagen, DK: Danish Industry Foundation.
Dalkey, N., and Helmer, O. (1963). An experimental application of the Delphi method to the use of experts. *Management Science*, 9(3), 458–467.
Danish Industry Foundation. 2016. *INSPIRE16: Ide- og Udfordringskatalog*. Copenhagen, DK: Industriens Fond.
Nielsen, R. K., Hjalager, A-M., Larsen, H. H., Bévort, F., Henriksen, T. D. and Vikkelsø, S. (2018). *Ledelsesdilemmaer – og kunsten at navigere i moderne ledelse*. Copenhagen, DK: Djøf Publishers.

Nielsen, R. K., Mogensen, M., Bévort, F., Henriksen, T. D., Hjalager, A. M., and Lyndgaard, D. B. (2019). *Ledelses-GPS til en ny tid – Håndtering af ledelsesparadokser og dilemmaer i praksis*. Copenhagen, DK: Copenhagen Business School, University of Southern Denmark, Aalborg University and Network of Corporate Academies.

Nielsen, R. K., Mogensen, M., Bévort, F., Henriksen, T. D., Hjalager, A. M., and Lyndgaard, D. B. (2020). *Både& – værktøjer til effektiv paradoksledelse*. Copenhagen, DK: Djøf Publishing.

Revans, R. W. (1982). What is action learning? *Journal of Management Development*, 1(3), 64–75.

Revans, R. W. (1998). *The ABC of Action Learning: Empowering Managers to Act and to Learn from Action*. London: Lemos and Crane.

Chapter 4
Phase 1: Choosing and shaping your focus area – paradox choice and qualification

The first step in paradox navigation is for you to uncover whether the challenge that you face can be considered a paradox or not. Chapter 2 offered a distinction between three conceptions for diagnosing managerial challenges – problems, dilemmas, and paradoxes – and Chapter 3 presented you with 10 fields of paradoxical tensions in leadership that you may take as your point of departure. In this and the following four chapters, we will zoom in on managerial challenges as paradox, which implies managerial challenges of a complexity that makes them worthwhile in this context.

When working with paradox, certain steps are crucial for getting off to a good start. You will have to choose a paradox that you find meaningful to work with by exploring:
- Why is this a paradox?
- How is it a paradox?
- How does the paradox manifest itself?
- How does it affect your everyday leadership practice?

In this chapter, we present a selection of tools to support this work, supplemented by narratives from managers who have worked with paradox firsthand and experienced the hurdles and opportunities of their endeavors. This brings us to the phase in paradox navigation that focuses on identifying and elaborating on the paradox to prepare it for practical elaboration, as illustrated in the phase model (Figure 4.1) introduced in Chapter 2.

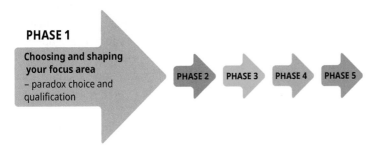

Figure 4.1: Five phases of paradox navigation – Phase 1.

https://doi.org/10.1515/9783110788877-005

The first task is to choose your paradox. This can be difficult as it is likely to be selected among several and competing challenges. Second, comes the testing of your choice before committing yourself to your chosen paradox. In this phase, it is especially important to involve others such as colleagues and discussion partners, but also people you may not usually perceive of as stakeholders, perhaps from outside your department or organization. This involvement can be helpful for getting a broader conception of the paradox before moving on. When you are satisfied that you chose a relevant paradox, it is time to move on to the subsequent steps. These steps consist of narrowing down, and describing in your own words, how the paradox manifests itself for better and for worse. You can state in an initial way how it might be handled properly, and how you could imagine going about implementation. Eventually, it is about keeping track of the balance between pros and cons of each pole of the paradox.

But first we need to identify the paradox and give it a name. To this end, this chapter contains these tools:

- Tool 4.1: *"The Paradox Springboard":* five questions for helping you identify your paradox.
- Tool 4.2: *"Use a Lifeline! Three game-plans for finding outside inspiration"*: three pathways for understanding your paradox using the inspirations of people and other sources.
- Tool 4.3: *"Paradox Exhibition – Tell us your paradox"*: suggestions to how you can share your paradox with management colleagues and explore it together.
- Tool 4.4: *"The Paradox Quiz"*: Pick something relevant – and have something at stake.

The use of these tools is illustrated by practical cases, demonstrating how managers have worked through this phase of paradox navigation in practice.

- Case 4.1: *"Not everything keeping you up at night is a paradox"* is on how this part of the process can lead to "disqualifying" the selected challenge as paradox.
- Case 4.2: *"From a cultural conflict to a division of labor paradox"* is about how a collaboration issue is turned into a centralization-decentralization paradox, thereby transforming the manager's understanding of it and his/her subsequent approach to the challenge.
- Case 4.3: *"Unfolding your paradox. Getting inspiration in your network"* shows how a manager can get a better understanding of the paradox through coffee meetings with colleagues and competitors from the business field.
- Case 4.4: *"The leadership team kickstarts its paradox by reading a management book together"* shows how a management group can develop a shared frame of reference for working with paradox by reading a management book together.
- Case 4.5: *"Managers identify relevant paradoxes with the assistance for HR and top management"* describes how a management group finds inspiration for selecting and working with their paradoxes, and how insights into fortunes and failures in the organization can emerge.

The chapter concludes with five learning coordinates for selecting and elaborating leadership paradoxes. These learning points act as a prelude to the next phase of the paradox navigation process.

Case 4.1: Not everything keeping you up at night is a paradox

Wendy is a chief accountant in a medium-sized enterprise. When she first considered working with one of her leadership challenges as a paradox, one specific challenge sprang to mind: Does it make sense to hope that the employee Marco will come onboard in the ongoing change, or would it be necessary to dismiss him? A key consequence of the change is more cross-organizational collaboration and the alignment of the organization according to business processes rather than functions. This means that more coordination between employees becomes necessary to ensure efficiency. Not all employees share the same enthusiasm or openness for this new organizational format, including Marco, who is a competent, but also very introvert, accountant, who often blocks the workflow because he holds on to his own tasks too long and fails to communicate with colleagues. The several one-to-one conversations that Marco and Wendy have had on this issue, have not had the effect Wendy had hoped for. Marco is quite competent in his field and has been with the company for many years. Even though this is the type of unpleasant situation that can keep most responsible managers awake at night, Wendy decides to act. After a discussion with her management colleagues and an external consultant she recognizes the situation with Marco is in fact a problem, and she needs to decide how to resolve it. As Wendy sees it, the challenge with Marco is not a sign of paradoxical tensions, but instead a situation that requires her to make a call, rather than dragging matters out. Wendy is aware that the new workflows will impact numerous employees and managers throughout the organization, not just finance. Upon this realization, Wendy turns to reconsider what is her actual challenge and paradox. Eventually, Wendy proceeds by identifying a new concern, namely a paradox concerning stricter performance management while taking into consideration not to "kill the passion by spreadsheet" throughout the organization.

Tool 4.1: The Paradox Springboard

Working with paradox in practice starts by identifying what paradoxes are at hand, prioritizing the most relevant one, and then starting the examination of this paradox. As organizations are ripe with paradox, there are usually plenty to choose from, but perhaps not all of them appeal to you in an energizing manner. Allow yourself to invest the resources necessary and give a special consideration to those choices that you are able to affect through you daily management. To get started with your paradox requires you to make a distinct choice.

The questions listed below can be used for you to identify a springboard from which to jump into your paradox. It is your itinerary to the process. In our experience, some of these questions require much reflection, and it would be highly beneficial for your process to frequently revisit and reconsider these questions.

One approach to working with paradox related to your leadership practice would be to begin by identifying what paradoxes are presently pressing, prioritize the most relevant of them, and then elaborate on that specific paradox. To begin with, lots of paradoxes might appear to be relevant for the process, but not all of them will appeal to you to as challenging enough to motivate you sufficiently. In addition, you may lack access to the resources, or they do not align with an opportunity to affect them through your leadership practice. We would recommend choosing a paradox that you have an opportunity to act upon, one that you feel motivated by, and one that is within your sphere of influence.

To set the stage for your paradox, complete the following sentences and answer the listed questions:

–   "It is a paradox to me that . . ."
–   What is your paradox? And how is your challenge a paradox and not just a problem that you can solve?
–   Describe why you think your challenge is a paradox:

   –   What is it that makes it a paradox?
   –   And how does this become evident in practice? (Please provide some examples.)

–   Why is it relevant for you as a manager to work with this paradox? What is your motivation?

Answering these questions should be done at the first step in your process, and you can revisit and reconsider them frequently to help guide and adjust the process. To begin with, it is important to choose a paradox. Leadership paradoxes are intermingled and mutually dependent, and if you attempt to manage them all at the same time, you risk ending up in paradox paralysis. We recommend selecting a starting point that appears substantial and get started. The process might lead to you reconsidering your paradox focus, and eventually choose another, or you will find yourself reformulating or refining it.

We see this as a natural part of the process. Even a brief pause to stop and reflect upon your fundamental challenges can lead to new ideas and new paths to follow. Systemizing such thoughts or analyzing them in a structured manner allow for the problems to emerge in new, meaningful manners, which makes it easier to assess what actions would bring the process forward. The five areas of attention help you focus on what you are fundamentally motivated to do, and they invite you to consider what other parties in your organization share the same challenge. Your surroundings can be important sources to understanding your paradox in new ways and providing alternative perspectives and views on your challenge. This will be a theme for the proceeding chapters.

Case 4.2: From a cultural conflict to a division of labor paradox

A manager at the Scandinavia-based headquarter finds herself challenged in the collaboration with one of the East European subsidiaries. She initially ascribes these challenges to cultural differences that she just needs to find a solution to. However, when diving deeper into her challenge, she discovers that it makes more sense and provides better grounds for a constructive approach to understanding the collaborative challenges as an expression of tensions between a local and global understanding of management. It appears to be more of a matter of centralization and decentralization that needs to be handled and managed. As it becomes clear for her that she is dealing with a paradox, she also realizes how the underlying tensions will continuously emerge and become subject to renegotiation. Had it "merely" been a problem, it could have been resolved through a culturally appropriate form of collaboration. By recognizing her challenges as inherent and naturally occurring tensions, and not just poor collaboration or reluctance on part of the subsidiary, she can start acting upon it as a paradox. The actions she takes may be similar, but the manager's modes of thinking and acting upon the challenge changes dramatically!

Case 4.3: Unfolding your paradox. Getting inspiration in your network

One of the managers in the company Pedersen & Bros is in the process of choosing how to focus his paradox and to better specify its inherent challenge. His immediate thought is that it makes sense for him to work with the tensions between various development processes taking place inside the company (so-called "inside–out") and such innovation processes that to a larger extent are taking place as co-creation with external competitors-colleagues, so-called "coopetititors" and others from the organization's ecological system ("outside–in"). To get an outside perspective, he invites two persons from his network, one with experience from similar challenges from another business, and one from a substantially larger company from the same line of business. The manager uses two coffee meetings to conduct informal, explorative interviews, which provide him with feedback on some of the assumptions and questions he finds difficult to deal with. The interviews also open his eyes to new challenges and opportunities, which makes him more confident in the paradox being sufficiently substantive and relevant to work with.

Tool 4.2: Use a Lifeline! Three game-plans for finding outside inspiration

At this point, many of those who embark on a paradox feel an itch toward problem solving. This pragmatic pull toward action can be felt a little extra if you are used to being a doer. Now is the time to go slow and linger on your paradox. Regardless of how easy you found it to answer the questions posed in the Paradox Springboard above, it is important at this stage to further test your paradox before choosing how you want to approach it. The next phase aims to qualify or elaborate your paradox, which implies describing and outlining it in your own words. In this process you will check out your challenge to make sure you are deciding on the right focus. It is often difficult to provide an exact answer to why a leadership challenge is challenging. What makes it challenging? Why is it a problem? To whom is it a problem, and how? This is about rephrasing the problem in a concise manner. You will most likely need to enquire information and draw upon the knowledge of others, both colleagues and from your network, to phrase your challenge.

In the following, three different game-plans for paradox "quality assurance" are presented. They will allow you to undertake the necessary service check on your own understanding of the paradox by using various sources: top management, your network, and management literature. The game-plans can be utilized by you as a manager to perform a personal reality check.

However, the tools focus on doing this in dialog with conversation partners in or outside the organization. Drawing upon whatever help is available through management literature is also highly relevant. Fortunately, it is unlikely that you would be the first to encounter a specific leadership paradox and, most often, inspiration from the thoughts and ideas of others are available through literature. There is no need to reinvent the wheel.

Gameplan #1: Consulting with top management

It is often a good strategy to get top management to bring clarity to what is expected of you as a manager in relation to your paradox, and to listen to suggestions. Below are a few guiding questions helpful in preparing such a meeting:
- What are the central concerns and competing demands involved in your current paradox sketch?
- What are top management reactions to your sketch? What do they find particularly interesting? What is missing?
- How will you capture your take-aways from the meetings? What are your most wanted take-aways?

Gameplan #2: Learn from your network and from someone outside "your box"

There is little need for reinventing the wheel, especially if someone else has already been through the motions. It is often useful and inspirational to seek advice from someone who has experience from fields like yours. However, it is a misunderstanding that you should only talk to people whose jobs greatly resembles yours, and who perhaps work for the same company. In contrast, people with experience from a different field, who can address your situation and challenge with new eyes, are often able to give the best advice. They may see the blind angles. Sending problems and questions to diffuse audiences through social media, allowing those who specifically do not have the same professional approach to come up with their creative ideas, often turn out to be productive. The point is, be open-minded when identifying those people from your network who can contribute good suggestions about how to deal with your current challenges. You may even ask them to bring a friend.

Below you will find a set of questions beneficial when considering who to include from your network:
- What kind of paradoxical challenge do you want to raise with your network, and what types of inspiration do you seek from them?
- Try to complete the following sentences:

 "My challenge/paradox is . . . and it is a challenge for the following reasons . . ."

 "Ideally, my network would help me . . . (be as specific as possible)."
- Make a list of those persons in your network who in your view would be able to provide interesting inputs for you. Try to be as inclusive as possible, rather than immediately ruling out persons in the periphery of your network. Try considering the following categories: colleagues from different functional areas, your personal life and extended family, friends, networks, or chance encounters at social functions.
- What good ideas, reflections, suggestions, and critique is produced by these persons? Try not to defend yourself by paraphrasing "We tried that", "It wouldn't work with us". Or "XX or YY would never agree to that".
- Discuss with the person(s) in question how their experiences might inspire you – or why they cannot be applied to your situation, and if this is the case, why not?

Gameplan #3: Learning from literature

There is little need to acquire the same hard-earned experience when others have been down that path before you. Obtaining knowledge from the management literature expands the range of experiences to learn from and contributes to managerial imagination. An easy approach to catch up with the practices of others is through studies and reports. The 10 fields of paradoxical tension in leadership presented in Chapter 3 may serve as a good starting point, including consulting the list of references for this book. Newspapers, magazines, (research) libraries, generative AI chatbots, or web search engines can all be sources of information. If you are not particularly keen on reading research articles, remember that many researchers also disseminate their research through digital outlets such as LinkedIn, Facebook, personal web pages, or YouTube channels.

Our point is that it is rarely sufficient what you know, or what your manager or top management think about your paradox. But you cannot be sure whether they know anything of relevance until you have asked. On the other hand, you can be certain that someone in your network has either faced what you are currently facing, or something much like it, and you can be even more certain that someone has an opinion about your situation worth listening to. It is worthwhile to find out what is already known about the paradox. But remember, you can rarely learn one to one from the experiences of others, but their contributions are often much better than just starting from scratch and guessing from there.

Case 4.4: The leadership team kick-starts their paradox by reading a management book together

Being able to identify and navigate paradoxes is a meta-competence, which can be used with all paradoxes. To have a meaningful dialog about a personal paradox and get in close with how it emerges on a day-to-day basis, a shared frame of reference is helpful. Without such frame, the conversation easily gets sidetracked and becomes shallow and abstract. To avoid such pitfalls, the management group at CapCore decides to have a shared point of departure in the form of a specific book on paradox leadership. As the whole group will read the book prior to their dialog, they develop a shared frame of reference and conceptual framework on paradox to help them elaborate and deepen their conversation.

Tool 4.3: Paradox Exhibition – tell us about your paradox

The inspiration from persons from outside your own company can help you in locating blind spots and help you uncovering blind angles. Although paradoxes appear in subjective and personalized forms, the management literature has proven useful to bring in inspiration and to provide anchorage in the form of a shared sets of paradoxes to take off from. Without such anchorage, discussions are likely to dwell on the contents of a particular paradox rather than focusing on seeing and describing how it specifically emerges to someone in a particular situation. The 10 fields of paradoxical tensions in leadership outlined in Chapter 3 can serve as such anchorage and provide the team with common grounds. At this point in the process, it is important to remember that the chosen inspirational paradoxes are to serve that particular purpose – inspiration! Subsequent steps might lead you to focus on a completely different paradox, or perhaps shift your focus in some other, unexpected direction. At this point, it is expected that the description of your chosen paradox is not 100% accurate, and it suffices that you find the paradox relevant and interesting to you on a general level.

You will need further inputs to proceed, but a shared point of departure can be the initiator for you to calibrate and explore further into your paradox's complexity. The generic, inspirational paradoxes might serve as working hypotheses, but they are not diagnoses. They must be tailored and polished to fit your focus. Perhaps you will even have to replace your paradox with another. This is not to be considered a failure, but rather in a wider sense beneficial, as this is part of the process this phase aims to facilitate. But first things first – the following process is designed to assist you in choosing a paradox that you wish to work with. We suggest that you "test" your current understanding of your paradox with relevant others – for instance, members of your team or department, managerial colleagues, or other close stakeholders. Your management colleagues can help you fine-tune this ability and take part in discussing the appearance of your paradox on a company specific and practical level.

Paradox Exhibition is a pathway for performing additional testing of your paradox by exploring it with your management colleagues. Collect a group of three to six managers, who will then ask insightful questions about one another's management practice. Their inquiry will be: "How can you recognize this paradox in your leadership role and work?" The tool provides a gameplan for a dialog. For the tool to work properly, it is necessary that all participants are committed to following the plan and help remind each other to try to stick to this agenda in the process. The purpose of this dialog is:

–   to be able to recognize paradoxes in your own practice and learn to see your own leadership practice considering paradox; this process unfolds partly through paradox presentation, and partly through paradox reflection
–   to be able to describe your own leadership practice in a paradox perspective and shift focus from generic examples, to your and your colleagues' day-to-day management. By discussing paradox in

the context of everyday practice, the management team co-creates a shared understanding of the contradictory considerations and tensions that produce the paradox, and through this it elaborates on approaches to its management.
– Seeing a problem in a paradox perspective includes recognizing its inherent complexity, with no easy solution available and to evaluate incoming suggestions from your management colleagues with special emphasis on how they match the complexity or the challenge. This discussion aims to create focus while simultaneously developing a sensitivity to detail and complexity. Easy or obvious solutions tend to either avoid difficult parts of the paradox, or simply fail to consider its complexity. However, such deviations and blunt readings are often valuable, not for solving the problem, but to further explore its complexity to gain a better understanding of the paradox.

Each person presents his or her own paradoxical challenge taking and receiving feedback from colleagues using the questions in the left-hand column in Figure 4.2. The process is concluded when the presenter reflects on the feedback received focusing on the questions in the right-hand column:

PARADOX EXHIBITION:
A collective look at individual challenges

For the exhibition visitor: Colleagues reflecting	For the paradox presenter: Presenting to colleagues
– What do you take special notice of in the paradox presentation you just heard?	– What was surprising?
	– What was important?
	– What caused most consideration for you?
– Do you see dimensions or tensions of the paradox that should be further explored or unfolded?	– What was problematic?
	– How did you become aware of new aspects of your challenge?
– Do you see significant parts, advantages, or disadvantages, overlooked?	– What would be your next steps?
	– How would you proceed from here?

Figure 4.2: Paradox Exhibition – a collective look at individual challenges.

When all participants have been through the process, all members should have received constructive in-puts to choosing a paradox of personal relevance. On top of this, the process creates a community on working with paradoxes. You can easily work with paradoxes in solitary, but we found great advantages associated with collaborating with management colleagues, especially on assessing how your work with paradoxes fits into what preoccupies the rest of the organization.

Case 4.5: Managers identifying relevant paradoxes with the assistance of HR and top management

Paradoxes have subjective appearances and are individually experienced. It is unlikely that your personal paradox is experienced in the same manner by others, especially from other parts of the organization. Others might not recognize your personal paradox, and it might not resonate with overall tensions that your company or organization is situated in. The management group in SASH Ltd.

attempts to find common grounds by entering a dialog with HR and top management in order to explore possible matches between their paradoxes and those of the company. In this process, they realize how pressing matters, as perceived by members of the company's top management, not necessarily overlap with those brought forward by the management group. This provides food for thought on how their perceived paradoxes comply with, or even come into conflict with, focused priorities of the upper management strata.

Tool 4.4: The Paradox Quiz: Pick something relevant – and have something at stake

Joining forces with others on paradox leadership really helps the process take off, both by heightening reflections on one's own paradox, but also by laying out a solid foundation for the latter parts of the process, which will include the support and sparring in the immediate environment. The Paradox Quiz can be used to identify common denominators in your management team.

The purpose of The Paradox Quiz is to stimulate each member to use the team to:
- describe and reflect upon personal management paradox
- realize why a particular personal paradox has been selected
- spar with management colleagues
- identify common denominators and differences in the team

Perhaps you are starting to feel more certain about your choice of paradox. However, it is advisable to look at your paradox considering how relevant it is when compared to the other paradoxes brought to the table by your management colleagues.

The Paradox Quiz consists of a series of questions, which give you an opportunity to reflect on and assess your own ability to handle the 10 fields of paradoxical tension in leadership. The result of the quiz forms a starting point for the discussion on the subsequent management team meeting. Before you meet, each member of the group considers the following questions:
- Which leadership paradox is most important to you? Why do you feel that your chosen paradox is the most important?
- Which leadership paradox is least important to you? What makes you choose that paradox as least important?
- To what extent do you consider yourself capable of navigating the individual paradoxes?
- What future paradoxes do you expect to become relevant for you? Where do you search for future paradoxes that you may expect to become relevant?

The questions aim to help you and your colleagues look at your own management practice in the long run. This opens a discussion concerning what factors will affect your options in the short or long run. On the basis of your preparation, the meeting aims to discuss your paradoxes, following this agenda:
- What are the individual manager's reflections on criteria and assumptions underlying the chosen paradoxes?
- Which of the discussed leadership challenges are relevant to us right now?
- What future management challenges are we facing or likely to face?
- What is our current capacity for managing the individual paradoxes?
- How can we develop the necessary capacity for working with the individual paradoxes, and how can we continue our work with the current paradoxes?
- What criteria and assumptions have the group agreed upon as shared when assessing what are considered important paradoxes?

– How do we view the company's challenges and capacity for managing them differently, and what do we agree upon?

The Paradox Quiz aims to provide the management team an eye for what are the individually important management paradoxes, and to facilitate a dialog on how they are intermingled in various ways. Paradox leadership is often a challenge to the individual manager but undertaking them as a team is to our experience a great help. The shared dialog makes it easier (but not easy) to clarify and define one's own paradox and feel better prepared for the task ahead. Perhaps you and your team aim too low, and your efforts might benefit from aiming a bit higher? Perhaps you need to dare venturing outside your comfort zone and work on something that appears a more difficult undertaking than you are used to?

Five learning coordinates for the first phase of paradox navigation – choosing and qualifying your paradox

At the end of this book we provide 25 learning coordinates for paradox navigation. This chapter provides you with the first five, summarizing the experiences from the first phase on choosing and qualifying your paradox:

1. All paradoxes are connected. Find a substantial place to start and move on from there. If you attempt to manage them all at the same time, you will end up in paradox paralysis, but if you focus on just one, you have a good starting point.

2. Paradox leadership is a meta-competence, which implies a general ability to manage paradoxes. But at the same time, all paradoxes are concerned with 'something'. To get started, the management literature often provides useful inspiration for finding appropriate and fresh paradoxes to work with when finding and choosing your own paradox. This chapter provides four such examples for inspiration – in addition to the 10 fields of paradoxical tensions in leadership presented in Chapter 3. A common starting point is vital when working together on your paradoxes. It helps you to make sure that your shared efforts do not end entangled in endless discussion of what belongs with which paradox.

3. A problem-solving itch is common among managers, turning paradoxes into something to be solved. The whole point of working with paradoxes is that they cannot be solved but must be handled or navigated on an ongoing basis. Often, it requires gearing down when viewing a management problem as a paradox. This phase requires you to dare to slow down, stop and reflect, dwell, and seek inspiration from others, both inside and outside your organization. If you happen to choose a challenge that you already know the answer to, then you might not have grasped the paradox and its complexity entirely. Or alternatively, you have chosen a paradox that you have already found a productive way to balance. In that case you will probably benefit more from looking into a different paradox.

4. Conflict avoidance and procrastination can prevent you from getting under the skin of your paradox. Be aware that uncomfortable choices that keep you awake at night are not necessarily paradoxes. Perhaps they are "merely" hard choices

that make you concerned and worried about communicating the consequences to the relevant parties.

5. All challenges are difficult, but seeing them as problems, dilemmas, or paradoxes makes a significant difference. While it might not be as important which label you start with, it's vital that you decide on focusing on a paradox, and not a dilemma or a problem. The space for action and your options are determined by how you understand your challenge. Paradoxes treated like problems will reappear like a cork re-surfacing every time you think, "Got it!"

You are now ready to start the next part of the paradox navigation process, which is described in the following Chapter 5, "Phase 2. Know your paradox – paradox investigation", leading to five new learning coordinates for paradox navigation.

Chapter 5
Phase 2: Know your paradox – paradox investigation

In Phase 2 (Figure 5.1), it is important to learn more about what the chosen paradox implies. Getting to know your paradox is about identifying the embedded opportunities and challenges and relating them to your leadership challenge and situation.

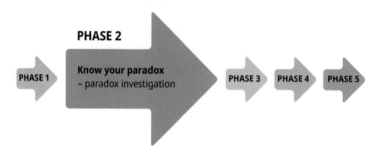

Figure 5.1: Five phases of paradox navigation – Phase 2.

When we use the term "investigation" it is for the purpose of signaling that you must stop and think twice. "Investigation" means that you will create an overview and describe how the chosen paradox appears in your role and context. However, investigation also entails seeking a better understanding of the paradox through an unfolding of all the relevant elements, relations, and conditions related to the paradox.

This chapter presents two tools:

– Tool 5.1: *"The Paradox Quadrant"*. The Paradox Quadrant (see Figure 5.1) is an effective method for unpacking the content of the chosen paradox and unfolding the possible consequences for yourself and your organization while prioritizing the two poles of the paradox. The model is accompanied by a roadmap that will assist you in analyzing your paradox.

– Tool 5.2: *"The Paradox Kaleidoscope – uncovering related paradoxes"*. One paradox rarely comes alone. The Paradox Kaleidoscope allows you to uncover other paradoxes related to your current paradox. Becoming acquainted with related paradoxes allows you to expand your understanding of your paradox even further.

The chapter contains five cases, which all illustrate how an investigation of your paradox bring you toward a deeper understanding of your position as manager, of you as a person, as well as of your leadership team or your organization.

– Case 5.1: *"Getting up close and personal with the paradox – Tony is filling in the Paradox Quadrant"*. In this case, we follow a manager as he gradually completes the model.

https://doi.org/10.1515/9783110788877-006

- Case 5.2: *"Same paradox, individual perspectives"*. Two managers work with the same paradox, but they have very different personal preconditions and therefore stress different aspects.
- Case 5.3: *"Two managers in owner-led organizations: same paradox, individual perspectives"*. Two managers work with the same paradox in two owner-managed companies, but from two different organizational starting points.
- Case 5.4: *"Diana's paradox knot – one paradox rarely comes alone"* is about a manager who uncovers adjacent paradoxes to her main paradox and revisits the Paradox Quadrant.
- Case 5.5: *"A collective leadership challenge – a paradox mix"*. In this case, a management team works with a variety of individual paradoxes and explores how the paradoxes are interrelated and interact in practice.

Exploring your paradox using the Paradox Quadrant and the Paradox Kaleidoscope paints a more complex picture and simultaneously provides more roads to future actions. This is exactly the strength of "paradox investigation": it unfolds the complexity of the situation and provides more ideas on potential actions. It provides a starting point for formulating ideas and for arguing for certain choices when the poles of the paradox are balanced off against each other. They may require (for example) competence development or enhanced involvement of new partners. The understanding of a leadership paradox is strengthened by systematically describing both sides of the paradox and uncovering both the positive and negative aspects.

Working with these tools clarifies the management development needs for the individual manager, the management team, and the organization. This solid understanding of your paradox creates the basis for you to select appropriate areas of action and to act in the next phases. From experience, however, it is also one of the most difficult phases in paradox leadership, because it is a phase that demands careful dwelling on your paradox, allowing it to unfold and for there to be reflection and resistance to acting. This can be particularly difficult for "professional problem solvers", "executers"; that is, such managers find it difficult to "sit on their hands" and reflect. This second phase is simply a matter of contemplation, curiosity, and nurturing a critical, yet caring, look at their own practice. The presentation of the chapter's two tools is accompanied by five cases detailing the stories of specific managers' experiences with the two tools as they work to unravel and get closer to their paradox. The chapter concludes with five learning coordinates for this second phase of paradox leadership.

Tool 5.1: The Paradox Quadrant – a paradox has two sides, each with positive and negative aspects

When you describe a paradox as a manager, it is about presenting two alternatives, each of which is important to the company and to you, and where a choice between them will affect the other. This model is inspired by Barry Johnson's Polarity Map (Johnson 2014, 1992) that we have developed and revised based on our experiences with using this line of thinking for development purposes in relation to paradoxical leadership.

With the Paradox Quadrant, you must identify the positive and negative effects of both paradox alternatives/poles. For example, consider the paradox of *development* or *operation*. A focus on development is positive for the organization because it creates new growth opportunities, but driving development is also costly, takes resources from production, and can risk eroding earnings. A focus on operations, on the other hand, is a way to create efficiency through routines with low(er) costs and thereby increased earnings. However, at the same time, this puts the organization at risk since it stalls innovation and new technological opportunities. As can be seen, both sides of the leadership paradox each have both positive and negative effects that simultaneously affect the other pole. The Paradox Quadrant is a way to create an overview of these effects and their interdependence. You can use the paradox model as a clarification tool for yourself, or you can use it with your management team.

The purpose of an investigation process using the Paradox Quadrant is basically for you to qualify the handling of your chosen paradox. The Paradox Quadrant is shown in Figure 5.2 in a filled-in version, to give you a sense of what it might look like once you are done with your investigative work.

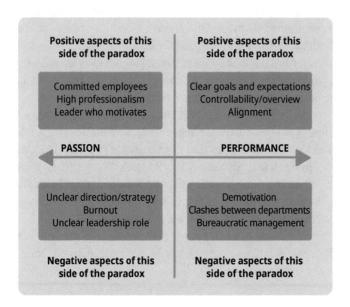

Figure 5.2: The Paradox Quadrant.

The Paradox Quadrant in Figure 5.2 provides an example of the pros and cons of both sides of the paradox. In this case it is about the tension between passion (higher purpose/meaning engagement) and performance (concrete results and performance management). The poles of the paradox are outlined on either side of the horizontal axis in the middle of the model. The vertical axis indicates the pros and cons.

Accordingly, the left side shows the pros and cons of the passion side of the paradox. Here, the manager states that the advantage of focusing on passion is that it creates commitment among employees, and it nurtures employees who are passionate about their professional approach to work and appreciate their manager's motivational leadership style. On the negative side, this focus on passion can lead to an unclear strategic focus, burned-out employees, and a lack of clarity about leadership roles because there is a large element of self-management.

The right side of the figure shows the pros and cons of the performance side of the paradox. A focus on performance can potentially lead to an experience of clarity in strategy and objectives, coherence, and common ground. However, it can erode motivation and commitment, create unnecessary competition, and waste resources on follow-up and documentation.

When you complete your own Paradox Quadrant, you can proceed as follows:

Instructions for completing the Paradox Quadrant

The model is filled in by writing your paradox in the horizontal axis; for example, there will be "Passion" versus "Performance". The left part of the model shows one side of the paradox "Passion", and the right side of the model shows the other side of the paradox, "Performance" (see Figure 5.2).

Then, fill in the pros and cons on each side of the paradox. Benefits are written at the top of the model, so that the benefits associated with the left side of the paradox are written at the top left, and correspondingly for the right side of the paradox. Similarly, the disadvantages are written on each side of the paradox in the lower part of the model.

Once you have completed the model, you can then make three kinds of comparisons and analyses – a vertical, a horizontal, and a diagonal – as described in greater detail in Figure 5.3. The idea is that you become more focused in the way you understand the choices, priorities, and derived managerial consequences of the paradox.

You can then present your Paradox Quadrant and your analysis to one or more colleagues. Involving sparring partners serves to qualify and challenge your immediate reflections. It is typically very rewarding, especially since most people have areas in the model that they find difficult to complete.

Suggested discussion points in your conversation with a colleague:

What preferences do I have?

How do my preferences affect my leadership practice?

What blind spots should I be aware of?

How can I address my blind spots (perhaps you have areas in the model, that you found it difficult to complete)?

What aspects of my leadership practice do I need to develop as a result of the analysis?

Suggestions for summing up:

How do my choices reflect the preferences that I personally have as a manager? How do they correspond with the values and norms of the wider organization?

How have I/we become wiser about the paradox?

How can I continue working with the paradox based on my new knowledge?

By evaluating and comparing the different relationships within the model, you increase your understanding of the paradox and its potential consequences. In this way, you will obtain navigation points for the paradox.

To retain what you have learned about the paradox, it is important that you make notes directly in the model. Since the tool is going to be used to reflect on a leadership issue later, your written notes can help to retain and thereby qualify your reflections. Your written notes can also support your further work when approaching the coming phases in handling your paradox.

Paradox Quadrant safety check - vertical and diagonal analysis

By filling in the Paradox Quadrant, you force yourself to make a preliminary assessment of the properties and content of the paradox. Simultaneously, it becomes possible to compare, combine and relate the positive and negative aspects. As mentioned, it makes a lot of sense to talk about the completed quadrant with colleagues or sparring partners, but you can also make a "safety check" of your completed quadrant yourself. The point is that you check whether you remembered to include everything of importance, and you do this by two simple analyses, namely horizontally and diagonally, as shown in Figure 5.3.

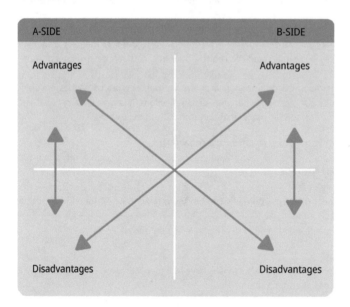

Figure 5.3: Vertical and diagonal comparison/analysis.

The *vertical analysis* considers the advantages and disadvantages of each side of your paradox, and it serves to reveal whether there are spaces in the model where you "need" to add something. It is often easiest to fill in only one of the spaces, while it can be more difficult to do justice to both the pros and the cons at the same time. Here, keep in mind that the coin always has two sides. Even though you may have a keener eye for the positive aspects of one of the dimensions of the paradox, it does not mean that there are only positive effects. It is a bit like the package leaflet of a package of painkillers, where the description of the possible side-effects takes up much more space than the positive effects for your headache. The point is, if the drug works, it probably also has side-effects that you will have to deal with, even if you are concerned mainly with the positive effects. However, it is not always the negative aspects that are difficult to spot. It may well be that you have been blinded by the negative aspects, and you cannot see the possible positive aspects. Regardless of whether it is the negative or the positive side that acts as your blind spot, the vertical analysis serves as an eye-opener to see what might otherwise be difficult to spot.

The *diagonal analysis is* another trick to leave no stone unturned in considering your paradox and possible blind spots. In the diagonal analysis, you look at what you have filled in on the negative side of the right side of the paradox and compare it with the positive side of the left side of the paradox and vice versa. The negative aspects of one pole of the paradox are often a mirror image of the positive sides of the other pole. You can therefore say, as a rule of thumb, that you must fill in the same number of points in both fields. If there is an imbalance, it gives you a clue of the fact that there is probably something you have forgotten.

These two analyses are especially needed if you are using the quadrant by yourself. If you use the Paradox Quadrant together with your management team or other sparring partners in your network, your conversation partners will usually be able to shed light on the aspects you may have missed.

The following case illustrates how a manager worked with a specific leadership paradox, namely the contradiction between innovation that comes "from the inside–out", that is, counting the closed knowledge flows within the company, and innovation that comes "from the outside–in", such as through open co-creation processes with external stakeholders (Figure 5.4).

Case 5.1: Up close and personal with the paradox – Tony is filling in the Paradox Quadrant

The manager Tony and his organization are at a point where, on the one hand, external impulses and partners are needed for their organization's development, while at the same time it is necessary to capitalize on their well-honed business model and the internal relationships that have been built up over several years. It is a company that, so far, had a successful but rather quiet existence with a solid customer portfolio. Tony himself is employed to provide a new "outside" inspiration for the company, and he was only part of the organization for a short period. Tony is therefore placed right in the middle of this paradox: How should he look outwards, as is part of his job description, while at the same time seeking to gain from the resources and strengths that already brought the company success?

Tony takes the Paradox Quadrant as his point of departure and as a way to systematically approach his leadership challenge and to gain an understanding of what is at stake. By using the model, Tony identifies the two sides of his paradox and how they are connected. At the same time, he clarifies what the paradox more precisely entails in his present context. Below are the principles of Tony's paradox analysis using the Paradox Quadrant (also see filled-in quadrant on the following page).

Referring to the quadrant, Tony describes his paradox in the following way, and it can be compared with the keywords written in the quadrant:

The sunny side, the positive aspects of the "inside–out" end of the paradox: The company's strong first-generation identity has created success by matching the needs of the market and continuously following the market development. Employees and managers can rightly say, "If it ain't broke, don't fix it" about the way the company has been operating so far. The company can carry out its commitments for customers in the niche that it has been in from the beginning. This means that it operates in a relatively simple and familiar world. The company is competitive and has grown to a considerable size. The company does what it is used to and good at, thus avoiding unnecessary uncertainties.

The flipside, the negative aspects of the "inside–out" end of the paradox: The company is beginning to show signs that it is stuck in its own success and has trouble in terms of renewing itself. New customers in the market expect products and services to be better integrated into combined solutions. The company has difficulty in overseeing and dealing with this with the existing "inside–out approach", which is based on well-known methods and partners. The company risks getting stuck in a rigid operative role and culture that limit it from progressing to more lucrative tasks and customer relationships. The customer-facing employees, who work directly with the users of the company's services, have built up extensive knowledge of customer needs and wishes. That knowledge is difficult to translate into development and use elsewhere in the organization. The company's customers signal that they see great value in involving the company in an "outside–in" approach, for example in collaborations with other suppliers. However, it has proven to be difficult because the "inside–out" way of thinking continues to have a great influence on the company.

After having put into words one dimension of the paradox, "from the inside out", Tony begins to fill in the right side of the paradox.

The sunny side, the positive aspects of the "outside–in" end of the paradox: In recent years, the company managed well to adapt its services and products to customers' demands with a relatively simple "outside–in" approach. The starting point is having conversations with a customer "over a cup of coffee". However, with the increasing volume and sophistication of the legal framework of business, negotiating over a cup of coffee is no longer enough. New inspiration and the application of knowledge is required to ensure that the company can understand its market and its customers' current and future needs. The company must strengthen its ability to observe its own actions from the outside, that is, from a customer perspective.

The flip side, the negative aspects of the "outside–in" end of the paradox: The company has not yet developed the competencies to handle this approach, and therefore it currently must use external suppliers to create this perspective. Brokers or intermediaries come on board, and that can be difficult for the organization and leadership to handle. If the desired future corporate identity is not clarified before applying an external perspective, there may be a risk that the company completely loses its identity in the pursuit of meeting the needs and wishes of external partners and customers. The "outside–in" thoughts are contradictory to the well-established culture where "he who lives quietly lives best". Historically, the company's place in the value chain has been as a producer, for some reason considered and ranked lower in the market hierarchy. To enter equally into an "outside–in" dialog, the company must sometimes take a more proactive position. This development, in turn, requires resources and new internal competencies. In fact, the company has previously tried and wasted a lot of resources on similar endeavors, and there has not been any additional business, rather extra costs.

In the above analysis, Tony discusses many elements of importance. Contemplating the company from the "outside–in" was his comfort zone, but it is also evident that there are several challenges connected to this side of the paradox. Tony discussed the completed model with his colleagues, and this led to his greater awareness of some positive aspects of working "from the inside out", a perspective that was largely hidden from him because of his position as an external change agent. His new and more nuanced understanding of the company's challenges led to, among other things, his ability to identify development paths as well as more familiar strategies.

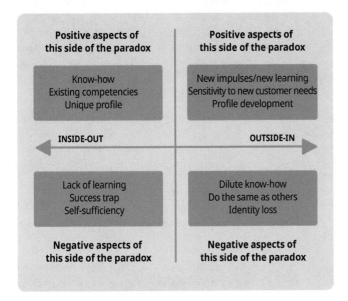

Figure 5.4: The Paradox Quadrant for the paradox "inside–out" versus "outside–in".

Tony's case above shows how to act to come to the point of residing well in the paradox, considering all the relevant elements. It also shows that the definition of the paradox depends to a large extent on the manager's personal capabilities, but also the specific situation of the company. In the next sections, we will dig into an example of how concrete differences in persons and situations can affect your understanding of your paradox and how you can best work with it. The point here is that the model is not "one-size-fits-all". You must therefore be careful when comparing yourself with others. A mindful attitude increases the potential of acquiring inspiration from others who are faced with the same paradox, even if they are confronted with entirely different circumstances.

One paradox – different managers

The experience and handling of the same paradox can be expressed very differently from one manager to another, even within the same company. It depends on personalities and abilities, but also on the choice of which pole of the paradox needs to be strengthened reflecting on the specific experience and development as a manager.

Case 5.2: Same paradox, individual perspectives

The company NowTech develops and produces knowledge-intensive and highly specialized niche prod-ucts for a wide range of industries. Sam and Karen are both executives at NowTech. They are in their mid-30s and represent the "new blood" and the new vision for NowTech as a company. Both managers thus share the same terms and the same paradox, namely having to lead a company undergoing changes in such a way that they *both stand out as individual managers and know how to manage in close interaction with the employees*. Accordingly, their paradox revolves around the tension between personal leadership as opposed to a collective and distributed leadership style. However, the two managers also differ from each other and are at opposite ends of the two poles of the paradox. They possess very different degrees of leadership experience, they work in two very different parts of the company, and they are at the same time very different as individuals.

Their ways of "being" in the paradox are not alike and can be sketched out as follows: While Karen is strong and accustomed to an individual leadership style, she also experiences an increasing need to strengthen the organizational part of her leadership. Sam leads primarily through a close and professionally meaningful collab-oration with his skilled employees, but there is an increasing request for him to step into character as a man-ager and through a stronger individual decisiveness set a clear direction for the overall team.

These managers' starting points and conditions for dealing with the paradox are thus immensely dif-ferent, and so are their concrete coping strategies. In Karen's case, strengthening the organizational di-mension of her leadership is executed by giving her deputy head a much larger part of the daily responsibilities and direct leadership of the employees.

Sam, who is relatively new to the leadership role, spent most of his first year as a manager in "hid-ing" and is only starting to take on board the leadership role. Initially, he moves into the role by creating alliances, partly upwards, and partly through an implementation of new technology. Instead of complain-ing about a very absent boss, he decides to book a meeting with his boss and, on that occasion, he obtains input and support for his plans for the department. Coincidentally, he gets the green light to attend leader-ship training to be able to move out of his previous (and preferred) position as an expert and into a full-blown leadership role.

This case demonstrates how a paradox can play out in very different ways depending on the individual manager's situation, experiences, and individuality. The way in which a paradox is understood can be fundamentally different between managers even in the same organization. It may be true that you can learn from the way your colleagues are dealing with their paradox, but it is equally important to be aware whether this in fact suits your own personality and situation. When working with the analysis of the Paradox Quadrant it can be tempting to reflect on the advantages and disadvantages of the two sides of the paradox in general terms. However, an important point is that a paradox always appears in relation to a specific situation and a specific manager's personality.

Hence, the same paradox can appear differently for two managers with different personalities and developmental challenges. Furthermore, managers working with the same paradox may have experienced a significant variance in contexts and condi-tions for working with the paradox. This means that you as a manager cannot be sure to have the same resources and limitations when working with a given paradox com-pared to other managers. Therefore, clarifying how the chosen paradox is manifested differently for you than for your management colleagues inside or outside your organization is an important part of the paradox investigation.

Taking the specific situation into account is central for maneuvering the paradox. The tension between individual and organizational management are experienced differently depending on the leadership situation. The paradox is about balancing between leadership as something that originates from the (top) manager as a person, or as something that is distributed to other managers and executed within the larger organizational system. The organizational dimension of this paradox challenges many managers, including how to become better at delegating leadership from powerful top managers to other managers. This is the theme and starting point of the following case.

Case 5.3: Two managers in owner-led organizations – same paradox, individual perspectives

The company ProdTech provides specialized production equipment and technical support within the food industry in a global market. The company focuses on high technical quality and is successful. The company relies on a professional board of directors, but is still characterized by the owner-managers, who are strongly committed to daily operation and still act as daily (albeit unofficial) managers. The department heads talk about the owner-managers as a kind of "shadow organization". The manager at ProdTech has been there for the past 20 years. Over the years, he has steadily risen in the ranks, and in his current position, he has been given responsibility for strengthening the standardization, professionalism, and strategic direction of the company. The challenge is that he never feels that he has sufficient time to give the longer-term commitments enough attention, as he is often pulled in as an expert in various production problems. The manager of ProdTech himself formulates his challenge as a matter of becoming better at delegating downwards to sub-ordinates in the hierarchy. At the same time, it is clear that his paradox reflects and is inextricably linked to what the owner-management does (or rather does not) do. The lack of trust, which the owner-management indirectly conveys by regularly issuing counter-orders, tends to undermine local communication, coordination, and leadership.

Another manager, Tina, experiences the same paradox as in ProdTech, but her conditions for paradox leadership are markedly different. The owner-manager in EstateServicePartner is a second-generation owner-manager. The family business specializes in providing real estate services but has expanded over the years into a wide range of sub-businesses. The manager has gradually established a small management group of three persons, supplemented with an active chair of the board. Like the manager of ProdTech, she has an ambition to strengthen the organizational dimension of the paradox. She herself formulates her managerial challenge as "[moving] from leading others in person to delegating leadership to others". Over the years, the employees in the company have adopted the habit of coming to the manager's office daily to ask for help and instructions on current issues and problems, and Tina has always had an "open door" policy. However, after the changed focus, the employees now must either solve the problem themselves or go to their immediate manager. Although the manager understands very well the need for increased professionalism and thus a radical change in the ways she has enacted her leadership role thus far, in practice it is difficult for her to give up control. It challenges her usual ways of acting and understanding of herself. When she is no longer physically available, it forces the other managers to step in, size up the situation, and find solutions together. She as a manager must find ways to exercise her managerial power, where she re-assigns management power and responsibilities to the rest of the managers, while at the same time staying available as a person and resource.

> The owner-manager for EstateServicePartner needs a manager such as the manager for ProdTech, who takes on some managerial responsibilities, while also delegating management to others further down the organization. Conversely, the manager of ProdTech is equally dependent on an owner-manager who has wider "moral" capacity to delegate managerial power. As it stands, there is a need for him to set an example by stepping down and putting aside the ingrained individual leadership habits. Bringing the stories of these two managers together and making them reflect on each other's paradoxes serves to illustrate the existence of co-dependency up and down the organization. Such endeavors can illuminate the actual differences between them in the context of their room to maneuver and to act on their paradox.

A paradox, such as individual versus organizational leadership, can, as shown above, have different expressions depending on the organizational context. If, for example, an owner-management does not want to give up responsibility to the hired professional leadership, it becomes more complicated to change focus from personal leadership to more distributed, organizational management. From an owner-manager perspective, the problem is delegation, while for a professional manager it may be the need for a clearer mandate to be able to serve the owner-manager's wish for a more organizationally anchored management. To explore your paradox is at the same time an inquiry into the context where you choose to make a difference. This considers both the capabilities of the managers involved and the organization in which the paradox investigation takes place.

Tool 5.2: The Paradox Kaleidoscope – uncovering related paradoxes

In the previous Case 5.1 of Tony investigating different approaches to innovation, we saw that by applying the Paradox Quadrant, he *widens* his paradox, so that both negative and positive sides on both sides of the paradox emerge more clearly. Although the picture has become more complex, it is also more tangible and manageable when it is put into writing in the template. As you fill out the Paradox Quadrant you may also discover that even if you have carefully followed the recommendations in Chapter 4 that presented you with the first phase of choosing your specific paradox, you will in the later step encounter different "interfaces" of your paradox. This is not surprising since paradoxes rarely appear alone; rather, they appear in "bundles". Maybe you observe that your paradox has "adjacent paradoxes", which you can use to understand better your chosen paradox (Henriksen et al., 2021). Or perhaps you will find out that your management colleagues have paradoxes that are "neighboring paradoxes", which in some way or other interact with your paradox.

The Paradox Kaleidoscope is a method for seeing "neighboring paradoxes" and "paradox bundles" without mixing them all together into a big mess. While maintaining focus on the paradox that you are particularly interested in mastering, you can expand your field of view to also include your own and possibly also your management colleagues' neighboring paradoxes. This is important since it offers you the opportunity to maintain sight of aspects that may not be immediately part of the chosen paradox. But they may in the grander scheme of things be decisive for defining the scope and actual possibilities for acting on the selected paradox. The kaleidoscope method is about looking at a leadership challenge through a particular lens and then changing the lens slightly to obtain a new perspective and see the paradox anew. A single paradox is comparable to one of the lenses in the kaleidoscope, as illustrated in Figure 5.5.

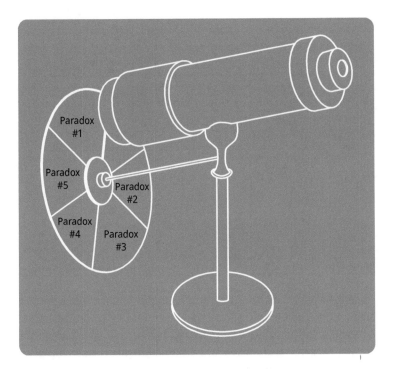

Figure 5.5: Paradox Kaleidoscope.

Case 5.4: Diana's paradox knot – one paradox rarely comes alone

The manager Diana starts her work with paradox leadership by looking more closely at the often-opposing management needs of respectively mobile and stable employees, where neither group can be dispensed with, and both groups must be catered for and developed, even if they want something different. To get even closer to her paradox (and become even more confident that she has chosen to put the most appropriate paradox in the center), however, she looks at her problems through the kaleidoscope. Here, among other things, she observes:

There are tensions when simultaneously she must lead highly mobile employees and the more stable and loyal colleagues. But the paradox also contains an element of another paradox, namely the opposing relationship between focusing on the elite versus the breadth of talent. Shall Diana go purposefully after the particularly high-skilled top formers, who in her case are also the most mobile? Or shall she give the attention to the reliable, solid performers, who admittedly do not set records, but on the other hand cannot be dispensed with? The highly mobile need attention to avoid attrition. At the same time, the loyal performers may feel that there is just a bit too much focus on the few top performers.

Diana turns on the kaleidoscope and becomes aware that there is also an extremely inconvenient coincidence between the mobile, talented, and younger employees, whereby Diana also must deal with a challenge that is about the field of tension between younger and older generations in the workplace. Competence and talent development requires both the ability for development-oriented leadership and control through management, and Diana understands she is strongest in management and systems. Still, she finds it challenging to focus on the development-oriented tasks. It becomes clear as she turns the kaleidoscope on to "leadership versus management", whereby she recognizes that her "anchor paradox" also contains this aspect. She continues to turn the kaleidoscope and now notes that she is in the situation that the specific talent and development needs addressing to include the attitudes of external stakeholders in addition to internal selection procedures of talents. Balancing external ideas of talent that find their way "from the outside–in" into the organization, where they must meet the organizational culture's more fundamental approaches, is to be counterbalanced with the understanding of who is a talent ("from the inside–out"). Conclusions from such different rounds of analysis far from always point in identical directions.

As she turns the kaleidoscope again, she is reminded that there is also another twist. Diana is the manager of a virtual team, where employees are geographically dispersed and of different nationalities. At the same time, she is in the cross-pressure between the employees who are co-located with her and those she needs to offer a visibility for at the distance. The fact that the dispersed team is located in different countries further adds to the complexity, because there are different subcultures and daily routines, just as there are variations in laws and general agreements that affect how she can act in order to ensure the retention and development of employees.

In a kaleidoscope, a series of light reflections causing beautiful patterns emerge from small, singular elements (for example, small, colored pieces of partially transparent material) when you turn it. In the same way, the "paradox kaleidoscope" offers the possibility to identify patterns and relations in an otherwise singular leadership paradox. This can be a way to qualify your understanding of the paradox, and it may serve as inspiration if you feel stuck. The kaleidoscope can be used to force a change of perspective that can provide new inspiration to understand a paradox more thoroughly. Once a perspective is exhausted, the kaleidoscope is turned to a new position.

The Paradox Kaleidoscope thus prepares you for a structured brainstorm. Depending on the paradox you have chosen as your starting point, you can choose to try two or three neighbouring paradoxes to see what can be learned from them. In Diana's case, the path through the kaleidoscope meant, among other things:

1) She became aware that there was an international challenge that she had not initially addressed.

2) It reminded her that she had a preference toward operational management as opposed to strategic employee development, which served to put her original paradox in a new light.

3) She saw that the geographically dispersed team posed specific challenges for employee retention, as some employees were situated physically away from her as a manager.

The Paradox Kaleidoscope deliberately provides the possibility to work with the tension that can exist between different leadership paradoxes as well as helps to further explore the individual paradox. With each new perspective in the kaleidoscope, a new image emerges and, from this, several new options for action can be identified. The basic idea is that a paradox is always located in a context of other paradoxes, which can have an influence on the possibilities of dealing with the paradox you have currently chosen to work with. You can, with the tool, work systematically to compare and possibly replace your chosen paradox, or you can reflect once more on the connection that your paradox has to related paradoxes. The Paradox Kaleidoscope can also be used to involve others, for example your management colleagues. In that case, is it about seeing your own paradoxes in the context of your managerial colleagues' paradoxes. Thus, you obtain an overall picture of your joint challenges as a management collective. Your "paradox mix" can give rise to positive as well as negative synergies as each of you also must deal with your own individual paradoxes.

Case 5.5: A collective leadership challenge – a paradox mix

Elfix is a technology and construction company that delivers specialist contracts within the fields of electrical engineering, plumbing, and safety installations for new buildings and renovations. Currently, there are about 850 employees. Although Elfix's strategies and visions include the vision to be able to guide everyone in the same direction, each individual manager is typically left with his or her own specific challenges. One middle manager in the group, Marianne, for example, experiences that the commitment of her employees is not always at the same level. This is especially the case of a small group of employees with whom she tends to spend an inappropriate amount of daily time and who receive a disproportionate amount of managerial attention. The other middle manager, Henrik, experiences a diverse constellation of the employees. Some are fiery souls, while others are working at a basic level of compliance. He wants to establish a small group of key workers who are stable and hard-working performers. The third manager, Stephanie, is the department manager, and she finds that many work tasks that could be solved internally are outsourced. Her challenge is to achieve better capacity utilization across departments.

The specific issues that the managers outline for one another in the group are the ones that they experience as their most burning current issues. However, it is only an expression of a small selection of the three managers' overall management tasks and challenges. There are additional administrative and operations-oriented management tasks as well as management obligations related to different types of development processes. The group of managers uses a paradoxical perspective as a common approach to identify the many cross-pressures that make up their specific leadership challenges. Taken together, this provides a picture of the leadership team's paradox mix.

The group identifies Marianne's challenge as a paradox mix consisting of the following three paradoxes: 1) individual *and* organizational leadership, 2) leadership *and* management, and 3) passion *and* performance.

The group jointly identifies Henrik's paradoxes as:
1) matrix versus specialization/silo, 2) employees *and* free agents, and finally 3) passion *and* performance.

Finally, they summarize the department head, Stephanie's paradox mix as follows:
1) innovation from the inside out *and* from the outside in, 2) leadership *and* management, and 3) passion *and* performance.

After identifying each paradox mix, each manager selects one paradox, which he uses as a starting point for exploring their joint leadership challenge.

Marianne chooses to focus his attention on the "individual *and* organizational"-tension, and thus concentrates on how she could both withdraw from operations while potentially increasing the commitment of his employees by becoming better at giving them additional responsibilities.

Henrik focuses on managing the differences between the very different employee groups via the "matrix versus specialization/silo" paradox.

Finally, the department head, Stephanie, highlights increased collaboration and knowledge sharing across departments via the "outside–in versus inside–out" tension.

The paradox perspective gave the three managers a better and more nuanced understanding of their own situation and a more focused starting point for embarking on some tensions contained in their paradoxes. They noticed that their leadership challenges had common features. They all had a leadership challenge that in one way or another was about dealing with the field of tension between passion and performance.

Five learning coordinates for the second phase of paradox navigation – paradox investigation

In this phase, the paradox investigation creates insight into the internal relations and contradictions of the chosen paradox, including a deeper understanding of the "hows and whys" of the chosen paradox. In summary, there are five coordinates that you may need to pay special attention to at this stage of navigating your paradox:

1. The "investigation work" related to your paradox is focusing on the internal dynamics of the paradox: what are the contradictions, what are the dependencies, and what effects are built into prioritizing one side of the paradox over the other? What is the contribution from each side, and what problems arise if one of them is downplayed? The Paradox Quadrant gives you an initial overview of the nuts and bolts of the paradox and your navigation of it. Specifically, our experience shows that the same paradox can have quite different individual manifestations. Managers have different responsibilities, professional backgrounds, experiences, and personalities and, for these reasons, they may share the same paradox, but place themselves in completely different places in relation to the two poles of the paradox.

2. The Paradox Quadrant clarifies why and how your paradox is "both–and" and not "either–or". If your efforts with the model convince you that one side is the only right side for you and your organization, you are well advised to consider returning to Phase 1 to re-select a focus area. Your focus area must be characterized by constituting a persistent challenge.

3. The investigation of your paradox(es) is necessarily also an examination of your own situation or context. Paradoxes do not come with a one-size-fits-all to-do list. They must be understood and handled in relation to where you are as a manager, and therefore each leadership paradox has its own specific expression and content features. In some organizations there may be an inclination to communicate certain poles as having a higher value than others, for example leadership in

favour of management, or organizational rather than individual leadership. If this is the case, it is critical that you as a manager do not blindly follow organizational norms and instead recognize that both of the poles may make sense in the context, and that they express a balanced both–and view.

4. It may be useful to test whether you experience several overlapping paradoxes, which could also be useful to expand your understanding and your abilities to handle your key paradox. This might entail a change of your way of thinking about your current paradox or supplement your reflections with new angles that might complement your developmental efforts.

5. When working with leadership paradoxes on your own or in a management team, there will often be several leadership paradoxes at play. It may be appropriate to examine how the chosen paradoxes interact. When similar paradoxes appear across a management team, this may indicate that the paradox is not just individual, but organizational, and therefore strategically relevant to the company. From our experience, managers utilizing their individual strengths in relation to the same paradox can act as sounding boards and sparring partners for one another, as one person's weakness is typically the other's strength.

You are now ready to embark on the next phase in your paradox leadership process, which is presented in Chapter 6, "Phase 3. Charting a course of action – identifying and choosing appropriate actions".

References

Henriksen, T. D., Nielsen, R. K., Vikkelsø, S., Bévort, F., and Mogensen, M. (2021). A paradox rarely comes alone: A quantitative approach to investigating knotted leadership paradoxes in SMEs. *Scandinavian Journal of Management*, 37(1), 101135.

Johnson, B. (2014, 1992). *Polarity Management: Identifying and Managing Unsolvable Problems*. Amhearst, MA: HRD Press.

Chapter 6
Phase 3: Charting a course of action – identifying and choosing appropriate actions

When navigating paradoxes, it is important that you as a manager give yourself enough time to clarify exactly what the paradox consists of. In the clarification phase the many different quizzes, games, and not least the Paradox Quadrant that have been presented on the previous pages can be utilized. That is the foundation for this chapter. As illustrated in Figure 6.1, we start Phase 3, Charting a course of action. However, choosing actions does not mean that you absolutely must start acting right now. Phase 3 still calls for reflection and afterthought. For the action-oriented person, this moment can be frustrating, maybe even be a provocation. From here, however, the suggestion is to mobilize your courage and confidence. Embarking on wanting to deal with paradoxes is both a challenging and time-consuming process, but it is also an important and necessary investment. Once you have invested time and resources in getting to know your paradox well, you have created a solid foundation for your leadership practice, both now and in the future. During the process you have had the opportunity to not only get to know your paradox, but also yourself, your own ways of thinking, and your action preferences:

Figure 6.1: Five phases of paradox navigation – Phase 3.

In this chapter, we offer two tools that in different ways enable you to choose your action strategies in a reflected and systematic way. At the same time, you will have the opportunity to reflect on the possible actions and your action preferences:

- Tool 6.1: *"Paradox Reflection for Action – Step by step"*. This tool guides you through seven steps: Motivation, Focus, Actions, Inspiration, Benchmarks/Key Performance Indicators (KPIs), Check the Balance, and Reality Check to help you select and formulate meaningful actions.

https://doi.org/10.1515/9783110788877-007

- Tool 6.2: *"The Caricature Cabinet – the development of personal strategies for dealing with leadership paradoxes"*. The mirror cabinet helps you identify your own action preferences and consider whether you should break with "what you usually do".

The way you usually go about your management tasks can be quite efficient, but if you are in a paradoxical, and perhaps new, situation, it may be necessary to give your own leadership style a critical overhaul. If you are used to delivering solutions and generally being quick on the trigger, it can end up being a barrier to maneuvering in paradox-filled waters in practice.

The chapter also contains three illustrative cases:

- Case 6.1: *"Breaking away from your existing self-image as a manager"*. An experienced manager does away with his usual notions of self-management and chooses actions that open up new sides of him/herself.
- Case 6.2: *"Coping with paradox – head or tail wind?"* is about what consequences it has if the way you want to navigate your paradox is clashing with the settled traditions and cultures of the organization.
- Case 6.3: *"From ostrich to action hero – getting into the game?"* An inexperienced manager acknowledges that she must step up and find her inner "action hero" and assume the character as a manager.

The first tool, *"Paradox Reflection for Action - step by step"*, is based on the Paradox Quadrant (see page 72) taking one step further from paradox reflection to the choice of possible actions. This represents a move from uncovering the sunny and shadow sides of the paradox to an actual plan for how the paradox can be handled in practice. Although paradoxes are inherently complex, this does not necessarily mean that your path to designate concrete actions should be complex as well. Step by step the extended Paradox Quadrant helps you to "break down" your paradox into smaller components. That way, you can use the model to focus exactly on those parts of your paradox that you want to and are able to act on here and now. The quadrant also helps you to ensure that your actions are followed up by specific goals, and that you are mindful to not only shift from one pole to the other, but maintain a balanced view of both poles. You should not lose balance along the way. Finally, the model gives you the opportunity to make sure that your choices of actions are realistic, so that you do not crash before you have even started.

The second tool, the Caricature Cabinet, is a self-reflection tool that invites you to confront the action strategies that you as a manager usually use. The tool focuses on the fact that managers respond very differently to paradox. Some are "consensus seekers", others are more hardcore "action heroes", while others prefer to live a secluded life, and calmly wait for the "storm to subside". This tool offers you the opportunity to reflect on different types of personal strategies and to consider if other possible paths could be useful and more appropriate in your situation.

Case 6.1: Breaking away from your existing self-image as a manager

Karl worked at the same company for 20 years, and over the years he gained increasing management responsibilities. It is a responsibility that he accepts, but that, after his most recent appointment, challenges his usual way of leading. From having acted as a professional beacon and effective "action hero", in close contact with the employees, Karl must increasingly lead the company's long-term and strategic challenges. Karl is aware of his paradox, to balance his highly person-dependent leadership with a new focus on leading through others and to support the organizational processes. Karl knows his paradox, the question is, what should he do about it? Karl himself chooses to focus on the expectations that both he and his employees have for him as a manager. To break with the previous (self-)image and not least create legitimacy around the prospected change, Karl decides to do two things: 1) to organize a meeting with his immediate superior before the end of the month. It is about gaining moral support, but also specifically getting permission to introduce one weekly homework day and thus create time for new and more "desk-heavy" tasks. 2) To communicate the changed priority to the employees. Here, too, it is about creating an increased acceptance that the action hero will be replaced with a less visible manager. In this way, Karl manages to translate his understanding of paradox into a very concrete and basically very simple action plan. Although the chosen actions may not "fix" his entire paradox, they are steps on the way to changing the ingrained action strategies that Karl has previously used, and this is thus an important starting point for his further paradox navigation in practice.

Tool 6.1: Paradox Reflection for Action – "Step by step"

This tool is built around the Paradox Quadrant (inspired and developed from Barry Johnson's Polarity Map; see Johnson, 2014, 1992) and requires it to be completed before moving on (see p. 72–75). The extended Paradox Quadrant adds a process of seven steps: Motivation, Focus, Actions, Inspiration, Benchmarks/KPIs, Check the Balance, and Reality Check. These seven dimensions help to focus, deepen, and balance concrete paradox leadership efforts, and to identify specific measuring points as a follow-up to the efforts. The individual manager must use the tool to create an actual paradox action plan. By following the seven steps in the process, you will benefit from prior insights about a paradox's sunny and shadow sides. The seven steps create a starting point for practical paradox leadership, which is sufficiently delimited so that it is also realistic to proceed with.

In practice, the extended Paradox Quadrant can of course be used in relation to any paradox. However, below we take our point of departure from a paradox about talent development and the necessary balance that must be found between investing in the elite without forgetting the breadth at the same time. Based on a completed Paradox Quadrant, we describe the seven steps that follow.

Step 1: Motivation

As a starting point, you, like most managers, will tend to lean toward a "favorite side" of your paradox. This is a side that you would like to strengthen and promote rather than the opposite one. In a paradox leadership context, it is of course important that you do not uncritically jump on that hobbyhorse and ride toward the sunset. As the whole paradoxical mindset prescribes, it can prove fatal to bet so one-sidedly. But when it comes to getting started, it is crucial to rely on the desire and motivation to act. For this reason, it can be important, as a starting point, to focus on the pole in the paradox that you immediately "want more of", of course, in full awareness that there is still another dimension to consider. If we take the paradox "Talent development – elite versus inclusiveness" in Figure 6.2, then the motivation could be to focus more on the particularly talented employees in the company, because you as a manager believe

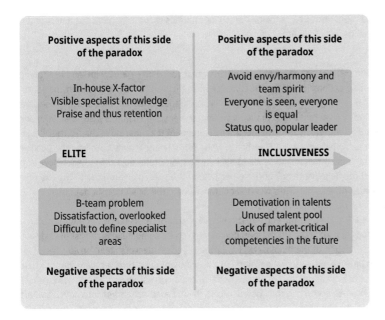

Positive aspects of this side of the paradox	Positive aspects of this side of the paradox
In-house X-factor Visible specialist knowledge Praise and thus retention	Avoid envy/harmony and team spirit Everyone is seen, everyone is equal Status quo, popular leader
ELITE	**INCLUSIVENESS**
B-team problem Dissatisfaction, overlooked Difficult to define specialist areas	Demotivation in talents Unused talent pool Lack of market-critical competencies in the future
Negative aspects of this side of the paradox	Negative aspects of this side of the paradox

Figure 6.2: Paradox Quadrant: An elite versus inclusive talent perspective.

that this will add much more value to the company in the long term. That is, here and now you may choose to focus and act solely on one pole of the paradox, namely the elite dimension.

Step 2: Focus
As clarified in the completed Paradox Quadrant even one pole of the paradox, including both its sunny and shadow sides, can contain many elements. When you have decided which pole in the paradox you are most motivated for, then there are still important steps to be taken to delimit your focus. Rather than expanding your view too much, it is about selecting some limited elements to dive into. In the example of talent development and elite versus inclusiveness, the Paradox Quadrant shows that the sunny side of the elite dimension can be linked to retention of employees in the department through increased "recognition", and it can also imply the opportunity to brand the department with a special X-factor and thereby increase its status in the organization. The first element primarily points to initiatives that are aimed at employees within the department. The second element draws attention to the wider internal branding and communication. Such quite different kinds of efforts confront you with a critical choice. It can be a difficult choice and therefore it is important to keep in mind that you can and should always return to your paradox model to address the remaining elements. In line with the example above, this means that if you initially choose to focus your attention on giving employees more recognition, then later the branding element will serve as a starting point for new choices of actions.

Step 3: Action – how?
Once you have chosen a particular focus, for instance retaining employees through increased recognition, then it is time to think about how. How can you, in a practical way, work to make the special competences of the employees visible? How can you motivate and retain employees by giving them increased recognition? Two specific efforts, which address our example and focus on the elite dimension of the paradox, could be: 1) Revise and differentiate current job descriptions so that it becomes clearer that employees do

and can do something different and 2) Work to link the job descriptions to formal job descriptions, or titles to be able, eventually, to differentiate in terms of salary.

Step 4: Find inspiration

Once you have chosen and focused on the part of the paradox that you want to work with, and in addition have identified your specific actions in relation to concrete elements in the model, it is with the fourth step time to collect further inspiration. Again, it takes the basic Paradox Quadrant as a starting point. As also described in the Paradox Quadrant in the previous section, the positive elements associated with one pole of the paradox will be reflected vis-à-vis the negative elements of the other pole, that is, the "diagonal analysis" of the Paradox Quadrant (p. 76). Therefore, when formulating actions based on the positive aspects of one pole of paradox, it may make sense to seek inspiration in the field diagonally below, that is, where you have noted the negative things at the other pole of the paradox. Returning to the example of the paradox, elite versus inclusiveness, this will be about increasing the awareness of potential actions in the negative aspects by promoting inclusiveness.

For example, in Figure 6.1 it could be the entry "Lack of market-critical competencies in the future". For the sake of possible actions, it could raise an examination of what those competences consist of and then linking them with the formulation of the employees' job profiles. Such endeavors could obviously call for the involvement of both internal and external partners. In this way, you get a broader view that can help you and your management colleagues to define the department's current strengths and weaknesses about a future market. Another action can thus be added: To involve external and/or internal customers as partners in defining the department's future competences and job descriptions.

Step 5: Beacons and Key Performance Indicators

If plans are not to remain just plans, it is essential that you commit yourself to implementing them. In a busy everyday life, where many things are fighting for your attention, it is also appropriate in the process to give that commitment a very concrete expression. In step 5, it is a matter of defining and formulating KPIs (Key Performance Indicators) or similar benchmarks (also see Chapter 7 for more on evaluation and follow-up). If we return to the paradox concerning exclusive *and* inclusive talent development, then it could, for example, be about measuring the extent to which the chosen efforts increase the retention and motivation of the employees. Specifically, simple measures can be established of how many employees leave the department, and/or how motivation or satisfaction develops in the annual employee satisfaction survey. However, it can often be difficult to make a direct link between an effort and quantifiable results, and therefore process goals can also be an option. Process goals can consist of setting deadlines for carrying out activities. In relation to the example above, you could, for example, set goals and follow up on whether you have completed job description workshops or presented revised role descriptions for HR and the Executive Board before a set date. Both goal and process benchmarks are essential to keep yourself on track in a busy work life. But it is important that the use of KPIs and benchmarks is kept at a reasonable level so that the focus remains on doing something rather than creating unnecessary bureaucracy in the form of excessive management of goals and follow-up.

Step 6: Check the balance

With a solid starting point in strengthening one dimension of the paradox, it is time for you to challenge the actions that you have chosen by looking at the opposite pole of the paradox. Only by insisting that it is not a matter of choosing between two extremes, but of doing both, can you navigate paradox in practice, namely a continuous balancing act. If you are betting on elite, then you also need to think about inclusiveness. If we address the positive aspects of working with inclusiveness, it is, as mentioned in the completed Paradox Quadrant above, also about ensuring a good sense of community, a "team spirit" among the employees. But individual job descriptions and thoughts about differentiated pay are potentially actions that directly contradict the ambition to build "team spirit". Step number 6 is about balancing the palette of actions so that they also incorporate the other paradox pole. It could, for example, be about 1) making joint employee workshops, where there is a focus on talking task distribution and interfaces and/or 2) introducing team development conversations as a supplement to individual development interviews, so that there is not only a focus on the individual (talent) development. As with the other actions, these require additions as well as revisiting KPIs.

Step 7: Reality check

At this stage, you have created a beautiful – and perhaps also very ambitious – action plan and the associated KPIs, each of which in its own way relates to the two poles of paradox. Step 7 is therefore about doing a reality check. Find out if it is really feasible to put all these fine ships in the sea, without at the same time ending up with a shipwreck or more in the fleet. In step 7, we suggest three parameters to check the project's real solidity. Against this background, you can decide which actions to prioritize here and now, which ones you should postpone, and which ones should not even see the light of day. It is about time, skills, and resources.

Time: You should choose actions that are possible to carry out in the foreseeable future. Excessively elongated projects are often ending up losing momentum and attention, both from yourself and from the others involved.

Competences: You should also ask yourself whether you really have the competences to carry out the project that you have committed to. In this context, competences need to be understood in more than one sense. First, it is about assessing whether you have the decision-making competence to carry out the actions that you have been given. If you can see in advance that (too) much depends on others further up the managerial rungs, or that you get into an organizational "headwind", then you risk just playing yourself off the field in advance. The actions you choose should preferably be within your decision mandate. You must have enough power to back off your intentions. As we shall see in the example below, it is possible to work with paradox leadership despite resistance. However, as the example illustrates, this presupposes that you can include the possible resistance in your reflections on choice of actions.

If we return to the second element of the competence dimension, it is about the knowledge and skills that you need to implement your plans. Have you thrown yourself into choosing actions that require you to act in a too unfamiliar role, for example as a process facilitator, when you are primarily used to acting as a manager based on your professional expertise? Paradox leadership will inevitably mean that you will have to learn and develop, but choosing a development path that necessitates development of (too) many new skills is not sustainable. This aspect is closely linked to the last point, namely the issue of resources.

Resources: You need to know your own limitations, or at least be open about the fact that you are not a superwoman (or superman). It is both about the professional competences, as mentioned above, but also about your personal resources and traits. Sufficient abilities, but also the necessary courage and energy, must be present. The task that you give yourself as a manager must be ambitious and at times it will bring you out of the comfort zone. However, your action plans must also be realistic in the sense that they should not end up knocking you off course. You may burn for it, but you must not burn out in the process.

The extended Paradox Quadrant is a support framework that helps you moving from reflection mode to defining and selecting relevant actions. Because the quadrant is based on the many good reflections from the completed Paradox Quadrant of Phase 2, you can ensure that the leadership actions you choose and design are based on paradoxical thinking, and that you relate to it reflexively and systematically to the specific context you are in, and the resources you have available as a manager, or the lack of resources. At the same time, it is important to emphasize that the process of the seven steps is not a one-off exercise. On the contrary. Precisely because the Paradox Quadrant is so rich in information, there is a basis for taking a tour around the quadrant several times. By repeating the process, you can be sure to get out into all the nooks and crannies of your paradox while keeping focus and direction in your paradox leadership.

Paradox leadership in headwinds – carefully choose your paradox

One of the things that can be extra demanding in paradox leadership, and challenge you on both competencies and resources, is if you experience "organizational headwind". Some leadership paradoxes provide opposition because they represent organizational change and conflict. Many managers or staff functions must not only be responsible for the day-to-day operations, but also drive major change processes. This place, where external demands and expectations meet the organization's current norms and routines, is a stormy place and it places great demands on the manager who wants to deal with them. It requires more personal resources, more time, and not least more collaboration with other stakeholders in the organization to deal successfully with paradoxes that meet "headwinds". On the other hand, paradoxical leadership in headwinds can be particularly valuable because, at least potentially, it can act as a catalyst for major processes of change.

Case 6.2: Coping with paradox – head wind or tail wind?

An example of paradox leadership in headwinds takes place with the HR manager in BuildForm, a medium-sized company in the construction sector. The company has been Danish owned until 10 years ago, when it was first acquired by a European company and then by an American private equity fund. In connection with the acquisitions and internationalization, there has gradually been a greater focus on HR. Previously, HR was "something you were used to do without", as the newly hired HR manager expresses it. The former HR manager served also the marketing director, and this meant that the HR portfolio was given low priority, and necessary tasks were largely outsourced to external suppliers.

Since the private equity fund emerged as a new owner, a consulting firm has streamlined and optimized the company in several ways. Eight strategic focus areas are identified, including talent development. In the HR manager's work with talent development, she has a special focus on balancing formalization and openness about processes, and criteria are added toward a more informal model, where talent development can operate a little more "under the radar". It turns out that when the HR manager formulates concrete actions she is greatly challenged by the fact that talent development is a potentially sensitive topic. Talent is a concept that is first and foremost brought into the company with the intervention of the new owners and the external consultants. According to the company's managers, highlighting some employees over others is far from the company's culture. As one of the managers puts it: "We have a strong community culture. Everyone is seen as equal. We all help to make the community run." They think and speak in "we" rather than focusing on the individual performance.

In a situation where the HR manager on the one hand has been given a limited task of introducing talent development and on the other is confronted with a culture that emphasizes community values inclusiveness she must proceed cautiously. First, she chooses to take the initiative to involve the management team in an open dialog about what talent is to them. Second, she chooses to include a form of development interviews, which is already used by the managers in the company to assess the employees' performance and potential. With the implementation of the two actions, the HR manager succeeds in taking a first step toward a more formalized approach to talent development, while respecting the company's culture and preference for community and equality. Paradox leadership, including choice of actions, is not just a matter of personal preference. When you must choose the actions to deal with your paradox, then you must necessarily relate to the organization and its culture. And not least the "headwind" issues.

Tool 6.2: The Caricature Cabinet – the development of personal strategies for dealing with leadership paradoxes

The second tool proceeds on the topic of identifying actions for navigating your chosen leadership paradox, but we step a little closer and focus on your personal leadership style and action preferences. By offering a total of nine images, nine metaphors, for personal action preferences, the tool acts as a mirror. What you see in the mirror is a caricature. Exaggeration, as you know, often helps you understand. This does not mean that you feel fully recognized and disclosed when you look around in this Caricature Cabinet. Nevertheless, just like with a cartoon, the nine images, with humor as a tool, manage to highlight the essence of the different types of management behavior. And don't you see a bit of yourself in the stereotypical image? In any case, you can understand the Caricature Cabinet as an invitation to reflect on your action preferences and identify available alternative action strategies.

When people experience a situation, they typically have a back catalog of actions and strategies for how to handle it. With this chapter's Tool 6.2, we focus on managers' "knee-jerk" reactions, that is, the ways in which managers unconsciously choose to deal with their leadership challenges. Often, a more experienced person has a more extensive acting repertoire, but he or she has developed habits and preferences. They constitute the person's typical reaction patterns, for example if he or she is thrown a ball or is confronted with an option. These are called reaction or action preferences, and they are activated automatically when people respond to an incident. As a manager, you have a similar backlog of action and reaction preferences. This is expressed, for example, in the form of communication preferences (do you prefer to call, email, or do you take the conversation face-to-face?) and decision preferences (do you make the decision yourself, do you delegate, or do you prefer to investigate the matter further?). When you encounter a paradox or are in a paradoxical situation, you will either tend to, for example, wait and see if the situation goes away on its own or you may roll up your sleeves and start solving problems or you could be in the habit of reducing the complexity by delimiting the problem. These are just a few examples of action preferences that managers (and maybe you too?) will typically take advantage of – additional examples follow.

Having clear preferences for action and problem solving as a manager is not necessarily the most appropriate thing when it comes to dealing with leadership paradoxes. However, the opposite situation is not much better. In that case you as a manager experience no options for action and therefore allow yourself to get paralyzed by being overwhelmed by a paradox. Between the two extremes lies the possibility of finding several (more) appropriate and effective approaches to dealing with paradoxes (Figure 6.3).

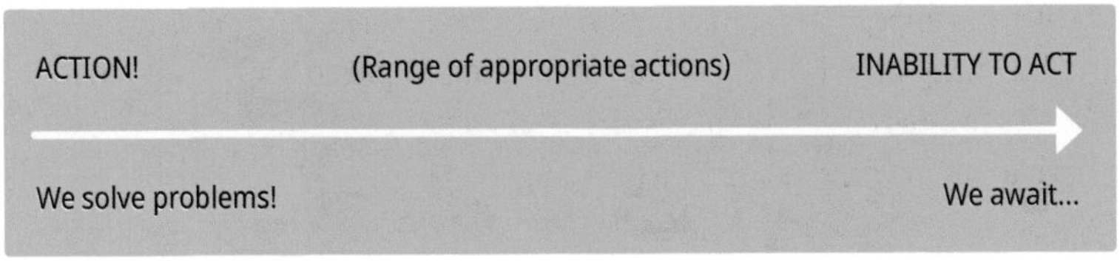

ACTION!	(Range of appropriate actions)	INABILITY TO ACT
We solve problems!		We await...

Figure 6.3: Between action and paralysis.

If you fail to act as a manager, those involved will have the opportunity to solve their problems themselves, with the built-in risk that something will go wrong in the process. On the contrary, the fact that you immediately "roll up your sleeves", act, and solve the problems carries the risk that those involved do not themselves develop a way to solve the problems in which they are involved. To hit that space instead for action offered between the two extreme positions, it is a prerequisite that you as a manager:

- become aware of your own, unconscious reactions and action preferences
- develop a personal repertoire of approaches that can be used strategically in each situation

Becoming aware of your own unconscious reactions and action preferences

The purpose for you as a manager in this is that you see yourself in the mirror and clarify how you react when you encounter a paradox. Here it is important to distinguish between how you should, in principle, react and how you in fact react. What you need to focus on is the unreflective reaction, which is expressed when you do not think about how you should react. This is what typically happens when you are emotionally pressured, for example need time, if you are tired, or if you experience the situation as a routine task. In these situations, the knee-jerk reaction will often be triggered, and you will act accordingly, with the pros and cons associated with the automatic reaction. Of course, to become aware of your own, perhaps less appropriate, reaction patterns, you need to be willing to acknowledge your own weaknesses and strengths. At the same time, it requires you to be able to, for a moment, suppress your urge to describe what you should do and really address what you habitually do. This process can be helped along by answering the following question:

Challenge A: How do you usually react when you experience a paradox?

You can explore this question through the gallery of characters below, which reflects nine caricatured rough sketches of ways of relating to paradoxes. The purpose is first and foremost that the nine images of leadership styles should inspire you to become aware of your otherwise mindless action patterns. It is important to note that our list is based on the typical reaction patterns that we have observed during our interventions in the Leadership GPS program and the list is not meant to be exhaustive (for further inspiration, see, for instance, Zhang et al., 2015). We are inspired by Jarzabkowski and and Lê (2017) highlighting how humor aid in responding to paradox, and so the following stylized, fun-house mirror-image are designed as a reflective device fostering self-critical, yet appreciative dialog and reflection.

Presentation of the Caricature Cabinet's action strategies

Here you are introduced to the Caricature Cabinet's personal gallery (Figure 6.4) to create (humorous) awareness of and insight into the individual strategies.

The action strategies of the Caricature Cabinet

The M/F action hero with a strong can-do attitude:
I can fix it!
You roll up your sleeves and get started , preferably
from one end. You solve problems.

The M/F master of non-action:
Hummmm...
You express acceptance and positive indifference to
suggested solutions. You actively non-act.

The optimist: Don't worry, be happy
You live by the saying: "if you have a problem
and you do not know what to do, then forget it, because
you do not know what to do anyway. If you have a problem
and you know what to do, then forget it, since you
know what to do."

The ostrich: I will wait until the storm passes
You bury your head in the famous sand and unnoticeably
wait it out. Sometimes a storm just needs to be allowed
to pass...

Share and share alike: Everybody gets exactly the same
you lead and distribute and ensure that everything runs fairly.
Everybody is treated exactly the same and gets exactly
the same.

The master of all shades of gray: Compromise on all fronts!
You are the master of compromise, who makes black
and white meet in a common compromise in a shade
of gray.

The change agent: Everything is a (well-planned) process!
You work in a continuous before-now-after continuum, where
gap analyzes between the current and desired situation set
the course towards the goal.

Figure 6.4: The action strategies of the Caricature Cabinet.

The common denominator: The fusion and the common "third way"

You love working with what unites: for example, working with "one company", best practices or an organizational culture, where gathering around common values brings difference and conflicts of interest together under a common third way.

The balance artist: Everything must be in balance

You balance considerations and believe that balances can be found, lost, and rediscovered through ongoingly being in touch with yourself and your surroundings - even if it may feel a bit "unfinished" or "messy."

Figure 6.4 (continued)

How to develop alternative action strategies

Once you have worked on the first question, it's about developing and expanding your strategic back catalog. Here, the Caricature Cabinet illustrated in Figure 6.4 again can work as a source of inspiration. The question you may ask yourself in that process is, as above, straightforward:

Challenge B: Could you react in a more productive way when you experience a paradox?

All nine different reaction patterns could be of interest for you, not only one of them. Particularly those that you find interesting and a bit exotic, or perhaps as outright revolutionary or ridiculous, compared to your own preferences can inspire you to add new reaction patterns to your existing repertoire. In this way, you develop a broader catalog that you can potentially choose from, of course always taking into consideration the given situation. Where some situations require non-action, other situations invite you to roll up your sleeves and act. That way, there are not some of the strategies that per definition are better than others. Each of the Caricature Cabinet's strategies has its strengths and weaknesses. However, it is important to emphasize that the pursuit of alternative action strategies is not intended to replace your current action preferences. Instead, it is about offering alternatives in those situations where the given paradox invites alternative solutions. To move from a theoretical to a practically applicable understanding of the strategies, it is necessary to test them in practice. Once you have chosen some strategies that inspire you, it is therefore obvious to try them out in practice. You can use the following questions to support you:

Questions for reflection:
- Which approaches from the Caricature Cabinet did you use?
- What was the situation and how do you usually handle it?
- Why did you choose this approach?
- What effects did this approach have?
- Would a different approach have had different effects?
- Are there other approaches that you plan to try in similar situations?
- How will you handle similar situations in the future?

Case 6.3: From ostrich to action-hero?

Maria has just been appointed head of a small department consisting of highly experienced staff. Soon, the department is facing major changes because of the introduction of new technology, and Maria assumes that it will become a difficult transition. Maria is young and professionally skilled, but she is inexperienced in the role of manager. She sets out to work with the paradox of individual versus organizational leadership. While this paradox for a professionally skilled manager is usually about strengthening delegation and organizational management in favor of a person-dependent approach that is often tied to professional expertise, Maria's situation is different: Like the ostrich, she chooses to stick her head in the sand and wait. Waiting for her to get some clearer messages from her own manager. Waiting for the new systems to arrive so that the change is more self-evident. Waiting to produce a slightly better plan. Waiting for. In the meeting with a management colleague, who experiences a similar paradox but of opposite sign, it becomes clear that Maria is most of all waiting for herself to act. When she finally becomes aware that her own preferred strategy is the ostrich and that she is hiding from action, she reaches a turning point. Strongly inspired by her colleague and by incorporating elements of her action strategy, Maria arranges a meeting with her boss to present her change plan. On that occasion, she expresses her need for leadership training, and she receives support. She walks straight to HR, so she can access sparring about her leadership role. With her inner action hero in hand, it suddenly becomes easier to do something and rise to the occasion. Maria realizes that despite her inner ostrich, she manages to act herself out of her rather unmanageable situation, one step at a time.

Having gone through this chapter, you are one step closer to being able to act upon your paradox. If you are an impatient action hero, this chapter might have felt more like a waiting position for you. But, as the third phase emphasizes, it is about choosing your actions carefully, not just about getting started. In the third phase of paradox navigation, you received concrete input on how you, step by step, can translate your understanding of your paradox into focused, concrete, and measurable actions. Your chosen action need not be rocket science or revolutionary change. On the contrary. Because any paradox potentially opens many potential actions, the third phase is primarily about narrowing down, focusing, and making a choice. In this context, your own motivation, resources, and competences are essential to include in the equation. When it comes to choosing your actions, it is of great value to know yourself and your own preferences: Do you usually act like the ostrich persona, or are you more related to the "master of all shades of grey"-persona? Your action strategies, conscious as well as unconscious, can potentially have major consequences for your handling of a paradox. Here, too, there are significant choices to make, and sizable gains to reap if you want to go new ways in dealing with your leadership paradoxes.

Five learning coordinates for the third phase of paradox navigation – identifying and choosing appropriate actions

Choosing actions is a phase where you consider different action strategies that match your paradox. It is a phase where you may be tempted to "short-circuit" the process and go into solution mode, but it is rewarding that you stick to the following benchmarks and stay on the "reflection track":

1. Prepare in the form of a prior paradox investigation a prerequisite for action. Your choices of actions must be based on the reflective work that you have already done to select and investigate your leadership paradox.
2. You cannot act on all the dimensions of the paradox at once. It is therefore important to focus your work. Go for what you are most motivated for and make sure to concretize your actions as much as possible.
3. Headwinds require more energy. Be aware that your choices depend on both your and the organization's resources. The more organizational headwinds you are in, the more energy your action plans will require from you.
4. Beware of your own action preferences. By knowing your own automatic reactions, you will be better able to make conscious and potentially better new choices as well, which can expand your action repertoire and thus lay the groundwork for new avenues in your paradox leadership.
5. A mandatory recurring task. Your paradox "does not go away" even with the best action plan. Look at your work of choosing actions as a recurring process, revisiting the different dimensions of your paradox. Only in this way do you ensure that you can also "keep the balance" between the two poles of paradox over time.

With these learning coordinates, you are now ready to put your chosen actions into actual handling of your paradox. This task is presented in Chapter 7, "Phase 4. Action in practice – grasping and handling your paradox".

References

Jarzabkowski, P. A., and Lê, J. K. (2017). We have to do this and that? You must be joking: Constructing and responding to paradox through humor. *Organization Studies*, 38(3–4), 433–462.

Johnson, B. (2014, 1992). *Polarity Management: Identifying and Managing Unsolvable Problems*. Amhearst, MA: HRD Press.

Zhang, Y., Waldman, D. A., Han, Y. L., and Li, X. B. (2015). Paradoxical leader behaviors in people management: Antecedents and consequences. *Academy of Management Journal*, 58(2), 538–566.

Chapter 7
Phase 4: Action in practice – grasping and handling your paradox

The three previous phases focus on selecting a relevant paradox in your leadership. There is a focus on developing your knowledge of and stress testing your paradox. Then the process continued with thinking about how and what actions you can (and should) choose to work with your leadership paradox. Accordingly in phase 4, the starting point is that you are aware of your leadership paradox and that you ensure that it contains some very central issues in your job and your organization (Phases 1 and 2). You should also be passionate about working with it. You have now chosen the actions that you believe will help you develop your ability to deal with the paradox (Phase 3). Now you need to implement your actions, without jeopardizing the more nuanced understanding of your challenges that you have built up so far. Overall, Phase 4 (Figure 7.1) is about anchoring and creating momentum in the actions you have chosen, through a systematic reflection on how they work. Preferably this is undertaken together with the stakeholders you depend on for your success.

PHASE 4

Action in practice
– grasping and handling
your paradox

PHASE 1   PHASE 2   PHASE 3   PHASE 5

Figure 7.1: Five phases of paradox navigation – Phase 4.

In this chapter, you will be introduced to two tools that can help you qualify how you work with the actions chosen:
- Tool 7.1: *"The 3D Cube Model"*. With this model, you can unpack key aspects of the selected actions. Is the task challenging enough to create real development? Do you have an overview of who are the relevant stakeholders, and to what extent they should be involved? Do you have the right methods to proceed constructively with the task?
- Tool 7.2: *"The Reflecting Team – the hot seat challenge"*. With this model, you can involve key stakeholders in a targeted reflection that can qualify the implementation of your actions.

https://doi.org/10.1515/9783110788877-008

There are also four illustrative cases in the chapter:

- Case 7.1: *"The paradoxical job description"* illustrates a way to initiate a process that creates dialog in a management team and makes it possible to deal with parts of the paradox that a top manager and his management teamwork with. A classic tool is use for this purpose, but now it obtains new meaning and application for handling paradoxes. Paradox management can easily be considered in existing tools in your organization, but usually some adjustment is needed.
- Case 7.2: *"Accounting for performance with 'passion' – financial accountability with an eye for passion"* is about a manager's concrete method of reconciling simultaneous focus on passion and performance through the active involvement of her internal stakeholders. It shows how the paradox interacts with the organizational context in which the manager gathers his or her resources, and which parts of the organization will experience the consequences the most.
- Case 7.3: *"Paradox synergy"* shows how a management team can work with several different individual management paradoxes and still create organizational synergy between them. In this case, we experience how a management team takes responsibility across the individually chosen paradoxes and actions, in the case of colleagues in the management team, in the case of the top manager, and when working with the next layer of managers and employees.
- Case 7.4: *"Hot seat challenge"* is about how a leadership team helps one another identify and create a breeding ground for appropriate actions to deal with their paradoxes as a reflective team.

You may be acquainted with similar models from other contexts, and it is important to emphasize that the models presented here are used with the specific purpose of dealing with paradoxes. Even if they may be familiar, please note that they may be used slightly differently now. Phase 4 is about actions, but actions are unique to the context in which they appear. Therefore, the tools are aimed at supporting your chosen actions. The cases used are illustrative examples of actions that managers have chosen in practice. They probably cannot be "copied" directly, but hopefully they can give you insights about how to move forward with your own actions.

Finally, the chapter summarizes and adds learning coordinates for this part of the Paradox Pathway.

Tool 7.1: The 3D Cube Model – clarify task, methods, and stakeholders

The 3D Cube Model, shown in Figure 7.2, is a tool for systematically relating to the selected leadership paradox in a practical way (This model is inspired by the learnings from an action learning intervention presented in Andersen, Bakka & Larsen, 1990; Larsen, 1990; Larsen, 1996);

The model aims to provide you with an overview of what you should be aware of when starting to act on your paradox. It is a kind of three-dimensional "safety check" before take-off.

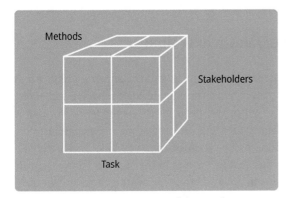

Figure 7.2: The three dimensions of the 3D Cube Model.

The purpose of the safety check is to ensure you have the best possible conditions for your paradox handling by considering three dimensions of the cube: *the task, stakeholders*, and *methods*. Each dimension is briefly described in the following:

1) First dimension: The practical task you ask yourself to do
This dimension involves formulation of the goal that your actions aim to accomplish. First you must relate to the paradox you are working with. If, for example, it is the competing demands between administration and operations-oriented management and development-focused leadership, and you specifically assess that there is a need to strengthen the leadership dimension, then a first step may be to talk to an experienced colleague. You can also simply decide to read an article or a book on the subject. As you become more aware of what leadership is and how you can strengthen your development-oriented leadership, you can set yourself the next task in a sequence. The point is that there can be many different tasks involved in dealing with the same paradox. The spectrum changes over time.

2) Second dimension: The stakeholders you want to involve
If you choose to start by reading a book, the concern for stakeholder interfaces is negligible. If, on the other hand, you can see that a significant obstacle to working a more leadership-oriented leadership style concerns the expectations for reporting that is embedded in the system, then relevant stakeholders could be your own manager or closest leadership colleague. It could also be the case that addressing a step in a sequence of action requires closer collaboration and greater trust with a neighboring department, or perhaps the support and involvement of HR?

3) Third dimension: The methods you want to apply
Methods should be understood broadly. It can be anything from gathering information, conducting conversations, organizing meetings, or giving presentations, or it could be a specific, however small, change in behavior. For example, a manager who was just working to strengthen leadership-oriented management decided to experiment with being more reluctant to give advice and to provide employees with more space to lead themselves. Her method was "to sit on her hands", as she put it. Specifically, this meant that she returned questions from her employees, with, for example: "What do you want to do? Find out and

come back to me." She experimented with a more reluctant role and, for example, let an employee speak in the meeting with a critical customer and, at the staff meeting, she had an employee make the summary on the board meeting. Small behavioral changes resulted in great effects in practical corporate life.

To balance the known and unknown over time

It is important to create the right tension between the known and the unknown. If you give yourself a task that is completely novel for you, decide to involve stakeholders that you do not normally interact with, and need to use methods that you have not tried before, then you have probably chosen a challenge that is too complex. Conversely, if you work in all areas within known territory, then you have with great certainty shielded yourself against new insights by staying in the comfort zone. As a rule of thumb, define the three dimensions in a way so that you will be in unknown territory regarding a minimum of one and a maximum of two of the three dimensions.

It is important to continuously, reflexively, and (self-) critically readdress the task, methods, and stakeholders. None of the three dimensions can or should be the same over time. The way in which the three dimensions change can be seen as an indication of the development that is taking place. The fact that you continuously change your task or methods is therefore not an expression of poor project planning, carelessness, or incompetence. It is a completely natural indication of the fact that you are on the move, and that you are learning something. Hence, paradoxes are not something you solve, but you will be precisely in a balancing act where you must continuously deal with and (re-)find the basic assumptions. The idea with the cube model is that as you try to handle your task, you also become wiser about your paradox. Figuratively speaking, the shifts may look like this (Figure 7.3), where the understanding and center of gravity changes, and the cube will roll as the work progresses:

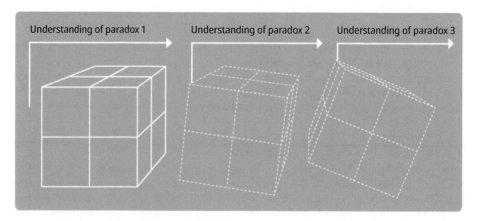

Figure 7.3: The 3D Cube Model in movement.

To ensure that you do not stagnate in the task and paradox understanding, it is crucial that you continuously re-evaluate whether you are still on the right track.

Below, we present cases of actions that managers have worked on in practice. They serve as inspiration for how you can work with the actions you plan to implement.

Case 7.1: The paradoxical job description – what does the boss need to do now?

A manager worked with the paradox between individual leadership and organizational leadership, that is, his own leadership vis-à-vis the leadership that otherwise took place in the organization. He and his management colleagues experienced that the manager's job description came into play. What are the manager's tasks today, and what should the manager do in the future when some of the tasks are built into the organization or delegated to others? When referring to the three dimensions of the 3D Cube Model, the task here is to change the distribution of tasks between the top manager and his management team and organization. The key stakeholders are the manager himself and the management team members. One of the methods to solve the task is to elaborate on the job description.

In principle, everyone knows what a job description is. It is defining key responsibilities, tasks, working conditions, and so forth. The example below shows basically what a job description for a manager could contain. As demonstrated, the technical or legal responsibility is not in focus in this understanding of the job description, but rather what tasks that the leadership role contains in the specific organization.

Example of elements in the manager's job description
Deliverables: What are the key results that the managers need to deliver, referring to the strategy and plans of the organization? To whom does the leader deliver?

Mandate: What decisions need acceptance from the superior manager and what decisions is the manager able to take on her or his own without asking others (superiors or the board)?

How should the manager prioritize her or his time among the tasks as described below following the responsibility and mandate as described above?

Recurrent meetings: For example, which meetings are "owned" by the manager. That is, which mandatory meetings are the manager responsible for and what is the role of the manager in the meetings?

People management: Which managers and employees are the manager responsible for and how? For example, what are the specific obligations involved for the performance of leadership (for example, one-to-one interviews)?

Which employees refer to the manager? How does the manager follow up on this, for example monitoring quality and quantity of agreed activities?

Role in general management: What tasks does the manager have in the organization in general, that is, in relation to their own leadership team or in relation to employees in other departments?

Roles in business development: What tasks does the manager have for business development, for example, concerning public authorities, external partners, and clients?

Other tasks: (specific for the organization in question)

The above description is an inspiration list of elements that are part of a specific leadership role. The list will be up for discussion when responsibilities and tasks are to be transferred from the top manager to the organization, for example, to other managers.

In the mentioned company, the former owner-manager needed to transfer a large part of the responsibility to his management group. His goal was to shift the focus away from himself as a person onto the organization that was in the making. The role and thus the job description had to be changed so that the owner-manager could achieve both the time and legitimacy to solve several external tasks, including business development and strategic customer care.

Some important questions for the job description were:
- Which meetings in the departments should the owner-manager join?
- What role should he play in them?
- Should he attend the regular management group meeting?
- And if so, for how long in the future, and with what role?

When beginning to define the new content of the leadership role compared to what it was before or relating to the expectations of the top manager, the paradox suddenly became much clearer. In this way, the reformulation of the manager's job description transformed into an important paradox action.

The main lesson from Case 7.1 about the manager's job description is that the conversation about what every manager should do and is responsible for automatically involves a discussion of the balance between what the top manager should be responsible for and should decide on and subsequently what should and could happen elsewhere in the organization. When considering the 3D Cube Model, the example focuses on the fact that working with the "task" (shifting focus from the manager to the organization) requires the involvement of the "stakeholders" (managers) and a choice of "method" (the job description). This is a way to initiate a constructive dialog in the management team on how the management could be arranged when the paradox has found a new balance.

Thus, a general point in Phase 4 in paradox leadership is that you can easily use well-known tools for paradox leadership, but in a new way. In other words, the paradoxical angle focuses on the principled managerial conditions in a way that elevates your understanding of your own situation. A job description for a manager is, seen in isolation, a rather unexciting administrative routine, but in this case, the job description becomes an important element in marking the relationship between the manager and the rest of the organization. It becomes a key tool for those involved to understand how a new balance between the top management's leadership behavior and the leadership and management that takes place in other ways can be achieved in the organization. It also becomes central to understanding some of the inherent unintended negative consequences that a new structure inevitably also entails.

In the next case, especially the "task" dimension will be in the focus area. The paradox was defined as the tension between, on the one hand, ensuring commitment and passion and at the same time creating motivation for performance and controlling that this performance is achieved. In the concrete example, the company had so far had great employee support in the form of loyalty, commitment, and hard work. On the other hand, there was very little support for the way in which a systematic financial follow-up had been established so far. This is a classic paradox, which translates into a practice where a remedy counteracts the goal. In this way, the case is illustrative of many management initiatives and actions that lead to other or the opposite results than those they were put in place to create.

Case 7.2: Accounting for performance with passion – financial accountability with an eye for passion

The finance manager, Katja, worked with her colleagues to create a financial follow-up that could create both "passion" and "performance". The task was to develop the new financial follow-up system in a way that could address the foreseeable paradox that may exist between following up on performance results and at the same time creating higher motivation and enthusiasm. The method included an examination of how employees and managers perceived following up on goals and financial targets. The stakeholders were the management team and their employees. The management team, who worked with leadership paradoxes, redefined the role of accounting from being a recording device to being a motivation and performance-enhancing tool. It was dubbed the "Passion Account". For years, the finance manager had been trying to introduce new KPIs to the organization, without getting much support, neither among the operational managers nor among the top management. It was paradoxical because the top management probably fully agreed with the idea of the new KPIs, but on the other hand did not enforce the use of them.

Katja was inspired by the paradoxical tensions between "passion *and* performance" (see Chapter 3), and she decided to turn the accounts' performance metrics and KPIs upside down. She started by researching what the individual working groups needed in terms of information and follow-up to become better at their task. Then the next question was: How can we best support the existing "passion" (enthusiasm and commitment to the work) and avoid undermining it in our eagerness to follow up and create sophisticated KPI systems? Finally, the last question: What information motivates and helps the colleagues in their daily practice?

In preparation for turning the performance accounts upside down, Katja started by increasing her knowledge about the production. She wanted to convey to the people in the production what her tools could do for them. Among other things, she and the employees had to acknowledge that this was not only a technical (management) exercise, but also a cultural (leadership) journey that would take some time. The ambitions had to be relaxed in relation to how advanced KPIs could be introduced and when.

A "passion account" is, according to the manager in question, a financial follow-up that supports and renews the professional enthusiasm and commitment in the company. How did the manager do it in practice? The manager worked with her management colleagues to identify the needs of the specific employees and the individual department. The "passion account" is therefore not about "measuring" passion, but about "creating the best possible support framework" for passion. Below are several questions you can ask yourself when developing your own "passion account".

The "Passion Account": Ideas for questions you may ask yourself about the way you do performance management in the organization
How do the employees benefit from our measurements?
How do measurements generate motivation/commitment/passion?
How does each measure (for example, a KPI) affect the employees measured?
What specific measures can lead to more motivation/commitment/passion?
What measures are reducing motivation/commitment/passion?

What measures could we do without?

How could we design the performance data (collection) in order to make them most useful for the employees who are measured?

How is it possible to create a greater common understanding of the usefulness of the performance management (for example, KPIs)?

How can we involve the measured employees in the design and follow-up on the goals in a way that supports motivation/commitment/passion?

To what extent do the existing performance management contribute to creating the level of performance we wish for?

How is the amount of time and energy we spend on performance management measuring up to the effect we achieve by doing it?

The example shows that success with this type of action requires that everyone – managers, specialists, and employees – believe in the good intentions and understand the motives of others. There must be a confidence that the follow-up is about collaborating and creating common results. The work takes time, but it is also a cultural development process.

More generally, the example shows that paradoxical thinking can be used to shift the discussion of a management issue. Before, the finance manager and the management team took for granted that performance management and the finance system should just "get up and running". Now, they became aware of the built-in contradictions between passion and performance and their interdependence. On the one hand, it made them more patient. It became more important for the management team to understand how the system could work for the employees who were affected by it. The paradoxical point is that the goal is a system that not only measures but also motivates performance, two factors that sometimes counteract each other and in other circumstances are each other's prerequisites.

The "passion account" is an example of how paradoxical thinking can improve your understanding of your situation as a manager and help to increase insights into how you can handle complex issues in your everyday life. In relation to the 3D Cube Model's three dimensions, the "Task" in this case is changed by shifting the focus in the paradox from performance toward passion. The management team and the employees who had to report data to and be measured via the system were significant "Stakeholders". Finally, one of the "Methods" is to shift attention from the tool itself, that is, the "accounts", to the stakeholders whose behavior the manager wants to change.

The interaction with stakeholders and colleagues is crucial to the success of your selected actions. The point is that colleagues working on similar development projects can be key players in dealing with your paradox. It can be a method find the synergy between the leadership paradoxes that a management team works with. The goal is not necessarily for the group to define what you need to work on, but even if you and your management colleagues want different development points and interests, it is obvious that there will be overlaps and mutual opportunities to support each other's projects. The following case is about this.

Case 7.3: Paradox-synergies in leadership teams

This case illustrates how a leadership team can work with several different individual management paradoxes and still create organizational synergy between them. The company is the same small, family-owned service company that was the context of the *Job Description* and the *Passion Accounts* cases above, where the entire leadership team worked with paradoxes – individually and together.

All managers in the group including the owner Eric are involved in identifying and working with their paradoxes. Eric defines his paradox as individual leadership versus organizational management, which in his case is about delegating the leadership and management tasks to several managers and removing the focus of the managers and management tasks away from his person. The background is that he finds that he cannot spend enough time on the things that are important for developing the business, but instead he is constantly occupied with operational problems ad hoc. The entrepreneur Tobias works with the same paradox as Eric, only in relation to the managers who refer to him. Kasper has chosen the paradox of leading "digital natives versus analog generations", which for him is about leading "the new and the old", hereby establishing a sensible relationship of trust with and between both groups. Katja has chosen "passion versus performance" because she works to establish measurement systems that must be able to follow up on operations, without at the same time losing the employee's commitment in the process.

The management group's paradox work started with Eric, who wants to create more leadership in his management team. It is both about redefining his own role as boss and at the same time "empowering" the management team to address both new tasks as well as some of the tasks he has previously solved himself. How should the individual managers use him in the development processes initiated together with the rest of the leadership team? Kasper and Tobias are particularly dependent on new boundaries being drawn between them and Eric's leadership mandate. In Kasper's case, it is especially a matter of handing over the management responsibility to the "old" employees who have normally approached Eric for advice. In Tobias's case, it has been about the big tasks where Eric "naturally" has been involved. Eric and the two daily leaders have had to find a new common understanding of how to ensure mutual loyalty to each other's roles. In Katja's case, we are dealing with the development of KPIs and other measurement points that can better support production and work, but that can also create passion and commitment. It requires a specific commitment from Eric and the board; otherwise they may just end up doing the same follow-up as they usually do. Eric must support the changed "passion-oriented" model, and Katja must convince him that the accounts are still suitable for following up on performance, despite the new focus.

When you work with navigating leadership paradoxes in a leadership team, the team members can be linked together across and up and down the hierarchy. If a leadership team manages to collaborate based on their individual paradoxes and the roles in the company, this will enhance the chance of success. The way you and your leadership team manage to formulate and handle your needs and tasks together is interesting, and it is about how you chose to create a synergy between the paradoxes, a synergy that ultimately benefits the organization's long-term development. As a top manager, the interface between this and the other managers is particularly important in the process. But the interfaces between the other managers can be just as crucial to whether you succeed in creating a real "paradoxical synergy". The general learning is that there are good prospects in trying to get the chosen paradoxes and actions in a leadership group to intersect. This is not always possible, and the preconditions will vary. However, the probability of lasting results is significantly greater if as many members of the overall leadership team can collaborate in this development process.

Tool 7.2: The Reflective Team – the team as a development tool

As a manager, it is important for you to spend time reflecting on your own perceptions and leadership practices, but it is just as important to be challenged by listening to others' perceptions of your perceptions. Following the logic of the 3D Cube Model, the Reflective Team is a way to involve key "Stakeholders" in your focus area and the actions you want to initiate to deal with your paradox.

The Reflective Team is a systematic way of getting feedback in small groups. It could be a group of management colleagues or perhaps managers from an external network. The advantage of using the tool with managers outside your own organization is that you can typically be more candid in relation to what you currently find difficult – regardless of whether it is about yourself or the collaborative relationships you have with your colleagues. We describe the procedure for the Reflective Team in Figure7.4.

The Reflecting Team: In the hot seat - talk about the burning issues
You take a place in the hot seat and present your current paradox to the group. That is, you present a picture of your present situation and how you understand the paradox. If you have already defined specific tasks for yourself (for example with the 3D Cube Model or the extended Paradox Quadrant (see Chapter 5, Phase 3), the presentation can be structured accordingly. When you are in the hot seat, it is important that the focus is your "pain points" and where you need help.

Let the group reflect – while you listen
You then turn your back on the others, literally. This means that you and the rest of the team must avoid making eye contact. The group then talks together about what they have heard you say – and what they themselves think about it. When they talk about what you have said, it is important that they talk as if you are not present. So, they are talking about you and not to you. For example: "It sounds like Henriette thinks her team is the problem. I rather get the idea that she should focus upwards in the organization." When the others talk in the third person about you, it is easier to listen to what is being said, instead of giving in to the inevitable desire to react and respond. As you listen, take notes on what is being said about your challenge. The group finalizes its open talk after approximately five to ten minutes.

You put into words what you see as your key insights
Unless the group has some clarifying questions that they would like to ask before concluding their talk, it is now time for you to turn to the group. You must now put into words what you have been particularly impressed by. It is important that you do not allow yourself to be defensive. The point is that you want to get smarter about yourself – not stand up for what you already do and know. The group can comment on what you say or elaborate on some of the points they have made, but the group should in principle not try to convince you. What the group delivers to you is just an offer. It is up to you whether you really want to listen to their reflections and suggestions, and whether you would like to transfer some of it into practice.

Figure 7.4: Hot seat challenge: The Reflective Team approach.

What do I want to do now?
As a conclusion to the Reflective Team, you can choose to wrap up and tell the group what you intend to do as you proceed and what you want to consider more carefully. Again, it is important to remember that you are the one who is the main character, and therefore you decide what you want to do. It is not about making the group happy.

New person in the hot seat
The process can then start all over again with another in the hot seat. Remember to make sure everyone gets an equal amount of time in the hot seat. For a start, appoint a timekeeper in the Reflective Team and decide how long (for example 20 to 30 minutes) you will allocate per person.

Figure 7.4 (continued)

The Reflective Team is a very powerful tool for sharpening you and your management colleague's attention to their own practice (Andersen, 1987, 1991). Reflexivity is crucial to develop your ability to handle a paradox. However, the reflective team is special in the sense that it can also help to strengthen the understanding and the unity internally in a leadership team. Unfortunately, it is often the case that managers are very much alone with their experiences in their leadership practices and do not have that many opportunities to share leadership challenges.

Case 7.4: Hot seat challenge

In a company, a management team agreed to conclude their management team seminar by working as a Reflective Team. When the time came, the boss looked at his managers and asked: "Who wants to be in the hot seat first?" None of the managers really wanted to but said in return that they would be a very reflective team for the boss if he would take the hot seat. He did so, and it became a very long, intense, and instructive process, in which the three managers diligently discussed how they, individually and together, could help their superior and vice versa. The top manager became somewhat embarrassed but was overall very pleased with the input he received from his managers.

If you make the reflective team a recurring event among your manager colleagues, the tool can not only be used to strengthen your paradox leadership, but also support the development of a common leadership vision. (Common) Reflection is and will be a necessary starting point for successful action.

Five learning coordinates for the fourth phase of paradox navigation – grasping and handling your paradox

The following five landmarks summarize the key points of attention in relation to paradox leadership in Phase 4 of the Paradox Pathway:

1. What is the task, who are the stakeholders, and what methods will I use? When initiating action related to your paradox, it is necessary that you are attentive toward what actions move something for your paradox.
2. Be pragmatic – use tools you know, but in a new way: It is important that you focus the actions with some manageable methods. The preparation of the manager's job description is an example of how an action that seems straightforward can have major consequences.
3. Involve others in your work: It is important that you move the process from your own process of reflection and development to a broader process where you collaborate with your management colleagues and ultimately move the process toward the employees who need to be influenced to deal with paradox.
4. Multiple roles, multiple perspectives, and stakeholders: Managers, especially in small- and medium-sized enterprises or in subsidiaries/branches, have different roles, for example because they fill several different jobs and management roles simultaneously or participate in matrix or project organization. Each role gives rise to a particular paradoxical landscape and vantage point. The more perspectives at play, the more angles will typically arise on the same paradox.
5. Action and reflection are closely related, which may seem like a paradox within a paradox: Sometimes it is a prerequisite for success in the chosen actions that you meet the relevant people and communicate, even though you may feel that it takes time away from the urgently needed action you are focused on right now.

You have now rolled up your sleeves and are dealing with your chosen paradox through active action. But does it work as intended? Do you gain insights along the way? Do you need to change course or center of gravity in your understanding and actions? And how is it possible to keep an eye on the "side-effects" that your otherwise well-considered action plan necessarily also implies? A paradox cannot be solved, and there are always "shadow sides" to consider – a theme we consider in Chapter 8, "Phase 5. Evaluation and follow-up – keeping track of your balancing act".

References

Andersen, T. (1987). The reflecting team: Dialogue and meta-dialogue in clinical work. *Family process*, *26*(4), 415–428.

Andersen, T. (1991). *The reflecting team: Dialogues and dialogues about the dialogues*. New York, NY: WW Norton & Co.

Andersen, I., Bakka, J.F. & Larsen, H.H. (1990) Ledelsesudvikling i Undervisningsministeriet. Copenhagen, DK: Nyt fra Samfundsvidenskaberne

Larsen, H.H. (1996). The Ministry of Education: Action learning based management development. In J. Storey (Ed.), *Blackwell Cases in Human Resource and Change Management*, 206–215. Oxford, UK: Blackwell.

Larsen, H.H. (1990). Ledelsesudvikling i Undervisningsministeriet. In H. H. Larsen, (Ed.), *Lederudvikling på jobbet – der er fremtid i erfaringer*, 159–176. Copenhagen, DK: Forlaget Valmuen.

Chapter 8
Phase 5: Evaluation and follow-up – keeping track of your balancing act

Following up is essential when working practically with the paradox, as is ongoing reflection and assessment. In Phase 5 (Figure 8.1), we examine how to systematically approach paradox work and how to balance your navigation. In this phase, it becomes important to set goals, to follow-up, and on a continuous basis to assess progress, for then to be able to set new goals and identify a new course. Evaluating and following up are important for you as a manager and for your progress but serve also as a reminder in terms of involving your environment of stakeholders, as mentioned in Chapter 4. This involvement is about generating legitimacy for your project, both upwards and downwards in the organization, as well as providing opportunity to involve co-managers, colleagues, and employees as co-navigators in your development process:

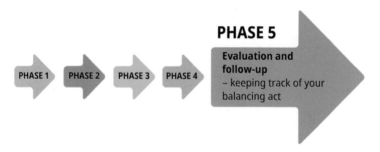

PHASE 5

Evaluation and follow-up
– keeping track of your balancing act

PHASE 1   PHASE 2   PHASE 3   PHASE 4

Figure 8.1: Five phases of paradox navigation – Phase 5.

It is important to emphasize that evaluating and following-up are not activities merely to be undertaken in connection with the finalization of a paradox navigation process. Evaluation should have an ongoing and formative purpose, and preferably it will be built into your paradox navigation strategy right from the start. It is important to navigate the process while continuously attempting to balance your leadership. Balance might be obtained, but only momentarily, as paradox navigation is all about continuously achieving it.

   To reach this in practice calls for you to systematically work with setting and revising goals, to identify significant indicators of imbalance, use them for navigation, and to ensure that both goals and indicators is successful in capturing both sides of your paradox. Keeping the balance in paradox leadership implies holding an eye on the various effects generated by your efforts, as such efforts tend to throw you off balance when tensions shift. If you, for instance, have placed your efforts on establishing a talent

https://doi.org/10.1515/9783110788877-009

program to support the elite, rather than focusing human resource development-efforts on the mass of the organization, it would be tempting to focus evaluation on the positive aspects of the paradox's elite-pole. However, it would also be relevant to keep an eye on indicators that would show whether negative aspects emerge if you, for instance, choose not to provide the company's majority workforce with the same attention as previously.

This chapter presents you with three different tools that individually, or combined, can help you in keeping on the right track:

– Tool 8.1: *Keeping Track of Paradox Performance* focuses on linking measurable objectives to those actions that you defined by using the 3D Cube Model from Phase 4 (see Chapter 7). Such measures can be output-, input-, or process-oriented, quantitative, or qualitative. It is important that measures connect your actions to your objectives to ensure your commitment. This supplements step 5 in the expanded Paradox Quadrant presented as part of the third phase of paradox navigation in Chapter 6.

– Tool 8.2: *Self Test of Paradox Preferences* provides an opportunity to evaluate your current balance and your current competencies for dealing with your paradox. Alternatively, the test can be used for staging dialog in the management team. By completing the test before, during, and after a paradox navigation process, it provides an indication of your development. The tool represents a rich source of inspiration for you to develop self-testing that fits to your needs and to your paradox.

– Tool 8.3: *"Paradox Pitstop"* helps you in sharpening your focus on what you have learned though the previous phases, and how this focus can contribute to setting new goals and push your process forward. Five questions aim to help you document your point of departure and understanding of paradox, but especially your new insights and actions, which have grown from your paradox exploration. With your five answers in hand, you hold a concise overview of your process and results, which are useful when having to explain the big picture to stakeholders in your organization.

This chapter introduces four cases illustrating how you can work with objectives and KPIs through:

– Case 8.1: *"When top management asks for an update"*. Experience from a management team demonstrates the importance of management inquiry, and how to utilize data on progress in development projects.

– Case 8.2: *"Key Performance Indicators – without 'deparadoxifying'"* paradox. A manager seeks to develop employees' ability to take initiatives and formulates process objectives to guide this endeavor.

– Case 8.3: *"Developing leadership with a self-test"*. A manager seeks to develop his own leadership capability and uses a self-test to support the process.

- Case 8.4: *"Setting goals for leadership objectives for a CEO".* A top manager seeks to change both his personal leadership style, and the leadership approach in the organization as such, and for that purpose he formulates leadership objectives for the whole organization.

The task of following-up and evaluating takes its point of departure in your individual actions and success criteria. However, it also requires an ongoing dialog with people around you. As you define targets and evaluate your efforts, it is important not to consider "the right balance" as a measure for you to determine very rigidly and alone. Assessing and finding the right balance is never an individual affair, but an ongoing negotiation with your organization: your immediate superior, your employees, your management colleagues, and most likely also other stakeholders. This collaboration between you as manager and your organization is a theme throughout the tools presented in this chapter. Overall, your ability to succeed is defined by the perspectives, conditions, and options provided by the organization.

Case 8.1: When top management asks for an update

Three managers in a tech-company were each working intensively with their paradox. Engagement had been high, especially toward the aim of making a remarkable change in their own management style and their relationship with their employees. Their endeavors with paradox development projects had been met with great interest from both the HR director and top management. To strengthen the company's and managers' ability to navigate paradoxes was already addressed at a strategic level and seen as a significant step toward more flexibility in an otherwise specialized and functionally divided organization. In practice, this attention toward the managers' projects affected the specific choice of paradoxes, and consequently a clear set of expectations for the managers to deliver on was established. The managers became obliged to communicate their findings and experiences to the rest of the organization. Rather than seeing this as a pressure or a limitation to their exploration, this commitment gave them a sense of meaning, and they could connect their individual work on paradox with current strategic challenges. This gave them purpose and direction in their work and helped them set up criteria for evaluating their progress. The company created a strategic platform, from which the managers could direct their efforts, and helped them to frame and focus their success criteria. In the subsequent evaluation, the individual projects could now be seen against the backdrop of strategically relevant challenges.

Tool 8.1: Keeping Track of Paradox Performance

Evaluation and follow-up require sincere commitment to concrete objectives. Being a manager, we presume that you are already competent in phrasing ideas and visions for your achievement. Perhaps you strive to become better at spotting and growing talents in your company (and not just a broad focus), and you probably already have ideas on methods for spotting which employees could be identified as talents. But subsequently, how would you evaluate whether you succeeded in your original objectives? And how would you make sure not to "lose balance" while overlooking the scope, taking carefully into account also the potentials among those employees who are not sticking out, but simply contribute to the important groundwork? To begin with, it is important to define how you would be able to examine whether your goal has been reached. Measuring progress only makes sense if the relevant indicators have been found and if they truly indicate whether you are on the right track. Second, indicators toward both positive and negative consequences of an effort must be effects.

The KPI table (Figure 8.2) provides a concise framework for linking actions to concrete and measurable objectives while keeping your balance in mind developed, as this is important to keep track of both positive and negative developments.

ACTION	KPI	
1.	Output goals	Process goals
2.		
3.		
Keep an eye on side effects (KPI):		

Figure 8.2: From actions to KPIs.

In the left part of the form, you will list the actions that you plan to undertake for navigating your paradox. We recommend that you revisit the expanded Paradox Quadrant presented in Phase 3. After having filled in your planned actions, it is time to consider the specific indications of progress that you are making. When defining your KPIs, you can distinguish between output and process goals. Frequently, output goals assume a quantitative focus, what can be measured or counted as result of your actions. Such indications may be based on existing data, for example, sales figures, employee satisfaction assessments, or statistics on sickness absence, but you may also define and produce your own measurable indicators. If you, for instance, are working with LEAN-processes in your company, and if you want to strengthen employee engagement and initiative, the number of employee suggestions on the LEAN-board might serve as indicative of a positive or negative development. Process goals include a framework for assessing your actions, and whether you succeed in getting something started, the extent of your actions, or the quality of what you do. A relevant indicator may be as simple as that you are to call for meetings at a particular frequency, or it could consist of the completion of a settled number of employee assessment interviews within a given time frame. While such process items can be measured in numbers, quality aspects are often more important.

If you have decided primarily to orient your actions toward one pole of the paradox, we recommend that you pay special attention to the field in the bottom of the form. Here you write the KPIs that are more related to the pole that got only little or no attention to begin with. If you, for instance, want to focus on strengthening the leadership dimension in your management practice, and you define KPIs toward this pole, the neglected management dimension would be in focus in the bottom field. You might have initiated an ambitious value-oriented process in the company and defined concrete goals for your efforts, and the indictors can then include how many employees you expect will recognize the values after three months, and how many of those do you expect to have taken them on board as personal values. At the opposite pole of the paradox, you will find a more bureaucratic focus, including legislative compliance, deadlines, and quality objectives. To monitor that the value work does not limit emphasis on such dimensions, we recommend defining KPIs, and especially warning indicators to that side of the paradox as well.

If the quality drops or if deadlines are neglected, this would indicate that your effort has "lost balance" and needs revision to ensure that the value work is complemented by sufficient bureaucratic attention.

Case 8.2: Key performance indicators – without "deparadoxing paradox"

Freya is a people manager for a small team of employees. Basically, she is a bit frustrated about them, as she finds that they lack drive and initiative. She is also aware that she is reluctant to assign them any real responsibility. She prefers to have everything under control to make sure that it is done by the book. Freya's paradox is about finding the right balance between providing employees' autonomy and responsibility without jeopardizing organizational procedure, necessary instructions, and quality standards. She decides to work simultaneously on both sides of the paradox, which is reflected in her approach to defining KPIs. First, Freya decides to formulate precise instruction for the employees that include, point by point, what circumstances to address and deal with when they manage projects themselves. Second, she decides to schedule frequent one-to-one conversation to keep an open dialog and manage her employees exactly where they are.

To keep track of herself and her plans, Freya sets up a deadline for completing her iterations of conversations, and she schedules a weekly deadline for when project plans need to be updated and puts the employees in charge of those updates. Freya's actions serve in many respects as inputs to her evaluation.

As her actions are not one-offs and as they require that she and her employees commit to certain actions within a given deadline, they also serve as formative process goals. Considering her paradox navigation, the process goal becomes "Employees update project plans each week", which directly supports the paradox pole on increasing employee involvement and self-management.

Tool 8.2: Self Test of Paradox Preferences – A, B, C

In the KPI track (Tool 8.1) you linked your actions to specific indicators to help you assess and adjust your initial actions. When you have had a good start with your paradox, the time comes for a check-up: How are you doing? For this check-up, we suggest performing a self-assessment, using one (or several!) of the varieties of self-tests presented below and exemplified through three different paradoxes.

The three variants share the same principle of self-assessment. The first two of them state different approaches to how you can test your progress, and the third provides suggestions to how your self-assessment can be used as a dialog starter with your internal co-stakeholders, allowing you to calibrate your self-assessment through the views of others. Using paradox-examples, the self-assessment tool aims to bring inspiration to how you can evaluate your paradox management.
-    Variant A: "The traffic light" – assessment of the bright sides of your paradox
-    Variant B: Balancing points – where do you put your emphasis right now?
-    Variant C: Dialog tool – ask you employees, your manager, and your management

You will assess your own and your organization's positioning at the beginning of your paradox navigation, repeating it midway, and finally upon completion. In that way, the self-assessment provides you both a here-and-now state-of-the art, and it illustrates your own and the organization's development. All three variants are suitable for making assessment at the start, halfway, and toward the end, thereby providing an overview of your progression. To inspire you to develop your own assessment tool, the tests are exemplified considering three different paradoxical tensions: local and global, exclusive and inclusive talent management, and individual and organization leadership.

Tool 8.2.1: Self-assessment variant A: "Traffic light" – assessment of the bright sides of your paradox

The concept of this tool is for you to start with the paradox that preoccupies you most, and then define its key paradoxical tensions. If you have started your paradox journey by filling out the Paradox Quadrant (first introduced in Chapter 5, Tool 5.1. The Paradox Quadrant), this can serve as inspiration for the specific types of opposite tensions entering into your assessment form.

If you, for instance, work with individual and organizational management (see Chapter 3), then you might already have outlined the positive aspects of the individual management-dimension. It could be that you enjoy the opportunity to use your own expertise, and that you enjoy a high degree of control. Turning to the other pole, you will have to look for the positive implications of letting go of control. In this way, you may move toward strengthening the organizational management and letting flourish new and diverse perspectives on matters when delegating management to others. You may conclude that you see new opportunities in showing your employees more trust. Use the form to fill in the development aspects of each side of the paradox, writing them up in pairs. An example is illustrated in Figure 8.3, showing how a manager, working with management *and* leadership, used the template to juxtapose tensions between an operational and administration-oriented management on the one hand, and the more development-oriented leadership on the other.

When you have defined your categories, use the positive dimensions of each paradox pole as a starting position for the evaluation of your/your organization's current balancing points. This tool can provide you with an overview of the current stage, and it also helps to assess you in your assessment of whether your and your company's current balancing is desirable or not.

A summary of your own paradox's inherent tensions serves as your starting point. The self-assessment in this example takes on board the management versus leadership paradox, and it states the positive characteristics of each of its poles. When you color code the individual statements according to your ability to perform the stated behavior, the tool can be used for assessing your current behavior and management of the paradox. Green indicates behavior where you show good abilities, yellow indicates behaviors that are less distinct or where you can improve, and red indicates behaviors that you by large do not perform and that require your additional focus. In this way, the tool provides a concise overview for areas of adjusting balancing efforts.

Self-assessment – step by step
1. Define those points of balance that characterize the problem field and write them in pairs in each of their columns. The Paradox Quadrant from Phase 2 and 3 can be used for inspiration.
2. Evaluate to what extent you find that the individual statements reflect your management and/or organization. Start with one side of the paradox, and then work your way through both columns. Color the statements according to how they describe your management style: green for a good match, yellow for a partial match, and red for those who do not match.
3. Reflect on the color dispersion and how it matches your current tasks, organizational characteristics, employees, and so on.
4. Use the result to define new actions and objectives (we recommend using chapters 6 and 7 for inspiration).
5. Repeat the test when you have finished your work with a particular paradox.

Management	Leadership
Manages	Renews
Maintains	Develops
Improves the present	Creates the Future
Looks inward	Looks outward
Focuses on the bottom line	Focuses on the horizon
Meets short-term demands	Meets long-term demands
Imitates	Creates original output
Manages and coordinates change	Creates change and development
Executes plans	Unfolds a vision
Focuses on systems and structures	Focuses on people
Uses authority and control as a steppingstone	Based on influence, trust and empowerment
Focuses on subordinates	Focuses on colleagues
Asks how and when	Asks what and when
Avoids conflicts	Uses conflicts
Is concerned with doing things the right way	Is concerned with doing the right thing

Figure 8.3: Illustration of "The traffic light" as a self-assessment of management versus leadership inspired by Bennis and Townsend (1989).

It is important to remark that the test does not indicate what is good or bad. The optimal balance between management and leadership, or individual and organizational management, is situational and cannot be determined universally. The assessment of the right balance between paradoxical poles is influenced by the specific management task, organizational placement, and organizational culture, and therefore not entirely up to the individual manager.

Case 8.3: Building a quick-test tool for your leadership paradox

Harriet manages the procurement department in a middle-sized company. Ten years in the same company had led her to focus on how to differentiate her personnel management. Some of her employees appreciate her well-known style, where she offers close and detailed sparring. However, in recent years other profiles have been employed in her department. She categorizes these as "strategic purchasers" as they have vast experience and ambition. These people drive for more, and they express clearly that they wish more self-responsibility over their tasks. Harriet is aware that she needs to find a new and more flexible balancing of her paradox about management versus leadership, and that it calls for her to strengthen her management competencies regarding the leadership dimension.

She starts by reading books on leadership, talks to the HR department about how it might support her process, and she uses the self-assessment tool to monitor her progression and make a status. Her self-assessment colors her green when it comes to "authority and control", whereas it colors her red on the other pole of "involvement, trust, and empowerment". Harriet decides to work with that pole. One of the actions (see Tool 8.1) is to literally "sit on her hands" when her employees express doubts and start looking for answers. Rather than providing them readily with her "right answer", she holds back and gives them the time and trust necessary to find answers themselves, remarking, "Most often, they end up figuring it out anyhow." With the self-assessment in hand, Harriet becomes able to pinpoint the dimensions she needs to strengthen. By repeating the test, it provides her with the opportunity to understand how she progresses, and she observes how the "red entries" in her self-test are turning into yellow or green compared to the previous self-assessments.

Tool 8.2.2: Self-assessment variant B: Balancing points – where is your emphasis right now?

This self-assessment uses a set of continuums to nuance your balancing abilities. It aims at addressing how your paradox navigation is progressing. This implies that you can position yourself according to a series of extremes that represent the poles of your paradox and provides an overview to help you adjust your paradox balancing between the juxtaposed tensions. The content of your continuums should represent the paradox you are working on, and the tool requires for you to identify sets of relevant poles to be used as continuum extremes. We recommend revisiting the Paradox Quadrant for inspiration as well as using the two continuum illustrations of talent management (juxta positioning of focusing competence development on the elite versus breadth) and global leadership (juxta positioning of focusing on local adaptation versus global alignment) below. As with the previous self-assessment tools, the illustrated paradoxes and continuum items are merely intended as examples, and we encourage you to adapt your content to your choice of paradox and the items to your particular situation.

The first example focuses on talent development, and ten items as balancing points (Figure 8.4 and 8.5).

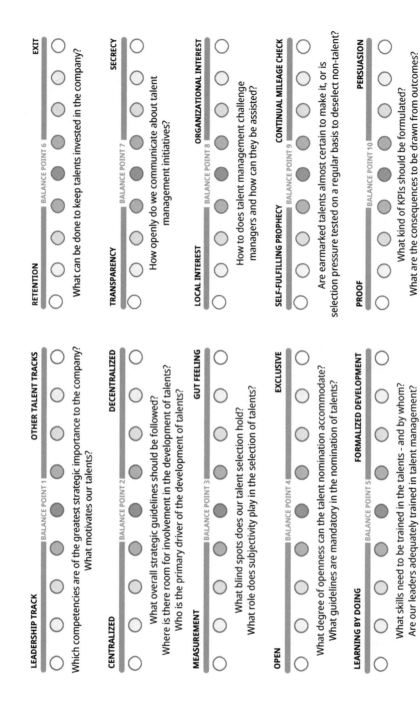

Figure 8.4 and 8.5: Self-assessment variant B: Talent management balancing points as point of departure.

Source: The figure is inspired by Maria Lindorf and Julie Lynge (2010) "Effektiv talentudvikling, praksis for praktikere", DEA; also see https://docplayer.dk/1982724-Effektiv-talentudvikling-praksis-for-praktikere.html. Reprinted with permission from the authors and publisher.

The second example of a self-assessment based on the continuum principle focuses on paradoxes in global leadership.

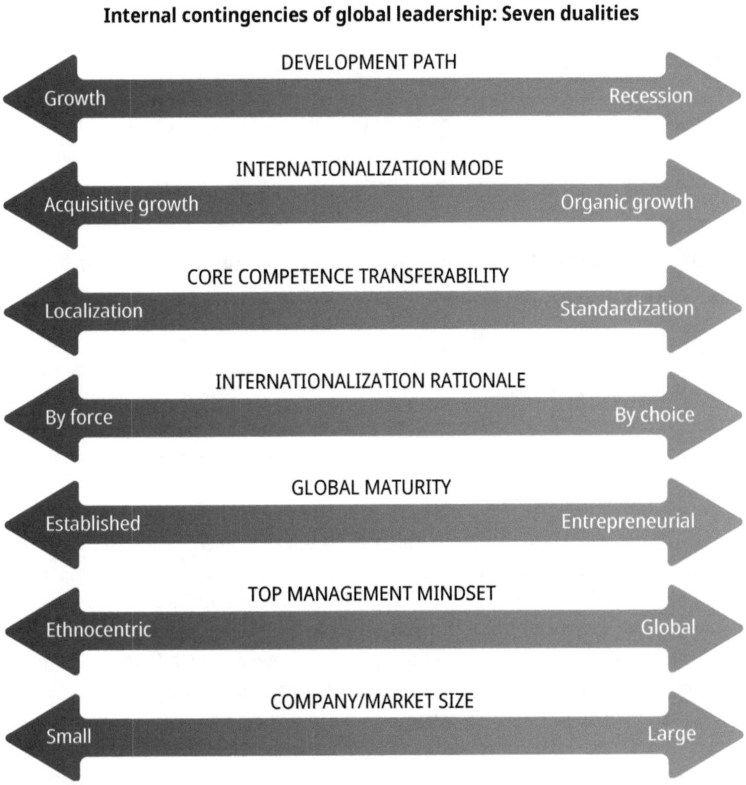

Internal contingencies of global leadership: Seven dualities

DEVELOPMENT PATH

Growth ◄──────────────────────────────────► Recession

INTERNATIONALIZATION MODE

Acquisitive growth ◄──────────────────────────────────► Organic growth

CORE COMPETENCE TRANSFERABILITY

Localization ◄──────────────────────────────────► Standardization

INTERNATIONALIZATION RATIONALE

By force ◄──────────────────────────────────► By choice

GLOBAL MATURITY

Established ◄──────────────────────────────────► Entrepreneurial

TOP MANAGEMENT MINDSET

Ethnocentric ◄──────────────────────────────────► Global

COMPANY/MARKET SIZE

Small ◄──────────────────────────────────► Large

Figure 8.6: Self-assessment variant B: Seven balancing points in global leadership.
Source: Adopted with permission from the authors from: Nielsen, R. K. with Nielsen, J. B. (2016). *Global Leadership Practice and Development Revisited. Exploring 3 roles – discovering 7 dualities*. Global Leadership Academy – Copenhagen Business School and Danish Confederation of Industry, p. 34. Also see https://www.globalledelse.dk/eng/chap11.html.

This example uses seven items to be balanced as continuums in Figure 8.6. Less focus is placed on the assessment of you as a manager, but instead on the position of your organization/team/department so as to be able to assess your room for maneuvering. This implies that the need to decide how you see the organization from your position.

For instance, the figure's third double-arrow and tension illustrate a key question in assessing to what degree your company or department operates from an alignment perspective, using standardized organizational recipes or whether it, to a larger extent, tends to leave it to the individual departments and subsidiaries to design their management systems, competence development programs, etc. If at this moment, you can immediately place your company in the standardization camp, your next task would be to evaluate how far the company can and should go to accommodate to local conditions.

The use of a continuum allows for a more nuanced self-assessment when compared to a categorical red, yellow, and green assessment. Regardless of the paradox content, the continuum also allows for an indication of your orientation toward the two poles, and thereby it is not a normative assessment. However, it is possible to add an ideal or desired position to the continuum, allowing you to use the continuum as a measure, either defined by you, or in collaboration with others. Continuum-based assessment can be used in two steps:

1) You place yourself where you think you are positioned right now.
2) You place yourself where you think you should/want to be.

Comparing the two positions would provide you with an image of how far (or how close) you are to your or your organization's objective.

Tool 8.2.3: Self-assessment variant C: Dialog tool – ask your employees, your manager, and your management colleagues

As assessments are dependent on their context, we recommend using the self-assessment (A or B) as a dialog starter among relevant stakeholders. By involving others in your assessment, different angles and perspectives can contribute to co-creating a "calibrated measure" for the benchmarking of the most optimal balance. It will have to consider how it would appear for you as a manager, for your department, for the division, and perhaps for the organization.

Regardless of whether you use one tool for self-assessment or another purpose, much can be learned from observing your results according to your surroundings' perspectives. As self-assessment indicates, the tool provides an image of how you as a manager, see yourself, and current situation. If you were to put paradox leadership into proper context, you have to dare to invite other views and opinions into the process. After completing a self-assessment, we recommend presenting and discussing your results with others in the company, either employees, your manager, your management team, or combinations hereof. If (surprising or significant) discrepancies come up between your and other's assessments, this might lead to you adjusting both measure and future objectives. Perhaps you realize that you, with the best intention, are overdoing and overrating your efforts in certain areas, while the opposite might be the case in other areas? After having completed your self-assessment, you can introduce the model to others by using the following steps as inspiration.

1. Show your completed self-assessment to your employees, your manager, or management team and explain to them why you have completed it as you have.
2. Invite employees, colleagues, or your manager to evaluate your management on the basis of your model, and initiate a dialog based on perceived differences.
3. Negotiate an agreement with your dialog partners on what dimension you and/or the organization should focus on the short and long run.
4. Repeat the self-assessment and dialog whenever you or others for a period have focused on making changes, attended courses, or found new inputs that might have affected you or the organization's balance points.

Case 8.4: Setting leadership objectives for a CEO

Harry is a CEO for a small, but very successful manufacturing company. He is charismatic, analytically bright, and quick to detect managerial problems, both with his three managers, and concerning his own actions. However, it is not until he seeks their council that he realizes his own paradox.

Despite his ambition to strengthen the company on a more strategic level, Harry spends much time and energy as an expert, especially within sales and marketing. Harry's paradox is about balancing his tendency to become too operational and focused on daily management with the need to focus more on strategic and visionary leadership. However, it remained quite unclear to Harry how to proceed toward this aim. He is convinced that he risk dominating his managers too much, and that is why he tends to hold back. Harry's understanding of the situation turns out to be far from that of his managers. When invited into the dialog, they all express a lack of managerial presence from him, and they would like to have him available as sparring partner daily. By starting to become more attentive to their perspectives and management needs, Harry's understanding of his paradox is better aligned with his colleagues. It provides new opportunities for finding a better balance. Setting the goal to become more leadership minded was to Harry not a matter of less management, as he had been led to believe, but on the contrary a matter of more management.

The previous tools are primarily focused on assessing and evaluating your paradox leadership capabilities throughout your process. We recommend using the self-assessment tools for defining your point of departure before you embark onto your paradox journey. When you have worked with your paradox some time, this allows you to measure progression by comparing it to new self-assessments. The Paradox Pitstop, which is presented as the last tool, is intended to provide (temporary) closure to a lengthy process. This tool aims to make and appraisal and to point toward the future. If you, during your paradox journey, have made use of the Paradox Springboard (see Chapter 4), we recommend comparing it with your Paradox Pitstop to make your progression more transparent, not just in the form of particular results, but also on how you now have come to understand your own leadership practice. As will be illustrated by the examples below, the effects of paradox leadership are not limited to knowing new tools and becoming better at managing in particular paradoxical situations. Just as important is the new perspective on your leadership as such and you as personality as a manager, as this has developed throughout your process.

Tool 8.3: Paradox Pitstop – taking stock of your development

When working with paradoxes, the process often evolves into a lengthy project and involves many different approaches, actors, and efforts. The following tool is a simple, five-question form that will help you to take stock of what you have done, what you have achieved, and what you have learned throughout your project. Some lessons might be earned the hard way, but the experience will most likely serve you well on the road ahead. When you have answered the five questions, we recommend using them as basis for presenting your project to your management team or other relevant stakeholders in your company, using a short, concise format. The following list illustrates the outcome for a manager who had worked with individual versus organizational leadership as his paradox, using this as an example on how it might turn out:

1) Define your leadership challenge:
    Individual _and_ organizational management

2) How would you describe your challenge as a paradox? What are the tensions to be balanced?
For my employees to become more self-managed and self-directed. For them to take on more responsibilities in terms of solving their tasks, but at the same time ensure that their efforts pull in the direction that the company wants regarding organizational frames.

3) What concrete, positive results have you accomplished through your project?
I have become more aware of the importance of me being clear on what I expect from my employees, and of the importance of clarifying frames and directions.

4) What has been difficult/challenging to your work on paradox?
Having to take on a much more visible management role to make my employees work more independently. I think I have become more rigid and demanding than necessary, but I can also see how it has, in fact, a positive impact.

5) What is the most important lesson you have learned from the project?
To be visible + setting clear frames and directions.

The manager in the example works in a company with overseas subcontractors, and for a long time she felt a frustration concerning how the workers abroad did not really meet her expectations. Even when they had every opportunity to come to her and ask for help, she repeatedly experienced how they eluded responsibility. They did not report errors or mistakes. Very close to the deadline, their deliverables often suffered from setbacks, or employees simply neglected quality standards. The idea of "freedom with responsibility" simply did not work for these employees. This became fully evident during a management team pitstop, and it was not until the manager succeeded in expressing her expectations in a much clearer way that the message came through about how the extended freedom and responsibility is a company framework that also accounts for the subsidiary.

Despite trying to promote more organizational leadership, self-management, more initiative, and more employee autonomy, it was not until she addressed its opposite pole that the policy really came to life. At that point she made her expectations clear and clearly stated the objectives and regulations that the employees had to oblige to. Following this, she was able to move toward her goal. The subsidiary employees started delivering on time and up to expected standards. As a result, the manager started to realize how the two sides of the paradox are intertwined as a yin to the yang. Taking this on board, the process not just leads to a better result, but also enhances the manager's awareness, and consequently her options. Paradox thinking helps her become aware of her own role in her challenge, and of her limitations. As noted in her reflections (see Figure 8.9), such insights are rarely comfortable as no one wants to appear "more tough than necessary". However, because she managed to overcome her discomfort and step out of her comfort zone, she managed to enter a dialog with her employees in a new and productive manner. Another manager paraphrases his key learning this way: "To me, working with paradox as a frame has given me an opportunity to see problems in more nuanced ways than merely being something that needs solving. Instead, I have increased my ability to weight its pros and cons against each other to find the right balance."

The potential of paradox leadership, and especially as accentuated by a Paradox Pitstop, lies in the development of a reflective competence. The various tools presented to you in this book are thought to develop reflexive competency from the beginning to the end of the process: from paradox choice and qualification to follow-up and assessment. These tools are important for both the result and process. However, it is in the mental imprint and awareness development caused by paradox thinking that we find the most important purpose and outcome of paradox navigation.

Five learning coordinates for the fifth phase of paradox navigation – keeping track of your balancing act

In working your way through this phase, the following five learning coordinates can guide your way:

1. Continuous follow-up and assessment are especially important in paradox leadership. This helps you ensure not to lose your balance by narrow-mindedly focusing on one paradox pole.
2. Evaluating your paradox leadership is conditioned by you defining specific and measurable objectives. Distinguishing between process and result goals allows you to work with both hard and soft data and utilize existing and newly generated data.
3. Setting assessment criteria for paradox navigation is not an exact science. The measure and indicators depend on what context you find yourself situated in. It will differ from manager to manager, and company to company, how an optimal balance might appear.
4. No specific evaluation result is particularly desirable in its own right – what is desirable is a product of your organization and your point of departure. This is central to paradox thinking as it rejects the idea of a perfect solution as "no cure exists without side-effects", and you will always end up being in the red somewhere at some point.
5. The best balance is often found together. You can evaluate your paradox navigation yourself, but it is important to involve a variety of perspectives and actors. Ask your manager, your employees, or your management team to join in on the reflections, and in the evaluation of how you might succeed and what to prioritize going forward.

Paradox navigation cannot and should not be evaluated merely on the basis of whether a leadership paradox has been successfully handled. A better measure would be on whether an enhanced capacity for dealing with paradoxes has been developed. To embark on choosing, qualifying, reflecting, and handling paradoxes is a learning process, whose most important impact is how it changes your awareness of your leadership task and role as a manager.

References

Bennis, W. G., and Townsend, R. (1989). *On Becoming a Leader* (Vol. 36). Reading, MA: Addison-Wesley.

Lindorf, M., and Lynge, J. (2010). *Effektiv talentudvikling, praksis for praktikere*. Copenhagen, DK: DEA.

Nielsen, R.K. with Nielsen, J.B. (2016). *Global Leadership Practice and Development Revisited. Exploring 3 roles – discovering 7 dualities*. Global Leadership Academy – Copenhagen Business School and Danish Confederation of Industry.

Chapter 9
The Paradox Pathway – 25 learning coordinates for paradox leadership in practice

At this point, you have almost come full circle with the Paradox Pathway of navigating leadership paradoxes. Although the five phases of the pathway have described it as a linear, progressive process, navigating paradoxes is in fact a cyclical process. Endings and beginnings merge with each other. Navigating paradox is not a mechanical process moving forward toward an end goal. Often, the experience is that you will need to go back to the start seeing the familiar with new eyes and starting over again.

This chapter addresses the general experiences of working with paradoxes with respect to the 25 learning coordinates highlighted in the paradox navigation phases (Chapters 4–8). In Chapter 1, we suggested that you begin with Chapter 2 and then follow the five phases of paradox navigation, possibly after getting inspiration from the examples of paradoxical tensions in leadership presented in Chapter 3 – or go straight to this chapter, where we connect the dots. That said, all managers' situations are unique, and all managers are unique. Thus, it is up to you as a reader to choose which coordinates and models to use and in which order, based on where you are. We have tried to provide hints and clues about what we think is important and what is effective based on what we know and have experienced having worked with managers in practice. Ultimately, the choice is yours.

The experience condensed in this part of the book is derived from the Leadership GPS action-learning research project introduced in Chapter 1. Our tools and coordinates for paradox navigation take their point of departure in the specific leadership paradoxes the participating manager chose to work on as well as the specific situations and competencies of the individual participating researchers, companies, and managers. In time, place, and space the cases, tools, and learning emerged from the specific group of 55 managers from 11 companies and 11 researchers/consultants from five different universities/organizations. Through various workshops and seminars held after and during the action learning project we also had the opportunity to use ideas and concrete tools from the book and the project in other contexts. This includes public organizations, non-governmental organizations (NGOs), professional associations, HR professionals, and other managerial professionals as well as function managers without personnel management responsibilities. Across all these contexts, we can see some common experiences that arise and reoccur in multiple leadership paradoxes and settings.

These are experiences that extend beyond the individual or organization, and thus are learning points of a more general nature.

We have presented paradox navigation as a series of actions that fall into five phases (Figure 9.1).

https://doi.org/10.1515/9783110788877-010

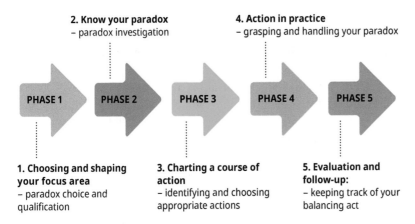

Figure 9.1: Five phases of navigating paradox (as previously introduced in Chapter 2).

Paradox navigation starts with choosing a focus paradox, verifying that it is indeed a paradox, investigating the paradox further, identifying and implementing paradoxical managerial actions, and finally incorporating the navigating of paradoxes as part of your daily management repertoire. This may appear straightforward, yet in practice we see that each of the phases come with not only a specific task, but also with several challenges and opportunities that managers should be aware of to either avoid them or capitalize on them. Our 25 learning coordinates assembled in the paradox GPS below are learning points from real-life managers' paradox work. The learning coordinates point to a paradox navigation that managers or development professionals assisting others in paradox navigation should be particularly mindful of when working through paradoxes to be able to harvest the benefits of paradox navigation and paradox learning.

A paradox GPS – 25 learning coordinates

Each of the five phases of paradox navigation has different points of attention and inspiring practices. Advice, tricks, and tips are discussed below in relation to their associated phase of paradox navigation. When we connect the dots, you get 25 coordinates, a "paradox GPS" to guide you on the journey:

Phase 1: Choosing and shaping your focus area – paradox choice and qualification

All paradoxes are connected. Trying to handle them all at the same time will paralyze you. Begin by choosing a paradox that seems relevant for you and take it from there. In practice, your choice of specific (content) paradox is less important than choosing one and getting started with the process.

Paradox navigation is a meta-competence. Dealing with paradoxes is a general skill that can be transferred across situations from one leadership paradox to another. Paradoxes are also about "something". Moving from a more general abstract notion of paradox is essential, and only when specificities are added can you start to flesh out the paradox in practice. You may think of, for instance, the general paradox between the simultaneous need for both decentralization and centralization, which has a specific expression in your organization. As you begin, it may be helpful to find inspiration in the management literature by identifying some well-described and evergreen paradoxes to juxtapose against your personal selections. In this chapter, we have provided examples to inspire you, and you can also find inspiration in the ten leadership paradoxes described in Chapter 3. A common starting point is particularly important when you need to collaborate with others on several paradoxes. This helps to ensure that your joint work does not suffer by difficulties in defining what belongs to which paradox or by lack of common vocabulary.

Many leaders have the "problem-solving itch". They see paradoxes as problems that need to be solved. However, the whole point of paradoxes is that they cannot be solved but must be dealt with on an ongoing basis. You will have to get used to considering your leadership challenge as a paradox. In this phase, you must dare to stop, linger, and seek inspiration from others inside and outside the organization. If you tend to choose a challenge that you already believe that you can easily handle, then you probably have not fully grasped the notion of paradox. You might have chosen a paradox that you have already become comfortable with, and in that case your time is probably better spent elsewhere.

For some leaders, conflict aversion and defensive routines can prevent them from getting into close contact with their paradox. Be aware that unpleasant situations that can keep you awake at night are not necessarily paradoxes. These may be "just" hard priorities, and your worries are only about having to communicate the consequences of your choice to the parties involved.

All challenges are difficult, but it makes a difference whether you understand them as problems, dilemmas, or paradoxes. While your initial labeling of paradox may be relatively unimportant, it is essential that you choose to focus on a paradox and not a problem or a dilemma. The room to maneuver follows from the problem understanding. A paradox treated like a problem will inevitably reappear to the surface like a cork. A problem treated as a paradox is tantamount to overcomplication.

Phase 2: Know your paradox – paradox investigation

Investigation of your paradox involves focusing on the dynamics of the paradox. What are its contradictions, what are its dependencies, and which dynamics are built in that require prioritizing one side of the paradox over another? What is the contribution from each side, and what problems arise if one of them is downgraded? The

Paradox Quadrant provides an initial overview of the pitfalls integrated in the paradox in relation to your leadership situation. Specifically, our experience has shown that the same paradox can come with very different individual expressions. Leaders have a variety of responsibilities, professional personas, experiences, and personalities, and they can therefore share the same paradox but place themselves completely differently regarding the two poles of the paradox.

The Paradox Quadrant specifies why a paradox is "both–and" and not "either–or". If you, after working with the model, are still convinced that one pole of the paradox is the only right one for you and your organization, that is fine. However, you might want to consider whether you should return to Phase 1 and choose a focus area that contains some long-term problems that typically have a paradoxical nature. Or you may want to consider that a unilateral focus on one pole will produce side-effects that are likely to grow over time. Knowledge and monitoring of side-effects will be central to your paradox work.

The investigation of your paradoxes is necessarily also an examination of the situation or context in which you find yourself. Paradoxes do not come with a list of facts. Each focus area and associated leadership paradox has its own nature and content that needs to be uncovered. In some organizations, there may be a tendency to prefer a particular pole of a paradox as better or more desirable than the other, for example, leadership in favor of management or one dimension of diversity or sustainability rather than others. It is particularly important that you as a leader do not allow yourself to be swept away by the current of management fads or the received wisdom, but work in the direction of the pole of the paradox that makes sense in the specific situation.

It can be useful to test whether there are other overlapping paradoxes that could also be useful for the understanding and working with the chosen focus areas. One paradox rarely comes alone. Paradoxes are often intertwined or entangled in knots. Although we have recommended that you face them one at the time, you may experience that as your knowledge of and familiarity with one paradox expands you are considering the same challenge in the light of additional interconnected, yet competing demands. It may help you to switch into a more useful way of thinking about your paradox or by supplementing your examination with additional perspectives that complement the development work.

When working with leadership paradoxes individually or in a management team, there will often be several paradoxes in play. It may be appropriate to examine how these paradoxes are interrelated. When paradoxes reoccur across a management team, it indicates that the paradox is not just individual, but organizational, and is therefore strategically relevant to the company. Occasionally, leaders who each have a strong position within the same paradox will be able to act as one another's sparring partners, as on person's weakness is typically the other's strength.

Phase 3: Charting a course of action – identifying and choosing appropriate actions

Your particular action must be based on the reflection work that you already completed when selecting and exploring your leadership paradox. This is important to consider at this stage of the journey, where many managers resort to classical problem solving and decision making. They leave behind the more nuanced understanding uncovered in the first two phases and do what they usually do, which is often to simply prioritize one of the poles in the paradox. Choosing appropriate actions implies such moves that will allow you to simultaneously keep competing priorities in mind, not jump to conclusions and decisions.

You cannot act on all aspects of the paradox at the same time. It is therefore important to focus your work. Go for what you are most motivated to tackle and make sure to concretize your actions as much as possible. Go for the obtainable, but be sure to check that your motivation is not tied to "the easy way out". "Deparadoxification" of a paradox – deflating complexity and adding simplistic shortcuts – is one of the biggest risks at this point.

Be aware that your choices depend on both your own and the organization's resources: The more you have organizational headwinds against you, the more energy your action plans will require from you.

Be aware of your own preferences. By acknowledging your own knee-jerk reactions and feelings toward a paradox you will be better able to make conscious choices, which can expand your action repertoire and thus lay the groundwork for new avenues in your paradox navigation.

Your paradox will not disappear even with the best course of action. Consider your work of choosing actions as a recurring process, where you will have to revisit the different dimensions of your paradox. Only in this way will you be able to ensure that you can also over time balance the poles of the paradox.

Phase 4: Action in practice – grasping and handling your paradox

When you act on a paradox, it requires that you pay attention to the fact that the actions you take are meaningful to the paradox. What are the tasks, the stakeholders, and the methods?

It is important to focus on actions with manageable steps. Although paradoxes are complex, actions directed at navigating the paradox need not necessarily be complex or complicated. The preparation of a manager's job description (Case 7.1, p. 105–106) is an example of how relatively small changes can have major consequences.

It is important that you move the process from your own reflection and development to a broader process in which you interact with your management colleagues and ultimately with those employees whom you need to influence to handle the paradox.

Managers, especially in small- and medium-sized companies or in subsidiaries/branches, have many different roles, as they typically hold several different management jobs simultaneously. This is also often the case for global or international managers or if you participate in matrix or project organizing. Each role gives rise to a paradoxical landscape and vantage point. The more perspectives in play, the more angles there will typically be to the same paradox.

Take time to make time. Remember that action and reflection are closely linked. Often, spending time meeting with the relevant people and talking with them are prerequisites for successful paradox navigation, even if you feel that it takes time from the urgent need for action that is your immediate focus.

Phase 5: Evaluation and follow-up – keeping track of your balancing act

In paradox navigation, it is especially important that you incorporate ongoing evaluation and follow-up. In this way, you can make sure that you do not become too one-sided in your paradox work and thus risk "losing balance" along the way.

Evaluating your paradox navigation presupposes that you set yourself specific and measurable goals. A distinction between performance goals and process goals may be helpful, allowing you to work with both hard and soft data. It may well be possible that the data you need already exist, but you will have to look at it in another way or procure information from new sources in your organization.

Setting assessment criteria for optimal paradox navigation and work is not an exact science. The scale and assessment criteria depend on your specific context. Therefore, the optimal balancing of the poles of the paradoxes will differ from manager to manager and from company to company.

Closure is not the goal – navigation is the goal. Hereby you will avoid short-sighted, ineffective "problem solving" or complexity paralysis. There is no cure without side-effects, so you will always have some issues emerging where you are "in the red". There will necessarily be considerations that were not optimally addressed, concerns or priorities that are currently not considered. But you are aware of them and ready to change your position if need be – and this need probably arises soon given the speed of change in modern organizations.

The best balance is found together with others. You can evaluate your paradox navigation individually, but it is highly recommended that you also involve additional perspectives and stakeholders. Part III of this book is dedicated to exploring paradox navigation with (and sometimes against) relevant others in and outside your organization. To start the process, you can invite your immediate manager, employees, or management colleagues to join you in reflection and evaluation of successes and future actions.

Coming full circle – the Paradox Pathway

As we mentioned at the beginning of this chapter, paradox navigation is a cyclical process. If you connect the 25 coordinates of the paradox GPS with the five phases and their management tools and cases, a Paradox Pathway is formed - a GPS or road map to guide your paradox navigation:

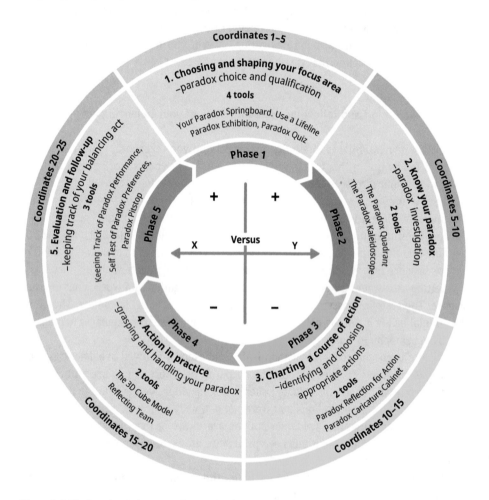

Figure 9.2: The Paradox Pathway (as also previously introduced in Chapter 2).

As illustrated in the Paradox Pathway, the center of the figure is left blank – this is where you come into the picture. It all starts with a challenge from your work life, a particularly difficult or reoccurring challenge in your organization as the objective of working through the paradox. As discussed in Chapter 2, it is important to distinguish paradoxes from problems or dilemmas, but if it is a paradox (illustrated in the figure by poles X and Y both with a plus and minus side), the Paradox Pathway is relevant.

Above we have described our experiences from working with paradox navigation in practice. These are experiences that go beyond the individuals or companies discussed. Further, it is also important to keep in mind that navigation of paradoxical leadership challenges cannot just be understood in relation to the different phases of paradoxical work or as something that is linked to specific leadership paradoxes. The navigation of a paradox must also be addressed based on the specific context. This is an aspect of paradox navigation to which we dedicate the remainder of this chapter.

Working conditions for paradox navigation: Coping with paradoxes in context

Context refers to the conditions in the company's and the manager's (local) environment, the outside world, as well as ownership or organizational culture, which have a significant influence on how the individual paradox can be handled in practice. Therefore, you need to consider the working conditions for paradox navigation, and you must know how such factors affect your room to maneuver and scope for action when navigating paradoxes. In this last section of the chapter, we discuss some of the contextual factors or working conditions that, in our experience, have had a particular influence on paradox navigation for individual managers. The context of paradox navigation will also be the central theme of the following Part III (Chapters 10–12).

Paradox – for others and for you?

When you as a manager work with paradoxes, it is important to be aware of the fact that there may, simultaneously, be several perspectives in play. It is a bit like the story of the blindfolded men characterizing an elephant, each blindfolded person touching a different part of the animal. The person touching the bushy tail extensively describes what he or she thinks, the person at the trunk has his or her own experiences, while the person sitting on the back of the elephant also has his or her unique interpretation of what he or she may be touching. In the same way, the different people and functions in the company will have different perspectives on a given leadership paradox. If you see the paradox from the customers' perspective, the pros and cons of the paradox will appear in one way. If you look at it from the employees' point of view, you will have a different interpretation, and if you go to management and take an overall organizational perspective, a third and completely different version will come up. When we talk about finding "the right balance" in paradoxical leadership, it is important as a leader to be able to consciously change your perspective. You have to ask yourself whether there are any stakeholders you tend to favor or conversely overlook. The premise is that in balancing the paradox, your interpretation of the sun and shadow sides are not necessarily the same as other stakeholders would prefer to emphasize.

What we have experienced in working with managers is that many people are very skilled and also tend to see their paradox from the perspective of employees or the departments and groups that are in their management scope. It is natural that you as a manager reflect on and deal with negative consequences for the employees, for example, what an increased elite focus in talent development will require. However, what about the negative consequences for the manager? In many cases, managers tend to ignore their own position in the leadership of the paradox. If you want to maximize the effect of your efforts, you must also increase your awareness of your own vulnerabilities when dealing with the inherent paradoxes of leadership. If, for example, you invest in an elitist approach to talent development to retain particularly career-focused high performers, you may risk becoming a less popular leader. Or you may train some of your employees so well that they are able to threaten your own position in the organization. Taking ownership also means that you understand your own stake within the paradox and recognize and what you risk losing.

The role of different leadership roles

When we have discussed leaders and paradox leadership in this book, we have done so without paying much attention to the fact that leadership happens at many hierarchical levels with different job content and so forth. Many companies, particularly small- and medium-sized companies, are operated by managers who own the company, and they have inherited the position and the family obligations through generations. Family management and/or fund ownership sets particular agendas for how decisions are made and paradoxes must be handled. Throughout the project, however, it also became clear that the specific characteristics of a manager's managerial role have an influence on the power of action – or lack thereof.

The individual personalities of leaders as well as their experience can also affect how they handle paradoxes. A manager who is new to upper management can, for example, find it riskier to throw himself into the deep water represented by paradox thinking. In other cases, the manager's experience, including experience that has come because of close partnership within the organization, can prove to be a stumbling block for change. For example, we know about experienced managers who crept into hiding in the face of paradoxical thinking when faced with new roles, hoping that the paradox would soon disappear. Conversely, we have also met experienced leaders who never really addressed paradoxes, despite being incredibly competent in other ways. Many years of experience as a manager can mask opportunities for organizational change, even in cases where you are surrounded by enthusiastic colleagues, who would provide support and encouragement.

The ups and downs

Growth or recession can initially be the cause of a leader's paradox but can also prove to be what ultimately puts an end to the paradox. In one company, perhaps everyone stands ready to collaborate to make things work. However, there is always the chance of drowning in one's own success. At the same time, it is precisely this success and blinding pace that creates many of the internal paradoxes and frustrations that managers experience in their everyday lives. There is an urgent need for common standards and procedures as well as a focus on building them. Leaders have often told us that both they and their colleagues constantly resort to the familiar resolution channels and patching solutions, particularly under increasing work-related pressures.

In sum, paradox navigation is a general capability, yet focused on working through a specific, reoccurring complex challenge through five phases. The Paradox Pathway in Figure 9.2 and associated learnings coordinates can guide your paradox navigation. Or perhaps – as a manager remarked – a roundabout, except for every turn you take the landscape will have changed.

Part III: **Paradox navigation 2.0 – working through paradox with stakeholders**

Modern organizations and the individuals who manage within them must operate in an increasingly volatile, uncertain, and ambiguous business environment. These conditions have helped foster an experience of ongoing complexity that presents a *stream of tensions that can pull the individual and organization in multiple-competing directions.*

(Jules and Good, 2014, p. 124, authors' emphasis added)

Until now, we have presented paradox navigation as a cyclical process involving different phases that paradox navigators work through in their efforts to cope with paradox. Yet, we have also seen how the managers in our cases from practice are increasingly made aware of and need the engagement of different stakeholders as they work their way through the phases (e.g., Case 7.3: Paradox-synergies in leadership teams). Our point of departure has been the individual paradox navigator dealing with their personal leadership paradox as a necessary starting point, yet paradox work does not take place in isolation. Paradox navigators are not alone on the road and rely on the companionship with and support of others on their journey. Where the middle part of the book primarily aimed at assisting the individual manager in navigating paradox on a more personal level, the following and last Part III of the book focuses on working through paradoxes with stakeholders – exploring paradox navigation as a "team sport" collaborating with internal and external relevant others. If learning to navigate paradox individually can be thought of as paradox navigation 1.0, paradox navigation with an explicit focus on the stakeholder landscape in which individual paradox is embedded can be cast as paradox navigation 2.0.

Our motivation for this change of scene to paradox navigation 2.0 is threefold:

First, we have observed in our work with managers in the Leadership GPS project how application of paradoxical thinking became increasingly difficult as they moved toward the last phases of paradox navigation, where paradoxical thinking is not only applied to understanding their everyday challenges in a different way, but also to implementing and taking paradoxical action. Such difficulties of transforming thinking into acting often arise because of failure to include or consider the impact of stakeholders on their individual efforts. Consequently, we wish to assist paradox navigators in considering their individual efforts as part of a larger eco-system of paradox navigation to capitalize fully on paradoxical thinking.

Second, we have experienced how most managers tap into paradoxical thinking with regards to "local" operational concerns in their individual team or department relatively effortlessly when given guidance. Yet, many managers find it difficult to move beyond that context and consider their own challenges in a broader organizational perspective of corporate-wide initiatives, such as strategy execution, organizational change, implementation of new technology, sustainable transformation, or co-creative innovation with customers or citizens. Individual efforts, however, are hampered if not connected to organizational challenges and objectives. Managers need to take overall responsibility, not only for the performance and engagement locally in the part of the organization the individual manager is responsible for, but rather for actively contributing to the navigation of the paradoxes of the entire organization. Taking on this responsibility and zooming out to consider the larger context can be experienced as quite overwhelming for many; this is particularly true for lower-level managers and other non-managerial paradox navigators, but by no means limited to these groups. This is the point where many resort to either–or thinking, identifying fixed compromises or retreating to what has been called "the avoiding zone" (Lewis and Smith, 2022; Smith

https://doi.org/10.1515/9783110788877-011

and Lewis, 2022), not because they do not experience paradox, but choose to abstain from considering the "bigger picture" and pointing to upper management or outside forces as responsible.

In our view, non-engagement with the bigger picture is not a sustainable position, however, particularly not in middle and upper-level management, because they are part of a management group who has a responsibility that goes across the organization and therefore similarly has a responsibility to navigate and balance the organizational paradoxes in collaboration with the rest of the organization. So, even if considering the bigger picture outside their own "silo" and span of (relative) control to engage with the wider sphere of influence can feel like losing control, this is exactly what is needed to tap into the friction energy of paradox navigation with others. The chapters in this part will provide insight into the practice, potentials, and perils involved in connecting individual efforts to organizational and eco-system challenges.

Third, we also wish to address challenges of more experienced and advanced paradox navigators who have already previously worked with paradoxes and help them take the next step. This also involves addressing the challenges of assisting others in developing paradox capability and working through paradox such as is done by development professionals (for example, HR), managers, or others responsible for helping others navigate paradoxes as part of their work.

To illustrate the connectivity between the paradox navigation and the context and collaborative environment, this Part III introduces knowledge and insights from research projects that have been undertaken after the completion of the Leadership GPS project that we reported from in Part II as well as ongoing research projects on leadership paradox. Consequently, we introduce new named as well as anonymized cases of organizational paradox navigation from public and private corporations working with paradox in practice that the authors have been working with for research or consulting purposes. Parts of this knowledge have been presented in white papers or academic conference papers, or (partially) published in academic journals, in which case, we reference these publications. In other cases, we invite readers into the "machine room" of data analysis from ongoing research projects in addition to relying on extensive field notes from our encounters with paradox practice as researchers and consultants.

References

Jules, C., and Good, D. (2014). Introduction to special issue on paradox in context: Advances in theory and practice. *The Journal of Applied Behavioral Science*, 50(2), 123–126.

Lewis, M. W., and Smith, W. K. (2022). Reflections on the 2021 Decade Award: Navigating paradox is paradoxical. *Academy of Management Review*, published online ahead of print, https://doi.org/10.5465/amr.2022.0251

Smith, W. K., and Lewis, M. W. (2022). *Both/And Thinking. Embracing Creative Tensions to Solve Your Toughest Problems*. Boston, MA: Harvard Business Review Press.

Chapter 10
Paradox navigation as a team sport:
Inter- and intra-organizational collaboration
on paradox

> [T]he two poles of a paradox may operate at different levels in the organization. A given dynamic may be true of individual behavior, but the opposite may apply at the organizational level.
>
> (Clegg, da Cunha, and e Cunha, 2002, p. 484)

Paradoxical tensions are experienced differently at different levels in the organization and the (attempted) response to paradox of one level may exacerbate (or alleviate) tensions at other levels. Our experiences from managers' paradox coping suggest that it is timely to engage paradox navigation as a team sport – a collaboration between relevant actors inside and outside the organization. This chapter explores paradox navigation as part of a wider ecosystem of collaboration with internal and external stakeholders presenting real-life examples of the ways in which different managerial levels may positively/negatively influence others' paradox work as well as how subordinates' paradox coping is influenced by managerial paradox navigation.

As the reader has probably come to realize by now from the previous chapters, there are no "best practice"-solutions to handling paradox neither individually nor as part of a larger collective, but we can extract valuable learnings from the ways in which others have (attempted) to navigate paradox collaboratively. In this chapter, we shall explore some of the ways that organizations experience and (attempt to) deal with paradox navigation together. In addition to our experiences from the Leadership GPS project, we will be introducing data from research projects and consultation activities on leadership paradox that the authors are engaged with and focus on the collaborative and contextual dimensions of paradox navigation (for additional information about these projects, please see references at the end of this chapter).

Paradox navigation – from individual challenge to collective change

> [R]esponding to paradoxical tensions by some actors give rise to unintended or negative consequences that may actually exacerbate tensions for others.
>
> (Hahn, Jarzabkowski, and Knight, 2019, last paragraph)

Paradox exists and is understood in context and situation – it is influenced by the environment, the resources, and the actors. Even if engaging with paradox on an individual level is helpful, stakeholders play a large role for the individual's available action repertoire. If you revisit Part II, you will perhaps remember that we have heard about

https://doi.org/10.1515/9783110788877-012

individual managers whose paradox coping was seen as connected to, yet different from, a top managerial community of practice between the chairperson of the board, the CEO, and top management colleagues (Case 7.1: The paradoxical job description). Also, we have heard about managers considering if the paradox navigation they saw fit could expect headwind or tailwind in the organization, knowing that they would need more resources for "headwind paradox navigation" than navigation in calm sea (Case 6.2: Coping with paradox – head wind or tail wind?).

The 20 different mini-cases and exemplars you have been introduced to in Part II have primarily presented the ways the managers moved through the five phases with their chosen paradox zooming in on the individual opportunities and challenges encountered on their way. Yet, in our research data and experiences from the Leadership GPS project it is also clear that the participating managers differ in their roles, degree of experience, specific responsibilities, hierarchical level, and position in their corporations in general. These differences impact their power to act – or lack thereof – on paradox. For example, we can think of a top manager who works to strengthen organizational, distributed leadership and has an extensive degree of freedom to change the organization. If the manager wants to give his employees and managers greater room for maneuver and responsibility, he can – as one of one the owner-managers from the GPS project did – choose to stay at home or arrive late at work as an attempt to leave room for lower-level managers to rise to the occasion in his absence. This is a strategy that this individual can freely choose to pursue, where lower-level managers – or employees – might need the approval of others to be able to engage their paradox in this manner. So, room to maneuver differs for different stakeholders.

We also observed that the possibilities for paradox navigation were affected by the degree of geographical dispersion of the organization, and whether the individual manager is in the head office or in subsidiaries and branches. Managers located at the head office typically had enlarged room to maneuver, as they often have the task of formulating common standards and processes, while managers in subsidiaries and branches were further from the centre of power. This group typically had to follow what was defined by the HQ as "corporate best practice" – even if this practice was not "best" in the individual subsidiary or branch. In such cases, the local paradox navigation is spun into a series of decisions at group level, which, depending on their nature, can be useful or make the task more difficult by the limited room for maneuver.

These observations resonate with an increasing interest from the paradox research community not only in managers' handling of paradoxes, but also in the consequences – positive and negative – of paradox leadership for employees or other stakeholders participating in or influenced by paradoxes navigation. For example: How and how much can employees be involved in paradox leadership? How can sharing of paradox with others avoid becoming a de facto evasion of responsibility if paradoxes are left to actors who have little room for maneuver, resources, or decision-making competence to navigate them? How do managers and employees respond to this relationship? What are the consequences in practice? This perspective is particularly important at a time when leadership is increasingly shared, distributed, and collective, and is self-leadership. When managerial and leadership behavior is not solely the responsibility of persons formally entitled "manager" or "leaders", an increasing number of people are charged with the challenge of paradoxical leadership. This recent focus on the ways in which actors at different stakeholders and perspectives also comes to the fore in relation to organizational or societal transformation that foresees concerted action across a broad range of actors such as for instance sustainable transformation.

In paradoxical challenges grand and small, the individual manager is part of a web on interconnected paradox navigators. Understanding the ways in which individual actors' paradox coping strategies influence and are influenced by other actors' coping space and available coping strategy repertoire is important for navigating paradox as a collective. In the following sections, we shall introduce examples of paradox navigation demonstrating how different hierarchical levels and internal stakeholders are intertwined Also, we shall harvest learning points of a more general nature from these cases along the way.

Case 10.1: "Glocal" governance model: Inter-function navigation of the local–global paradox in practice

If you let business arguments guide you in how you organize different global functions, you will find that none of these functions operate in the same business circumstances and hence will end up being organized differently to varying degrees. In doing this. you accept that one size does not fit all, and that's okay.
(Organization design manager, case-corporation, personal correspondence with authors)

Our first illustration of paradox navigation as an organizational endeavor zooms in on the local–global tension involving the simultaneous pursuit of the contradictory needs for global, corporate-wide processes and consideration for local specificities (cf. Chapter 3's discussion of the local–global paradox). The case company is an internationally operating manufacturing company with approximately 10,000 employees located worldwide, sales companies in 40 countries, and 17 production sites in nine countries (a case inspired by and developed from Nielsen and Lyndgaard, 2023; Nielsen, et al., 2016; Nielsen and Lyndgaard, 2018). Coming from being a very locally anchored organization the organization saw the need to develop into a transnational organization aspiring to becoming globally "one company". The overall vision of unity in "one company" was, however, operationalized with a *dual* "glocal" focus on local *and* global: *"We operate as one company with a dual focus on our local customer interface to retain local market responsiveness and global integration and processes to enhance global efficiency."* This principle was intended to allow the corporation to remain local and differentiated in the different markets and, on the other hand, it set the direction for optimizing all areas of the business globally. Given the corporation's past this represented a significant change where the company worked intensely to become an integrated global company with both organizational changes sparking off new ways of working and training of managers across all functions and business units. It also involved a new governance model foreseeing a differentiation approach of different mixing ratios of "local" and "global" for different functions, as illustrated in Figure 10.1.

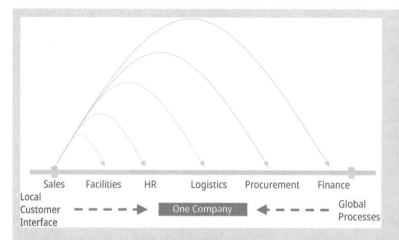

Figure 10.1: Balancing the local–global paradox – organizational mixing ratios.

What we see is that different functions such as "Sales" or "Logistics" have different mixing ratios of global and local – or formulated differently: Their local–global navigation mode differs according to their mode of operation and objectives. Starting in the highly local left side of the figure, we can think of a regional sales director in a solid market: As the case corporation saw it, this manager would *"need to know and understand she is part of a global organization, and maybe why she cannot get a specific product variation just for her customers, but other than that her business, customers, service staff etc. are all local"*. Moving right along the bottom line, we find "Facilities", the logic in the case corporation being that *"facilities are located, where they are located"*. Running the facilities is a local matter, yet optimizing the global portfolio and regional optimization is possible as is global common ways of working, knowledge, and best practice sharing across sites and so on. Consequently, much remains local in this function although a corporate-wide outlook and knowledge sharing is demanded. At the other end of the continuum of local–global mixing rations, we might find a national finance manager who is fully integrated in the global organization, reporting globally, observing global processes and standards, collaborating seamlessly with outsourced accounting in other parts of the world. This manager needs to know this setup and have a global outlook every single day, even though his primary internal customers are all local.

Now, the different mixing ratios might be different for other companies, industries, or sectors. The general learning point we wish to extract from this exemplar is that even if the corporation experienced an overall movement from multi-local to global integration, the integration of the two opposing forces of "local" and "global" did not foresee a synthesis of the two. Rather, a differentiated approach was condensed in the model allowing for different mixing ratios in different functions, while also insisting on a mixing ratio – that is, not allowing for any one function to choose either "local" or "global". The model can be seen as a map bringing together a diversity of paradox navigation modes, a collaborative tool for balancing the local–global paradox. In the case corporation, the explication of the local–global balancing acts in the model paved the way for productive dialog about differences in-between functions facilitating a more constructive and informed debate shifting the focus from "the right balance" between local and global to "balances". The map provides managers, employees, and other stakeholders with a starting point and conversation starter supporting a dialog of complex organizational processes. The case also shows that "the better balance" must be seen in relation to business objectives and tasks.

While the model's potential for inter-functional collaboration was appreciated in the organization, challenges were also present, however. Many managers complained that even if the model was a true and fair representation of the (intended) governance mode, it was also (too) confusing and complex. Indeed, communicating about navigation of paradox is a challenging task (a point to which we shall return in Chapter 11) as paradox per definition escapes the principle of clear, unequivocal messages. Partially in response to such criticisms, a group of matrix managers and hybrid support employees was appointed in the case corporation to assist in the working of the new model. The idea was that expert local–global paradox navigators would help other paradox navigators who might not need to exert the same level of competence. This also points to an additional take-away from this case: It might not be realistic or appropriate for all managers – or employees – to develop the same type of paradox navigation competence or develop this capability to the same extent – one size does not fit all in this respect as well. Although we contend that returns to investment in developing paradox navigation skills would always be positive, we do not expect them to be uniform. The value added by the ability to work in fields of paradoxical tensions comfortably and competently, and the value subtracted by the absence of such ability, is likely to be strongest in the case of those individuals who are directly responsible for managing cross-functional activities, followed by those who must interact frequently with colleagues from other functions or otherwise span and bridge internal and external boundaries of the organization.

Case 10.2: Paradox navigation crossing hierarchical lines

> [W]hat seems paradoxical higher up appears confusing and absurd lower down.
> (Czarniawska, 1997, p. 97, cited in Berti and Simpson, 2021, p. 253)

Paradox navigation resulting in virtuous rather than vicious dynamics do not rest solely in the leader's hand, but are also closely tied to the followers, subordinates, and superiors and their experience of the paradox. In our next case from the public sector illustrating paradox navigation in collectives, we are not looking at paradox navigation across functions, but spanning different hierarchical levels. As we shall see, paradoxical tensions are experienced differently by different managers at different hierarchical levels and contexts. In addition, tensions also interact between levels and in this respect the aspect of power in terms of resource access, mandate, and competences becomes important. Interpretation of paradoxical tensions may differ, but the degree to which actors are equipped and able to choose an appropriate course of action also differs. The room to maneuver is unevenly distributed among hierarchical levels, and so lower-level managers or non-managers may be confronted by paradox but have little opportunity to cope. The individual managers' coping strategies also impact their stakeholders such as, for instance, their subordinates or immediate superiors and they are in turn influenced by these actors' coping strategies. This begs the question of how managers experience and cope with the consequences of their own paradox navigation and that of their subordinates and superiors.

In the following, we report from previous as well as ongoing research exploring the interaction between three levels of managers and their experiences of navigation of leadership paradox in the Royal Danish Defence (Nielsen and Hansen, 2020; Hansen, 2013; The Royal Danish Defence Academy, 2008; Holsting and Damkjer, 2020). The Royal Danish Defence, consisting of approximately 20,000 employees of which 15,000 are in uniform, is an interesting case, as this organization has been actively and explicitly working with paradox thinking and theory for more than 10 years. Their leadership philosophy, leadership training and evaluation is based on selected core paradoxes deemed particularly relevant for the Royal Danish Defence. We aim to highlight the consequences of "sharing of paradoxes" across managerial levels, and how this is experienced in practice by paradox managers.

To cope with the increasing complexity and often opposing demands, the Danish Defence decided to implement a Leadership Codex, which builds theoretically on paradox theory in general and is hugely inspired by Cameron and Quinn's work on the competing values framework (Quinn and Cameron, 1988; Cameron and Quinn, 2011; Cameron, et al., 2022), the main paradoxes arising from the tensions between focusing on the relations (employees) and results (performance) and from focusing on creating organizational stability or change. The goal was to strike a proper balance between the tensions, in effect a "both–and" solution instead of an "either–or" solution. In 2008, the Leadership Codex was implemented with the purpose of creating a shared understanding of modern leadership for all employees. The codex builds on three levels:

1. philosophy (underlying assumptions)
2. ethics (values for good leadership)
3. norms (actual leadership behavior)

The Leadership Codex was developed through a combination of strategic policy making and an involvement of the organization through 20 representative focus group interviews, 176 participants in all. The interviews aimed at identifying a collective understanding of the leadership roles and values that constituted good leadership behavior in the Danish Defence.

More than a decade later, the general feedback from internal Danish Defence surveys is that the managers of the Danish Defence see a lot of appreciation of the paradox-based Leadership Codex at all levels in the organization. They do, however, also observe some challenges and opportunities as voiced in the organizational leadership courses where participants bring and work on their own cases. Central challenges and opportunities can be summed up in three main types, all emphasizing the collaboration (or non-collaboration) between hierarchical levels:

1) When paradoxes are perceived as having been delegated too far down the hierarchical line unaccompanied by the necessary resources to pursue a "both–and" strategy.
2) When a both–and approach has been communicated from upper-level management, yet the experience further down the line is that the approach is in fact one-sided.
3) Unexpected activation of paradox coping strategies by subordinates can mitigate inability to navigate paradox at higher levels.

The first *challenge* of cross-level navigation occurs when the navigation of paradoxical tensions is perceived of as having been pushed too far down the organization, and the person or group designated to handle the paradox finds themselves in a position where they do not have the capacity/competencies nor the mandate/power to do anything about the challenges at hand. This often leads to frustration or even stress among the implicated participants. This could be in cases where the task is to step up production and at the same time reduce costs, for example, train the soldiers to do more challenging tasks in a wider spectrum of combat scenarios but with less time to train them and without the capacity to manage this paradox. Another example is when the task is to coordinate with other branches of the Defence and get them to contribute with resources but with no authority to make them do so.

The second *challenge* is observed when paradox leadership is used as a promise to solve a problem that is the result of competing demands. This could be during a period of organizational change where the leaders promise to focus on both the changes at hand but also the stability of the routines in the organization. This is so the organization simultaneously can prepare for the tasks of tomorrow and keep the level of the present operations. Often the employees find themselves in situations where they do not have enough resources or the right competencies to make the necessary changes nor continue the level of operations expected of them. In this case, they feel that their managers have not fulfilled their promise of handling both criteria for success/demands. This often leads to a diminishing level of trust between superior and subordinates and in severe cases employees leaving the organization.

A recurring *opportunity* of collaborative paradox navigation as experienced by managers occurs when subordinates activate paradoxical coping strategies, in cases where their superiors are unsuccessful. Managers report that this may mitigate the negative consequences of failed paradox navigation at higher levels in the hierarchy. A case in point was a Colonel in the Airforce whose subordinates responded unexpectedly constructively when facing a major organizational change involving new tasks, but with fewer resources. The Airforce Colonel tried to implement more lean procedures to meet the budget cuts and expected a high degree of resistance in the organization. His expectation of resistance to change did not happen. Instead, he found that the shared understanding originating in the Leadership Codex among his officers of the challenges as paradoxes made them more resilient and able to navigate conflicting demands facing them with "both–and" solutions rather than "either–or" solutions. The Colonel's superior was very happy and a little bit surprised with the fast results and almost no "noise" from the organization.

So, collaborative effects are not exclusively negative in nature. Although we might intuitively associate consequences for lower-level stakeholders and followers with negative synergies, we need to stay open to possible unintended upsides of sharing of paradoxes across managerial levels and with employees. Indeed, this is a source of resilience and change capability when navigating contradicting demands.

Paradox sharing – learning from collaborative paradox navigation in practice

If one is to reap the positive results of paradoxical leadership, our experiences suggest that it must be done in a way that includes detailed knowledge about both the concrete challenges that modern management faces (such as exemplified in Chapter 3, What paradox? Introducing fields of paradoxical tensions in leadership), but also the way in which contemporary leadership is exercised in collaboration with many stakeholders and by actors who are not officially managers. Several learnings that facilitate this movement from individual thinking to collective action can be detracted from our two examples of collaborative paradox navigation in this chapter as well as from the cases presented in Part II.

First, we often experience managers express concern that sharing paradoxes with subordinates is too complex and confusing, and that employees are best spared the conundrum. While this might (also) be true, the experiences from the Danish Defence demonstrate that employees sometimes are the better complexity copers and paradox navigators capable of assisting and supporting managerial paradox navigation. Employees are not always resisting paradox – indeed paradox navigation can be assisted by employees when the manager runs out of steam. This resonates with experiences from a study conducted in the Swedish defence by Bergström, Styhre, and Thilander (2014) showing how employees can develop paradoxical sensemaking resources as a way of coping with seemingly meaningless and (unrealistically) one-sided organizational change initiatives. So, sometimes the courageous expert paradox navigators are the followers, not the managers. Indeed, employees or lower-level managers may be better positioned to handle the paradoxes since they have a rich understanding of the manifestations and consequences of paradox in everyday practice and therefore can approach paradox navigation with a more creative and domain-specific manner. At the same time, this chapter's case example from the international manufacturing company shows the other side of the story. Presenting organizational reality as paradoxical and fraught with competing demands may be portraying management as it is rather than how we hope it is; yet "telling it like it is" it may also be experienced as confusing by employees – a point to which we shall return in Chapter 11 about paradoxical communication.

A second central learning is the simple, yet often overlooked fact that a paradox takes different forms in different parts of the organization. Organizational tensions are made salient and experienced differently among different stakeholders in the organization and manifest themselves at several levels. Indeed, what appears to be a paradoxical tension between local and global demands in headquarters may manifest itself and be experienced differently but also as an entirely different tension in other parts of the organization. Different hierarchical levels and functions have different room to maneuver, and when delegation of paradox navigation responsibility is not accompanied by the mandate or resources to actively navigate the paradox, this creates a negative effect. Also, as we see in the case of the international manufacturing company not all managers or employees are exposed to a paradox in the same way or to the same degree. As suggested by the presented governance model, all managers were not equally exposed to the global business and hence did not have to have the same degree of local–global paradox navigation capability. The value added or subtracted by ability to navigate paradox was diverse and differed in different functions.

Third, we also observe that both organizations had used extensive resources on employee and management development when introducing both–and organizing and collaboration. In the case of the manufacturing company, all managers had participated in leadership development activities and numerous strategy implementation workshops had been organized. In the case of the Danish Defence, an organization-wide leadership codex had been developed following an organizational bottom-up process and was later the basis of leadership training, development, and performance reviews. So, paradoxical leadership and followership was accompanied by training and development as well as organizational guardrails in the form of a leadership codex and governance model supporting organizational navigation.

Fourth, both cases also suggest that organizational paradox navigation may benefit from the help of expert paradox navigators or other organizational "helpers". The difficulties of not only navigating your individual paradox, but also collaborating with others with different perspectives and balancing points, can be enabled by supporting or third-person actors assisting others in coping with paradoxes. Third-person actors include supporting actors such as HR professionals, professional peers, or network connections (Pradies, et al., 2021; Deeds Pamphile, 2022; Keller, Wong, and Liou, 2020; Mormann and Sender, 2022) that can act as "substitutes" (Nielsen et al., 2019) in the navigation of paradoxes as well as internal or external consultants (Fairhurst, 2019). In the case of the Danish Defence the internal corporate academy drives the development process; in the case of the manufacturing firm, special "matrix managers" were given the role of leading and assisting the organizational balancing efforts. In the case of the companies participating in the Leadership GPS project, they joined a research project where an external consortium of researchers and consultants designed and implemented a development program for groups of managers. (Also see chapter 12, dedicated to discussing opportunities and challenges of paradox navigation helpers.)

Fifth, our exemplars also suggest that paradoxical collective action is an ongoing endeavor, a journey that constantly evolves and takes turn. For instance, our case from the Danish Defence suggests that practice makes perfect in the sense that managers across managerial levels were at times able to help one another navigate paradox productively. It also, however, suggests that even 10 years down the road of organizational paradox capability building, paradox navigation is a complex co-creative process that can never be perfected in a standard operating procedure or best practice. Not only do new managers enter the organization, change jobs, or hierarchical level, and so must acquire paradoxical insights through corporate programs or in a new context. The central paradoxes presented as particularly pertinent and reoccurring, change in content and stakeholder set-up over time. So, even if you are an experienced paradox navigator in one type of paradox, changes in the external or internal environment can alter the concrete specificities of that paradox leading to a need to rethink and regroup.

Finally, these co-creative research experiences lead us to suggest that the Paradox Pathway presented in Part II can not only be a useful tool for grasping individual paradoxes, but also as a dialog tool for engaging with others. For example, we have experienced managers that have used the cases in the book as conversation starters for getting groups of employees thinking and talking about paradox. As we saw in Chapter 7, one of the participating companies in the Leadership GPS project chose to participate as a group consisting of CEO, chairperson of the board, and top management team working with both individual leadership paradoxes as well as exploring their challenges collectively. We have also seen managers fill out the Paradox Quadrant (presented in Chapter 5), have employees or other stakeholders or sparring partners in their external network fill in the model too and subsequently have a discussion on that basis.

Too often, individual efforts to navigate paradox do not produce the desired results, because central stakeholders do not subscribe to a paradoxical view leaving "lone wolf" paradox navigators frustrated and disillusioned. Although the individual navigator is important and individual thinking and deliberation about paradox is essential, paradox navigation is a team sport. This is particularly the case in the phases where managers, followers, and other stakeholders move from paradoxical thinking to paradoxical action – where the individual's understanding of their own paradox meets with other groups' understanding of their paradox. Consequently, we encourage readers and supporting actors to consider paradox navigation as a team effort where a web of stakeholders is involved in a paradox coping eco-system handling interconnected demands and objectives.

References

Bergström, O., Styhre, A., and Thilander, P. (2014). Paradoxifying organizational change: Cynicism and resistance in the Swedish Armed Forces. *Journal of Change Management*, 14(3), 384–404.

Berti, M., and Simpson, A. V. (2021). The dark side of organizational paradoxes: The dynamics of disempowerment. *Academy of Management Review*, 46(2), 252–274.

Cameron, K. S., and Quinn, R. E. (2011). *Diagnosing and Changing Organizational Culture: Based on the Competing Values Framework*. Hoboken, NJ: John Wiley and Sons.

Cameron, K. S., Quinn, R. E., DeGraff, J., and Thakor, A. V. (2022). *Competing Values Leadership*. Cheltenham, UK: Edward Elgar Publishing.

Clegg, S. R., Da Cunha, J. V., and e Cunha, M. P. (2002). Management paradoxes: A relational view. *Human Relations*, 55(5), 483–503.

Deeds Pamphile, V. (2022). Paradox peers: A relational approach to navigating a business–society paradox. *Academy of Management Journal*, 65(4), 1274–1302.

Fairhurst, G. T. (2019). Reflections: Return paradox to the wild? Paradox interventions and their implications. *Journal of Change Management*, 19(1), 6–22.

Hahn, T., Jarzabkowski, P., and Knight, E. (2019). Sub-theme 09: [SWG] Change for good? Organizational paradoxes and unintended consequences of transforming modern societies, Egos.org, https://www.egos.org/jart/prj3/egos/main.jart?rel=de&reserve-mode=active&content-id=1564449184268&subtheme_id=1542700474982, accessed October 14, 2022.

Hansen, M.P. (2013). How to lead complex situations. *Military Studies Magazine. Contemporary conflicts*, 1 (1), p. 1–6. Copenhagen, DK: The Royal Danish Defence College.

Holsting, V. S., and Damkjer, A. (2020). *Militært Chefvirke: At skabe handlekraft i komplekse situationer*. Copenhagen, DK: Samfundslitteratur.

Keller, J., Wong, S. S., and Liou, S. (2020). How social networks facilitate collective responses to organizational paradoxes. *Human Relations*, 73(3), 401–428.

Mormann, H., and Sender, A. (2022). Breaking up order through temporal role taking: HRM professionals as jesters in navigating paradoxes. In *Academy of Management Proceedings* (Vol. 2022, No. 1). Briarcliff Manor, NY 10510: Academy of Management, p. 10, 352.

Nielsen, R.K., and Hansen, M.P. (2020). *Exploring the Unintended Consequences of Managerial "Paradox Sharing" with Subordinates and Superiors. The Case of the Royal Danish Defence*. Paper accepted for European Group of Organization Studies 2020 Colloquium, Hamburg.

Nielsen, R. K. with Lyndgaard, D. B. (2018). *Tackling Global Leadership Practice*. Copenhagen, DK: Global Leadership Academy – Copenhagen Business School and Danish Confederation of Industry.

Nielsen, R.K.; Mogensen, M.; Bévort, F.; Henriksen, T.D.; Hjalager, A.M. & Lyndgaard, D.B. (2019). *Ledelses-GPS til en ny tid – Håndtering af ledelsesparadokser og dilemmaer i praksis*. Copenhagen Business School, University of Southern Denmark, Aalborg University & Network of Corporate Academies, https://www.industriensfond.dk/Ledelses-GPS.

Nielsen, R. K., and Lyndgaard, D. B. (2023). Developing Global Leaders in Denmark via Academic-practitioner Collaboration: Lessons for Educators and Consultants *Advances in Global Leadership* (Vol. 15), 255–268.

Nielsen, R. K, Maznevski, M., Poulfelt, F., Broundal, M., Hansen, P. G., Mortensen, E., and Bird, A. (2016). Exploring the individual-organizational global mindset nexus: An MNC-practitioner-academia dialogue. In *Academy of Management Proceedings*, (Vol. 2016). Briarcliff Manor, NY:The Academy of Management.

Nielsen, R. K., Mogensen, M., Bévort, F., Henriksen, T. D., Hjalager, A. M., and Lyndgaard, D. B. (2019). *Ledelses-GPS til en ny tid – Håndtering af ledelsesparadokser og dilemmaer i praksis*. Copenhagen, DK: Copenhagen Business School, University of Southern Denmark, Aalborg University and Network of Corporate Academies.

Pradies, C., Tunarosa, A., Lewis, M. W., and Courtois, J. (2021). From vicious to virtuous paradox dynamics: The social-symbolic work of supporting actors. *Organization Studies*, 42(8), 1241–1263.

Quinn, R. E., and Cameron, K. S. (1988). *Paradox and Transformation: Toward a Theory of Change in Organization and Management*. New York, NY: Ballinger Publishing Co/Harper and Row Publishers.

The Royal Danish Defence Academy (2008). *Forsvarets Ledelsesgrundlag*. Copenhagen, DK: The Royal Danish Defence Academy.

Chapter 11
Let's talk about paradox! Communicating consistently inconsistent about paradox with stakeholders

[I]n the past, the terms tension and contradiction have had negative connotations, perhaps we need to think about how organizations and their management might use tension and contradiction in a beneficial way?
(Grant and Cox, 2017, p. 197)

In this chapter, we present communication about paradoxes as a particular form of leadership communication (Fairhurst and Connaughton, 2014) and a rhetorical problem (Gabrielsen and Christiansen, 2010) that not only calls for intensified communication efforts (Smith and Lewis, 2012), but may also call for a different thinking about effective (leadership) communication than many managers and other paradox navigators may be used to. Paradox theory delivers a framework for managerial action that is robust and resilient yet accepting of vulnerability as a precondition for change and a sense-making resource for dealing with change and complexity for managers as well as other organizational actors (Benbenisty and Luria, 2021; Sparr, van Knippenberg, and Kearney 2022; Backhaus et al., 2022). Yet, the sensemaking and decision-making potential of paradox theory in assisting managers in navigating paradox can only be harvested if the individual paradox navigator can communicatively relate to the relevant others with whom the individuals need to collaborate to act on the paradox. Even if coping with paradox on an individual level is helpful, stakeholders play a large role for the individual's room to maneuver and the available action repertoire for responding to paradox as discussed in Chapter 10 on paradox navigation as a team sport.

In this respect, managers can play a leading role as the orchestrator of a third space, a symbolic site where actors engage paradox through mutual learning and collaborative dialog with the end goal of deriving "thrive with tension" (Miron-Spektor,Ingram, Keller, Smith and Lewis, 2018, p. 26; Schad et al., 2016) and sensegiver (Gioia and Chittipeddi, 1991) for co-navigators of paradox. This places a premium on leaders' ability to communicate paradoxical situations, decisions, and strategies to and with followers and similar relevant others. Communication plays a central role as a glue that keeps navigators together, but also as the way in which collective meaning is created around the paradoxes and in relation to how paradox is labeled and framed. This is not least the case when the manager increasingly collaborates with employees on management, where matrix constructions and agile organizational design across are given the task of breaking down silos, and where co-creation with external partners (colleagues, educational institutions, users, customers, citizens) is widespread. In the remainder of this chapter, we discuss

https://doi.org/10.1515/9783110788877-013

and demonstrate the potentials and pitfalls of communicating consistently inconsistently about interconnected, opposing demands involved in paradox.

Admitting to uncertainty is part of paradoxical leadership communication

> I do not believe in the opposition between health and the economy that some would like to establish. There is no thriving economy in a degraded health situation with a virus that is actively circulating. And, I tell you very clearly, there is no health system that will hold up if there is not a strong economy to finance it. So, it is a fair balance that we must constantly seek.
> (President Emmanuel Macron, in a speech to the French nation during the COVID-19 pandemic, October 28, 2020, cited in Lê and Pradies, 2022, second paragraph)

The COVID-19 experience is a reservoir of collective, practical paradox experience that paradox navigators can tap into – a "grand narrative" and "textbook example" of paradox navigation in action and the need for leadership to admit to uncertainty. Paradoxes create uncertainty, reduce line of sight, and challenge "best practice" thinking. In turn, paradoxical leadership challenges a traditional understanding of managers as pillars of certainty and "final" decisions. If the overall strategic direction and higher purpose of an organization is both–and how do you as a manager come across as decisive and in control? During COVID-19, political leaders, corporate leaders as well as representatives of health authorities have shown – for better and for worse – how admitting to uncertainty while still accepting responsibility is part of paradoxical leadership. For instance, the Danish prime minister has stressed in numerous state-televised national addresses during COVID-19 that *"we are likely to make mistakes on the way"* and *"we may change our guidance very soon as new information come to light"* (The Prime Minister's Office, 2020). These are inspirational examples of paradoxical leadership communication that we can learn from going forward.

At the same time, the COVID-19 crisis has also demonstrated the difficulties associated with actively and openly pursuing a "both–and" strategy. Although paradoxical leadership strategies may make sense at the level of the individual manager, the media may have little room or understanding for paradoxical decision making or communication. The journalistic genre is keen on yes–no, right–wrong, good–bad. The media thrive on tension, but they also expect tensions to be resolved, not left open for ongoing balancing acts. Paradoxical balancing can easily be construed of as zigzag-course, indecisiveness, or outright incompetence. In our experience, less media-exposed paradox navigators may also experience similar reactions from stakeholders such as top management, shareholders, employees, or customers that demand certainties and directions, not probabilities and perhaps.

While the COVID-19 crisis has made the concept of paradox more relevant and resonant by surfacing the "invisible currents of paradox" (Quinn and Nujella, 2017, p. vii), the crisis, however, also highlights the need to explain and translate paradox.

Crises and change may increase the demand for short-term solutions and clear answers; at the same time highlighting interconnectedness, calling for flexible, concerted action and consideration for contradictory relationships. While employees and stakeholders may request simplicity and clear accountability, change also exacerbates mutual dependencies, demonstrating that sustainable coping must involve a broad group of stakeholders. This places an emphasis on the ability of managers to be able to translate paradoxical strategies to stakeholders, to harvest the potential benefits of paradoxical leadership beyond positive effects for the individual manager.

Engaging demands for clarity/compliance as well as professional creativity and empowerment

While the corona-crisis is (hopefully) a 100-year event and an example of radical crisis, let us consider next a "normal" change initiative. Working with paradoxes requires not only new or changed competencies and leadership role of the leaders, but also of the employees and other stakeholders inside and outside the organization who contribute to paradoxical leadership. Similarly, strategy implementation and change initiatives such as sustainable transformation not only foresees collective paradox coping among actors internally in the organization but point to the interconnectedness between actors inside the organization and actors outside of the organization. Let's consider employee responses to a sustainable transformation initiative in a public organization foreseeing not only maintenance of a high standard for using organic raw material, but also introducing additional demands of sustainably produced raw materials (Jacobsen, Nielsen, and Eskjær, 2021). Some employees wanted clear answers, guidelines to comply with, and a clear signal from top management as illustrated by the following quotes:

> But one can say the frame is set. I do not question whether we should go for [specific standard X]. I also do not question whether we should financially bring it down [to a lower standard Y] because it would give us more leeway in the budget, because there I have a manager who has stated quite clearly that we are aiming for this. So that's what we're aiming for. (Employee interview 14)

> When we got this conversion from traditionally produced raw material to organically produced, it was heavily problematized, and then the decision was made, and in my view – the next day, everything I ordered of raw materials was organic . . . . It's just a matter of, that we make the decision about sustainable raw materials too. And then just do it. (Employee interview 9)

By contrast, other employees were critical of the efficiency of organizational guidelines, which they saw as paternalistic and did not demand or utilized the creative and professional capacities of employees:

> I believe that in a modern world with intelligent people, you cannot dictate people what to think . . . . If I start talking about and saying that 'you have to, because it's good', then I think that 'I have to decide for myself, damn it', and then it does not happen. (Employee interview 2)

People they are not stupid, young people are not stupid. They know very well what it takes for us to create a better world and for us to create a more just world. (Employee interview 4)

Working with sustainability and sustainable raw materials was a journey toward a moving goal, where new knowledge about the interconnectedness of different aspects of sustainability constantly must be absorbed and related to existing strategies and knowledge. Also, green conflicts within the environmental aspect of sustainability arose as it quickly became clear that use of organic and sustainable raw materials were not necessarily objectives that aligned with one another; indeed, sometimes they were perceived of as negatively impacting each other by employees. It is a transformation for which there is no definitive solution, but that the organization, manager, and employees can determine a specific course or attitude to how the built-in contradictions in sustainable raw materials must be balanced in practice. However, a common course was difficult in a field where it is a matter of sometimes internally conflicting and mutually exclusive priorities. Just as different aspects of sustainability are balanced differently in different situations, under different degrees of resource scarcity and by different disciplines, we also saw that employees had very different opinions about the way in which management could most suitably help them navigate this paradox as well as the degree to which they felt able and willing to partake in the navigation of paradoxes involved in sustainable transformation.

The value of inconsistent communication for paradox navigation

> While most teachers, researchers, and practitioners of organizational communication encourage clarity, a critical examination of communication processes in organizations reveals that clarity is both nonnormative and not a sensible standard against which to gauge individual or organizational effectiveness. People in organizations confront multiple situational requirements, develop multiple and often conflicting goals, and respond with communicative strategies which do not always minimize ambiguity, but are nonetheless effective.
>
> (Eisenberg, 1984, p. 227)

As outlined in the opening quote, communicating strategic ambiguity may be an essential component of paradox navigation involving numerous stakeholders in that communication of such messages facilitate organizational action on paradox through what Eisenberg (1984, p. 227) labels "unified diversity". This view of inconsistently inconsistent, paradoxical communication runs counter to much thinking about communication placing a premium on certainty, accuracy, and consistency in everything organizations say and do. As remarked by Christensen, Morsing, and Thyssen (2015, p. 12), "[o]rganizational messages about corporate values, in particular, are expected to accurately and unambiguously depict the organizational sender 'behind' the words. . . . Lack of accuracy in organizational messages – including inconsistencies between what organizations say and what they do – may be an important driver of organizational and social change, because such differences have potential to raise expectations and apply pressure on organizational actors to improve their practices." Communication of paradoxical both–and messages may be construed of as inaccuracy or ambiguity or expression of ambivalence that may impact conversations partners negatively (Rothman and Wiesenfeld, 2007). At the same time, ambiguity and ambivalence may foster capacity to change and act, while simplification and alignment may hamper the transformative potential of paradox.

For instance, the adoption of a governance philosophy or organizational values that embrace paradoxical decision making and action may ease the paradox work of the individual manager such as discussed in Chapter 10 and the cases of the Royal Danish Defense and an internationally operating manufacturing firm (for other examples, please see: The Municipality of Billund, 2020; The Municipality of Fredensborg, 2021; Schneider, Bullinger, and Brandl, 2020; Lewis, Andriopoulos, and Smith, 2014; Grant and Wolfram Cox, 2017). On the one hand, this form of simplification where managerial and employee paradox coping is fenced in by organizational guardrails (Smith and Besharov, 2019) cutting through Gordian paradox knots with normative guidance may be highly supportive in that managers are offered help in a challenging process. On the other hand, organizational guidelines narrow the outreach and action repertoire of the individual manager to cope with paradox. This is a source of taming the paradox that may deflate the paradox too much, in effect treating it as a problem or dilemma to be solved not worked through. Also, organizational guardrails, formulation of an organizational higher purpose, and structural/design choices to accommodate paradox may in fact be additional sources of taming resulting in routinization of paradox work.

Paradox interventions that are integrated into specific organizational change efforts or corporate academy programs with specified learning objectives are encouraged to be very mindful of a reductionist, taming tendency. Often, paradox development efforts are activated to develop complexity coping capability. Reducing complexity makes paradox more accessible at the outset yet may be tantamount to sabotaging the opportunity to develop the very competency that activation of paradoxical thinking was intended to facilitate the development of.

The dark and the bright sides of paradoxical communication

In the previous paragraphs, we have stated the case for the positive potential of ambiguous, polyphonic communication and consistently inconsistent messages compared to a more traditional view of leadership communication emphasizing consistency, clarity, and alignment. At the same time, we have also seen how different stakeholders may demand and value consistent respectively inconsistent messages very differently. In addition, communicating paradox may not only have positive effects. As you would expect, paradoxical leadership communication involves paradoxical tensions in and of itself of opposing demands and positive as well as negative outcomes.

Taking our point of departure in research literature and our experiences as paradox interventionists and trainers, Table 11.1 highlights illustrative examples of bright (functional) and dark (dysfunctional) aspects of managers' paradox communication. The table highlights bright and dark sides of managers' framing and communication of paradox individually and in relation to paradox co-navigators. In effect, we distinguish between managers as the lead paradox communicators and employees as interlocutors in managerial paradox communication. The top part of the table highlights bright and darks sides of managers' framing and communication as lead communicators, while the bottom part of the table shows the bright and dark sides of managers' paradox communication as experienced by paradox interlocutors:

Table 11.1: Functional and dysfunctional uses of paradoxical communication – lead communicators and interlocutors.

Managers: Lead paradox communicators	
Dark Side	**Bright Side**
Paradoxical communication as impression management and complexity washing (Gaim, Clegg, and Cunha, 2019). Maintaining ambiguity for organizational protection (Cappellaro, Compagni and Vaara, 2021).	Durable decision-making style (Smith, 2014). Painting a realistic picture (Johansen, 2018). Using organizational hypocricy as a vehicle to expand opportunities and experimentational work-in-progress mindset (Brunsson, 1993; Christensen, Morsing, and Thyssen, 2020).
Mixed message as organizational defensive routine (Argyris, 1990; Lüscher and Lewis, 2008).	Unleashing creativity by legitimizing and including a diversity of points of view (Miron-Spektor et al., 2011; Keller, Wong and Liou, 2020)
Paradoxical communication as a prolonging strategy for managers wearing their tensions as a badge of honour (Cheal, 2020) or as expressions of "fancy footwork" (Argyris, 1990, p. 45).	Signaling constructive controversy between different co-navigators as driver of paradox coping (Johnson, Johnson, and Tjosvold, 2000). Using polyphonic communication and aspirational talk to instigate action (Christensen, Morsing, and Thyssen, 2013, 2015).
Promotion of acceptance of tension as ideal may silence critical, disempowered voices (Berti and Simpson, 2021).	Inviting stakeholders to contribute with their views to not neglect opposing demands (Sundaramurthy and Lewis, 2003; Johnson, 2014).
Paradoxical communication may be at odds with interlocutors' demand for clear answers and line of command (upwards/downwards, internally/externally) (Grote et al., 2019; Waldman and Bowen, 2016).	A common language for understanding VUCA-world (Bennet and Lemoine, 2014). Organizing in times of turbulence (Quinn & Cameron, 1988). Ability to capture complexity and ambiguity (Schad et al., 2016).

Table 11.1 (continued)

Managers: Lead paradox communicators	
Dark Side	**Bright Side**
Paradoxical communication may be perceived of as decision-making "zigzagging", indecisiveness, or incompetence – by the manager or interlocutors (Nielsen, Cheal and Pradies, 2021).	Sense-giving (Gioia and Chittipeddi, 1991AQ.): offering sensemaking resources in chaos (Sharma and Good, 2013; Sparr, 2018), empowerment through reflexive sense-giving (Robert and Ola, 2021). Creating discursive resources for paradox transcendence (Bednarek, Paroutis and Sillince, 2017).

Interlocutors' reception of managers' paradox communication	
Dark Side	**Bright Side**
Individuals with an underdeveloped paradoxical mindset may experience anxiety, paralysis, and disengagement when confronted with paradoxical communication (Miron-Spektor et al., 2018).	Paradoxically minded individuals may feel energized and positively challenged (Miron-Spektor et al., 2018).
Task coordination experienced as too complex and conflict-ridden (Broundal, 2016; Smith and Lewis, 2012).	Communicating that management is humble and appreciates local complexities (van Dierendonck, 2011), diversities, and professions.
Overchallenged interlocutors may disengage and reduce expectations (Li, 2020) and subsequently lower quality standards to make ends meet.	Emotionally invested co-navigators feeling greater urgency vis-à-vis paradox may experience affective change when able to cope actively with tensions (Cheal, 2013).
Experiencing that multipolar communication from management is in fact one-sided (Nielsen and Hansen, 2020; Argyris, 1990).	Empowerment and activation of local resources, contributing to a multifaceted action and strategy (Eisenberg, 1984).
Pandora's Box-effect: unleashing of additional and knotted paradoxes when people engage in paradox coping (Cunha et al., 2019; Sheep, Fairhurst, and Khazanche, 2017).	Invitation to act in a difficult change situation and avoid paralysis (Beech et al., 2004). Fostering non-naïve organizational positivity (Cunha, Simpson, Rego and Clegg, 2022).
Stress and confusion as result of limited resources and room to maneuver paradox (Berti and Simpson, 2021. Paradox communication may be perceived of as managerial ambivalence (Rothman and Wiesenfeld, 2007).	Activation of interlocutor resources that may assist the manager in paradox coping (Nielsen and Hansen, 2020; Schneider, Bullinger, and Brandl, 2020; Rennison, 2017).

As Table 11.1 shows, some of the positive outcomes (right-hand columns in the table), also discussed previously in this chapter, can also be associated with negative intentions and outcomes (left-hand column in the table). Claiming paradoxical tension can be nothing more than a cover up for questionable practices or misleading information. Presenting problems and dilemmas as difficult paradoxes may be deceptive and evasive, leaving receivers of such communication confused and demotivated in deadlock.

In the table, we have taken our point of departure in employees as the primary interlocutors and co-navigators of paradox, but you can think of similar bright and dark sides of collaborative communication between others and additional groups of stakeholders in and outside the company. Managers have often pointed out to us that their employees need to be spared too many paradoxes, which is a sympathetic trait. We have seen in previous chapters examples of employees reacting negatively when they feel that a paradox has been delegated to them that they really have no opportunity to act on. At the same time, we have seen examples of employees and other stakeholders contributing their expertise and experience and helping leaders with paradoxical navigation. However, we have also experienced that managers try to shield themselves, rather than their stakeholders. In an interview on organizational tensions and change management, Putnam calls for "dialectical sensibility" – a term that *"refers to becoming aware of contradictions and oppositional tensions, but also having a sense of reflective practice. One in which tensions are acknowledged, explored, and used as stimulus to raise awareness of options, multiple voices, and alternative meanings."* (Grant and Wolfram Cox, 2017, p. 197). Leaders may communicate clearly and unambiguously, even though they are aware that it is an illusory representation of reality, thus ignoring tensions and conflict. This approach may seem just more manageable – in the short run. We will therefore argue that managers – and others who communicate on behalf of the organization – take a self-critical look at their own motives and emotional investment before they simply conclude that "the others" are unable to cope with the complexity of paradoxes or shy away from difficult decisions in a fog of alleged complexity.

Again, we see that paradox navigation is a team effort that benefits from several different forms of assistance. Such help may come from a variety of sources – sometimes from the staff, other times from professional helpers to which we shall turn our attention in Chapter 12.

References

Argyris, C. (1990). *Overcoming Organizational Defenses: Facilitating Organizational Learning*. Boston, MA: Allyn & Bacon.

Backhaus, L., Reuber, A., Vogel, D., and Vogel, R. (2022). Giving sense about paradoxes: Paradoxical leadership in the public sector. *Public Management Review*, 24(9), 1478–1498.

Bednarek, R., Paroutis, S., and Sillince, J. (2017). Transcendence through rhetorical practices: Responding to paradox in the science sector. *Organization Studies*, 38(1), 77–101.

Beech, N., Burns, H., de Caestecker, L., MacIntosh, R., & MacLean, D. (2004). Paradox as invitation to act in problematic change situations. *Human relations*, 57(10), 1313–1332.

Benbenisty, Y., and Luria, G. (2021). A time to act and a time for restraint: Everyday sensegiving in the context of paradox. *Journal of Organizational Behavior*, 42(8), 1005–1022.

Bennett, N., & Lemoine, J. (2014). What VUCA really means for you. *Harvard Business Review, 92* (1/2), https://hbr.org/2014/01/what-vuca-really-means-for-you, accessed December 24, 2022.

Berti, M., & Simpson, A. V. (2021). The dark side of organizational paradoxes: The dynamics of disempowerment. *Academy of Management Review, 46*(2), 252–274.

Broundal, M. (2016). *One company, multifaceted governance. Balancing the local customer interface and global processes in the VELUX Group.* Unpublished teaching case, September 8, 2016. Hørsholm, Denmark: The VELUX Group.

Brunsson, N. (1993). Ideas and actions: Justification and hypocrisy as alternatives to control. *Accounting, Organizations and Society*, 18(6), 489–506.

Cappellaro, G., Compagni, A., and Vaara, E. (2021). Maintaining strategic ambiguity for protection: Struggles over opacity, equivocality, and absurdity around the Sicilian Mafia. *Academy of Management Journal*, 64(1), 1–37.

Cheal, J. (2013). Exploring the perceptions of efficacy of an NLP related intervention: a linguistic analysis of the 'Dilemma Integration Technique'. *Current Research in NLP*, Vol.3, pp 21–33.

Christensen, L. T., Morsing, M., and Thyssen, O. (2013). CSR as aspirational talk. *Organization*, 20(3), 372–393.

Christensen, L. T., Morsing, M., and Thyssen, O. (2015). The polyphony of values and the value of polyphony. *CHRISTENSEN, Lars Thøger, The Polyphony of Values and the Value of Polyphony, ESSACHESS – Journal for Communication Studies*, 8 (1), 15, 9–25.

Cheal, J. (2020). *Solving Impossible Problems 2nd Ed.: Working through tensions & managing paradox in business*, GWiz Publishing, Crowborough, UK.

Christensen, L. T., Morsing, M., and Thyssen, O. (2020). Timely hypocrisy? Hypocrisy temporalities in CSR communication. *Journal of Business Research*, 114, 327–335.

Cunha, M. P. E., Simpson, A. V., Clegg, S. R., and Rego, A. (2019). Speak! Paradoxical effects of a managerial culture of "speaking up". *British Journal of Management*, 30(4), 829–846.

Cunha, M. P. E., Simpson, A. V., Rego, A., and Clegg, S. (2022). Non-naïve organizational positivity through a generative paradox pedagogy. *Management Learning*, 53(1), 15–32.

Deeds Pamphile, V. (2022). Paradox peers: A relational approach to navigating a business–society paradox. *Academy of Management Journal*, 65(4), 1274–1302.

Eisenberg, E. M. (1984). Ambiguity as strategy in organizational communication. *Communication Monographs*, 51(3), 227–242.

Gabrielsen, J., and Christiansen, T. J. (2010). *The Power of Speech*. Copenhagen, DK: Hans Reitzels Forlag.

Gaim, M., Clegg, S., & Cunha, M. P. E. (2021). Managing impressions rather than emissions: Volkswagen and the false mastery of paradox. *Organization Studies*, 42(6), 949–970.

Gioia, D. A., and Chittipeddi, K. (1991). Sensemaking and sensegiving in strategic change initiation. *Strategic Management Journal*, 12(6), 433–448.

Grant, D., and Wolfram Cox, J. (2017). Using a discourse lens to explore tensions and contradictions in organizational theory and change: A conversation with Linda Putnam. *Journal of Change Management*, 17(3), 189–202.

Grote, G.; Sparr, J. L.; Smith, W. K.; Fairhurst, G. T.; Oliver, N. & A. Waldman, D. A. (2019). Paradox and Uncertainty, *Academy of Management Proceedings*, 1 Aug 2019, https://doi.org/10.5465/AMBPP.2019.11398symposium.

Fairhurst, G. T., and Connaughton, S. L. (2014). Leadership communication. n L. L. Putnam and D. K. Mumby (Eds.), *The SAGE Handbook of Organizational Communication: Advances in Theory, Research, and Method*, pp. 401–423. Thousand Oaks, CA: Sage Publications.

Jacobsen, A. J., Nielsen, R. K., and Eskjær, M. F. (2021). *Smag for bæredygtig fisk: Kortlægning og udforskning af barrierer og muligheder*. Copenhagen, DK: Department of Communication and Psychology, Aalborg University.

Johansen, J. H. (2018). *Paradox Management: Contradictions and Tensions in Complex Organizations*. Cham, SCH: Springer.

Johnson, B. (2014). Reflections: A perspective on paradox and its application to modern management. *The Journal of Applied Behavioral Science, 50*(2), 206–212.

Johnson, D. W., Johnson, R. T., & Tjosvold, D. (2000). *Constructive controversy: The value of intellectual opposition*. In M. Deutsch & P. T. Coleman (Eds.), *The handbook of conflict resolution: Theory and practice* (p. 65–85). San Francisco, CA: Jossey-Bass/Wiley.

Keller, J., Wong, S. S., and Liou, S. (2020). How social networks facilitate collective responses to organizational paradoxes. *Human Relations, 73*(3), 401–428.

Lüscher, L. S., & Lewis, M. W. (2008). Organizational change and managerial sensemaking: Working through paradox. *Academy of management Journal, 51*(2), 221–240.

Li, X. (2021). Solving paradox by reducing expectation. *Academy of Management Review, 46*(2), 406–408.

Lê, P., & Pradies, C. (2022). Sailing through the storm: Improvising paradox navigation during a pandemic. *Management Learning*, published ahead of print, 13505076221096570.

Lewis, M. W., Andriopoulos, C., & Smith, W. K. (2014). Paradoxical leadership to enable strategic agility. *California management review, 56*(3), 58–77.

Miron-Spektor, E., Ingram, A., Keller, J., Smith, W. K., and Lewis, M. W. (2018). Microfoundations of organizational paradox: The problem is how we think about the problem. *Academy of Management Journal, 61*(1), 26–45.

Miron-Spektor, E., Gino, F., & Argote, L. (2011). Paradoxical frames and creative sparks: Enhancing individual creativity through conflict and integration. *Organizational Behavior and Human Decision Processes, 116*(2), 229–240.

Nielsen, R. K., Cheal, J., & Pradies, C. (2021). Fostering Paradox Resonance: Exploring Leaders' Communication of Paradoxes during Crisis. *Journal of Management Inquiry, 30*(2), 157–159.

Nielsen, R.K. & Hansen, M.P. (2020). *Exploring the unintended consequences of managerial 'paradox sharing' with subordinates and superiors. The case of the Royal Danish Defence*. Paper accepted for European Group of Organization Studies 2020 Colloquium, Hamburg (virtual).

Quinn, R. E., and Cameron, K. S. (1988). *Paradox and Transformation: Toward a Theory of Change in Organization and Management*. New York, NY: Ballinger Publishing Co/Harper and Row Publishers.

Quinn and Nujella (2017). Foreword: Paradox in organizational theory. In W. K. Smith, M. W. Lewis, P. Jarzabkowski, and A. Langley (Eds.), *The Oxford Handbook of Organizational Paradox*. Oxford: Oxford University Press, pp. v–viii.

Rennison, B. (2017). Polyfon ledelse. Fra kakofonisk krydspres til kreativ polyfoni. *Lederliv*, March 16, http://www.lederliv.dk/artikel/polyfon-ledelse, accessed October 1, 2022.

Robert, K., and Ola, L. (2021). Reflexive sensegiving: An open-ended process of influencing the sensemaking of others during organizational change. *European Management Journal, 39*(4), 476–486.

Rothman, N.B. and Wiesenfeld, B.M. (2007), "Chapter 11 The Social Consequences of Expressing Emotional Ambivalence in Groups and Teams", Mannix, E.A., Neale, M.A. and Anderson, C.P. (Ed.) *Affect and Groups (Research on Managing Groups and Teams, Vol. 10)*, Emerald Group Publishing Limited, Bingley, pp. 275–308. https://doi.org/10.1016/S1534-0856(07)10011-6

Schad, J., Lewis, M. W., Raisch, S., & Smith, W. K. (2016). Paradox research in management science: Looking back to move forward. *Academy of Management Annals, 10*(1), 5–64.

Schneider, A., Bullinger, B., & Brandl, J. (2021). Resourcing Under Tensions: How frontline employees create resources to balance paradoxical tensions. *Organization Studies, 42*(8), 1291–1317.

Sharma, G., and Good, D. (2013). The work of middle managers: Sensemaking and sensegiving for creating positive social change. *The Journal of Applied Behavioral Science, 49*(1), 95–122.

Sheep, M. L., Fairhurst, G. T., & Khazanchi, S. (2017). Knots in the discourse of innovation: Investigating multiple tensions in a reacquired spin-off. *Organization Studies, 38*(3–4), 463–488.

Smith, W. K. (2014). Dynamic decision making: A model of senior leaders managing strategic paradoxes. *Academy of Management Journal, 57*(6), 1592–1623.

Smith, W. K., & Besharov, M. L. (2019). Bowing before dual gods: How structured flexibility sustains organizational hybridity. *Administrative Science Quarterly, 64*(1), 1–44.

Smith, W. K., and Lewis, M. W. (2012). Leadership skills for managing paradoxes. *Industrial and Organizational Psychology,* 5(2), 227–231.

Sparr, J. L. (2018). Paradoxes in organizational change: The crucial role of leaders' sensegiving. *Journal of Change Management,* 18(2), 162–180.

Sparr, J. L., van Knippenberg, D., and Kearney, E. (2022). Paradoxical leadership as sensegiving: Stimulating change-readiness and change-oriented performance. *Leadership and Organization Development Journal,* 43 (2), 225–237.

Sundaramurthy, C., & Lewis, M. (2003). Control and collaboration: Paradoxes of governance. *Academy of management review, 28*(3), 397–415.

The Municipality of Billund (2020). *Leder- og medarbejdergrundlag.* Billund, DK: The Municipality of Billund.

The Municipality of Fredensborg (2021). *Bæredygtigt lederskab – fælles for Fredensborg.* Ledelsesgrundlag 2021. Fredensborg, DK: The Municipality of Fredensborg.

The Prime Minister's Office (2020). Pressemøde om COVID-19 den 11. marts 2020, https://www.stm.dk/presse/pressemoedearkiv/pressemoede-om-covid-19-den-11-marts-2020/, accessed October 7, 2022.

van Dierendonck, D. (2011). Servant Leadership: A Review and Synthesis. *Journal of Management, 37*(4), 1228–1261.

Chapter 12
Facilitating productive interactions with paradox – the role of facilitators, peers, and professional helpers

In the previous Chapters 10 and 11 as well as in many of the cases of managerial paradox navigation presented in Part II, we have seen how paradox work is an individual endeavor embedded in a wider ecosystem of stakeholders whose paradox navigation may enable or hamper the individual managers' available action repertoire and room to maneuver. We have also seen how organizational support systems such as governance models or leadership codes may facilitate paradox navigation in practice. We have also seen extensive training and education accompanying organizational efforts to pursue both–and strategies and advancing both–and leadership behavior. This chapter is dedicated to the exploration of the role of organizational supporters or professional helpers facilitating others' paradox work, for instance HR, strategy execution officers, internal or external consultants, trainers, teachers, or managers wishing to involve other stakeholders in paradox navigation. We will explore this role by introducing examples of HR support for paradox work in practice as well as sharing the authors' experiences from paradox intervention-research and consultation captured in five learning thresholds that facilitators must cross themselves as well as assist others in crossing and three dimensions of facilitator paradox readiness.

Assisting others – experiences from HR professionals as paradox navigators by proxy

Some of the managers participating in the Leadership GPS program were HR managers – a group that we have already presented as a group with the potential to be helpers and facilitators of others' paradox work in addition to handling their own paradoxes (Chapter 10, p. 153–154). The specific paradoxes that HR managers chose to work with in the GPS program were as diverse as other participating managers, for instance the competing demands between inclusive and exclusive talent management, local and global processes as well as the attention to the needs of mobile high-performers and high-seniority solid performers at the same time. A common HR challenge across the specific paradoxes they chose to work with was how to best assist others in navigation of paradox at different levels in their organizations. HR professionals are often charged with the task of formulation of corporate-wide processes and policies yet are also acutely aware that much HR work is local and taken care of by personnel managers and employees in daily work and interaction. Therefore, a recurring concern was to figure out how they could

https://doi.org/10.1515/9783110788877-014

be organizational level representatives as well as local-level substitutes or proxy paradox navigators, that is, also representing and including local concerns and paradoxes.

As part of the program, substitute paradox leadership was pursued through different HR actions that can be summed up under the headlines of explanation, facilitation, feedback, and experiment, attempting to connect with different organizational aspects and stakeholders involved in paradoxical processes of which HR was a "caretaker" or "orchestrator" (Nielsen et al., 2019):

Tool 12.1: EFFE - Explanation, Facilitation, Feedback and Experiment

---

1) **Explanation:** The first group of HR actions centered on creating awareness of the organizational perspective on paradox, the balances involved, and how local, individual actions would be connected to the organizational level. Activities would include:
    - development of concepts and policies that ensure the overall division of labor so that all aspects of the paradox are considered in accordance with the balancing that the company wants
    - dissemination of the overall corporate strategy for dealing with organizational paradoxes
    - drawing of the "big picture" of which the individual paradox of the individual is a part
    - designation of local opportunities by being part of the "big picture" or "the other end" of the paradox

2) **Facilitation:** Organizational paradox navigators typically want to help the organization execute through the established organizational processes such as HR and strategy. At the same time, it requires a great deal of local knowledge to contribute in a meaningful way. This makes the collection of knowledge very important not only for the individual actors, but also for organizational actors to become aware of the local conditions. If the actors whose job it is to create corporate-wide processes do not have the knowledge to support the local actors, paradox leadership may end up being de facto left to the individual instead of being supported and recognized by a central paradox transformer station. Central support for paradoxical navigation can be "sending the monkey" further down the system wrapped nicely as "help" if not connected properly with a local perspective. Activities would include:
    - gathering knowledge about paradoxical leadership locally
    - sharing knowledge about paradox leadership locally
    - formulation of guidelines and other resources to assist paradox navigation locally

3) **Feedback:** Ensuring feedback from the local level about the nature and consequences of organizational paradoxes. Often the specific manifestations of paradox differ at different levels, side-effects are unevenly distributed among different internal stakeholders, and balancing points differ. Therefore, it is necessary to gather information about the actual working of the paradox in order to be able to help or organize. Activities would include:
    - collection and dissemination of feedback from local paradox navigators
    - dissemination of the existence and extent of side-effects of the chosen paradox navigation course
    - ambassador role for local and individual paradox navigators' point of view in organizational decision-for ang for a

4) **Experiment:** Experience with the work of HR as well as other staff functions in helping individual actors navigate the local implementation of organizational-level paradox shows that it is complicated to assist others in dealing with paradoxes. Therefore, HR participants from the GPS project suggested experimentation as a fourth HR action area, including:
   - workshops with managers and local HR partners experimenting with different forms of "road maps"
   - personnel development talks as a site for knowledge sharing, idea generation, and initiation of local experiment
   - work-in-progress formulation and testing of different key performance indicators matching cross-level paradox navigation

---

Across the many participants who have participated in the GPS project, the pervasive observation is that paradoxical navigation on behalf of others, "by proxy" as we have chosen to call it here, is not an easy place to start. It can be difficult to get it completely under the skin of a challenge when it is not part of your own practice and job task. Therefore, the call from HR managers participating in the Leadership GPS project: Start with yourself! Everything else being equal, it is easier to get others involved in paradoxical navigation once you have tried it on yourself first. Indeed, it was found that it was difficult to only design for paradox navigation, and that a more viable solution was to develop paradoxical capability in the managers themselves, seeing at they would have the local knowledge needed to act.

This is a point that holds true not only for HR professionals attempting to assist managers in paradox navigation in everyday leadership, but also for facilitators, consultants and teachers of corporate programs and similar types of formally designed learning experiences and development efforts to which we now shall turn.

Five thresholds in facilitation of paradox work

Helping others with anything at all is a complicated social process (Schein, 2009), and teaching and learning on paradox or any other topic is no exception. Yet, we believe that there are facilitator challenges that are particular to facilitating or helping others developing paradox navigation competence. Therefore, this part of the chapter explores pathways for productive interactions (Spaapen and Van Drooge, 2011) between paradox theory as an area of complex knowledge and actionable practice, in effect exploring "[p]aradox as the subject of pedagogy, or how to actually teach students the art of paradoxical thinking" (Knight and Paroutis, 2017, p. 529) and learning though paradox (Lewis and Dehler, 2000). The "students" we have in mind, though, are more likely to be managers, HR professionals, and consultants seeking to develop their skills in organizational practice. Echoing the five phases of paradox navigation presented in Part II, we now introduce five thresholds (Figure 12.1) in the development of general paradox navigation capability, key points of transformation that facilitators must cross themselves as well as assist others in crossing:

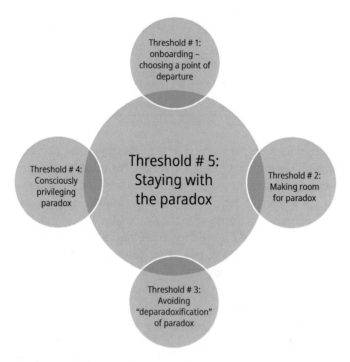

Figure 12.1: Five thresholds in paradox facilitation work.

In the following, we shall discuss each of the thresholds of paradox facilitation work.

Threshold #1: Onboarding – choosing a point of departure

An important learning from the Leadership GPS program as well as subsequent interventions in other settings is that paradoxical thinking is best based in a general comprehension of contradictions, yet it should preferably be applied to a particular challenge. This is the reason our Paradox Pathway foresees the formulation of a personal project with the 3D Cube Model introduced in Chapter 7, pp. 102–103. Our experiences also suggest that learning to navigate paradox should be tied to a particular paradox. In Chapter 3, p. 29–52, we have introduced the reader to 10 fields of paradoxical tensions that could be timely starting points. It is not important that paradox navigators work with one of these but it seems important to choose to work with a particular paradox, as domain-specificity is important for learners to understand paradoxical thinking in relation to their own practice and not only as an abstract concept.

An important feature of the action-learning program was the fact that the managers were presented 10 predefined organizational paradoxes. In the Leadership GPS research project facilitators conducted a literature review of each of the paradoxical tensions involved. This was a process of leaving behind an understanding of the identified challenges as problems to be solved, as contradictory elements to be synthesized, or as "old ways" in need of being replaced with "new ways". It also entailed a dedication to viewing paradoxes as inherently different from dilemmas. This literature review was condensed and disseminated for managerial readers and turned into a white book distributed to all participants. This white book served several purposes (Bévort et al., 2018). First, it was an academic ground zero for the exploration of paradox and a common frame of reference for the research project group. Second, the white book was a point of departure for recruiting prospective managerial participants, who were presented with the paradoxes when approached by the project group. Lastly, the white book was the starting point for working with paradoxes in the intervention phase of the action learning project, where all participants received a copy of the booklet and were introduced to its contents in a kick-off seminar. Although corporate facilitators are unlikely to have the resources to conduct a literature review, we do encourage facilitators to provide a paradox presentation as common ground. Chapter 3 of this book can be used as an inspiration catalog, but common ground can also be built on other leadership literature such as we have seen in the case of the Danish Defence (Chapter 10, p. 150–151) or in the formulation of organizational guardrails (Chapter 11, p. 159–161).

Compared to the intervention project conducted by Lüscher and Lewis (2008), which draws on an action research tradition and stresses a highly open research agenda "when the specific issues of study must be identified as part of the process" (p. 225), the focus as well as the design of the GPS project was more fixed to begin with. However, while the 10 paradoxes introduced were meant as concrete knowledge input, they were just as much a reflexive device, a mediator, from where the dialog between researchers/consultants and participants could begin. By introducing the 10 paradoxes to the participating managers, the intention was to make them actively engage with these, evaluate their relevance, and develop their own practice and managerial abilities considering the paradoxes. Introducing the 10 paradoxes, including the language and thinking of organizational paradox, served to productively stimulate innovative and constructive reflections and learning of the managers.

The researcher/facilitator team worried if the pre-selection of 10 paradoxes would be too limiting to the managers, for instance because their most pressing leadership challenge could not be included. Yet, this turned out not to be the case. Managers amplified and customized within the given frame, and the category of "Leadership vs. management", also introduced in Chapter 3, turned out to be a "catch-all frame". Although presented with the option to choose different paradoxes, all participating manager formulated their initial problem statement within the frames of the 10 paradoxes. Over time, these statements led in several directions. Some changed their paradox; others had forgotten their initial choice when participating in subsequent interventions; and all managers went on to personalize the chosen paradox in a variety of directions in effect leaving no one manager with the same paradox over time. So, it seems productive to fence in the initial discussion about paradox in other to start from a common ground that over time will evolve in a diversity of directions as learners consider their specific challenges and context in the light of a particular paradox.

Threshold #2: Making room for paradox – considering interaction with existing change and development initiatives

Organizations and corporations are generally very different with respect to how much leadership and management development is already taking place. Some of the larger companies participating in the Leadership GPS program already had long-standing tradition of leadership and management development conducted through already established programs and formats; others had not previously worked with formalized leadership development. The leaders who had not been enrolled in existing programs had a steeper learning curve but were also freer to implement the tools that have been part of the project as they saw fit. In larger or more development-matured settings, paradox leadership as a management tool can, on the other hand, be on a collision course with existing initiatives. For example, it can be difficult to pursue and involve others in a paradoxical course of action, if, for example, HR has development processes that go in a completely different direction or do not immediately support this type of thinking. In the Leadership GPS project, some of the participating managers were discouraged from using paradoxical thinking tools with others because it was thought by HR to be "too confusing" or would "interact negatively" with tools and ways of thinking advanced in an existing in-house leadership development program (first author field notes, August 19, 2018).

Organizations that already work with paradox may have an interest in maintaining a focus on specific paradoxes, or a particular pole of the paradox (Cunha and Putnam, 2019; Huq, Reay, and Chreim, 2017). As demonstrated in the road map for HR paradox substitutes presented earlier in this chapter, HR may see it as their role to promote an organization-wide (corporate) point of view in which a local view was to be aligned. Organizations may already have specified the "right solution" when working through paradox – in effect "de-paradoxifying" the paradox. Our participation in a corporate development program in an international engineering consultant company is illustrative of such a situation:

A workshop on paradoxical leadership was offered to project and program managers focusing on the tension between project-/program-specific objectives and specificities while at the same time contributing to operational concerns and corporate best practices. At first, HR development professionals and top management were very enthusiastic about offering sessions on leadership paradoxes as part of a corporate development program. This approach, it was thought, would allow participants to deal with interconnections and balancing acts between local concerns in the individual project and corporate-wide alignment and integration. Project managers participating in the program also appreciated paradoxical thinking as a lens for exploring and understanding the difficult balancing act of dual allegiance and multi-KPI pursuit at the same time. Indeed, session evaluations were positive. The evaluation made by requiring top managers and HR development professionals, however, was not so positive: It was believed that the workshop gave local concerns too much influence to the detriment of a clear message of compliance with corporate, global objectives.

Clearly, as facilitators we had failed to adequately convey the message that a paradox perspective would likely be inclusive, giving voice and legitimacy to a variety of points of view that might or might not be in alignment with a headquarter perspective. When the next cohort of managers participated in that corporate program, it was without the paradoxical leadership session. Instead, a new workshop on strategy execution was offered, focusing on the improved implementation of strategy and the value of strategic compliance. Although there may have been different or additional reasons for this HR and top management mandated change of curriculum, we suggest that paradox facilitators be mindful that a traditional change management logic "tend[s] to be one-sided", where "each reform invokes a single set of consistent values and perceptions of the world" (Brunsson and Olsen, 1993, p. 34). This is not conducive to paradoxical thinking and acting.

Threshold #3: Avoiding "deparadoxification" of paradox

The rise in the legitimacy of paradox thinking in theory and practice is a double-edged sword. On the one hand, there are far more tools available to help us understand issues facing managers in practice and how to aid their development. On the other hand, a growing separation between theory building and practice creates divisions based on different languages, methodologies, and social networks. This creates both an opportunity and challenge for paradox theorists and practitioners, particularly that development efforts labeled "paradox training" in organizational practice may not necessarily have much to do with a theoretically informed notion of paradox (Fairhurst, 2019; Nielsen et al., 2021).

The scholarly paradox community is vividly discussing the need for definitional clarity of the term "paradox", and we have suggested some practical ways of ascertaining that your paradox work is indeed dealing with a paradox in Chapter 2. For practical purposes, we see no need to be dogmatic about the definition of paradox, but at the same time also strongly encourage facilitators to be mindful of the fact that not all tensions are paradoxes. They may be "just" dilemmas or difficult problems. The value of using a paradox lens is greater in practice if the challenge at hand can meaningfully be characterized as a paradox. Similarly, it detracts from the value of using a paradox lens if the challenge is in fact a simpler problem – indeed, many managers might reach the conclusion that paradoxical thinking is tantamount to severe overcomplication. Not only would facilitators find it difficult to explain the value added of acquiring this leadership skill. Facilitators might also find it difficult to demonstrate how a paradox lens can help managers navigate their most difficult leadership challenges.

Facilitating managerial as well as other learners' passage across the thresholds of paradox thinking and action is a challenging task. Consequently, facilitators may be tempted to simplify paradoxical thinking in order to ease the passage to the detriment of the vibrancy of paradoxical thinking (Cunha and Putnam, 2019). Managers may often detect and experience paradox as sensation of uncertainty and confusion, experiencing what Lüscher and Lewis (2008, p. 227) has termed "mess". Indeed, one of the difficulties identified in the paradox literature is that managers rarely speak of their problems as paradoxes (Gaim, 2018). Even the ability to be able to identify and understand paradox thinking as well as acquisition of the vocabulary (for example, distinguishing paradoxes from "difficult problems" or challenges in general) is a difficult and for some managers insurmountable task (Sleesman, 2019; Nielsen et al., 2019). Identifying and naming a paradox relevant for managers' individual leadership practice took extensive effort on the part of both facilitators and participants (Mogensen et al., 2018) in the Leadership GPS project. Only at the end of the six months' intervention, a larger number of participants had familiarized themselves with the vocabulary and outlook involved in paradoxical thinking.

Yet, simplification of the concept may "deparadoxify" paradox thus defusing the energy and innovative potential of paradoxical thinking. At the same time, too much counter-intuitive thinking and complexity may overwhelm or put off managers or other learners from engaging with paradox or understanding its practical value added. Our learnings as facilitators led us to believe that it is not a question of either simplification or amplification of complexity. This apparent tension between tame(d) (complexity diminished) and wild (complexity amplified) paradoxes may not be a contradiction, but rather a question of a conscious balancing act. Fairhurst remarks that, in her view, "the message is not to refrain from taming paradox but knowing when to do so and knowing what else a change manager needs to do under complex organizational change conditions" (2019, p. 11). Indeed, our experiences show that strategies aimed at amplifying as well as simplifying the complexity involved in paradox thinking and action are present throughout the intervention, and we suggest that this might be a timely paradox to explore for facilitators (also see our revisit to the Three Cs of facilitator paradox work below).

Threshold #4: Consciously privileging paradox

Echoing paradox scholar Gail Fairhurst criticizing many other practical paradox interventions for privileging both–and management strategies as qualitatively better than either–or management strategies (Fairhurst, 2019), one much debated challenge among facilitators involved in the Leadership GPS project was the degree to which a paradoxical navigation strategy would always be best. Also, it was intensely discussed if program participant failure to pursue a paradoxical course of action should be perceived of as a "learning failure" or as a natural outcome of paradox navigation when evaluated in the short run at a distinct point in time.

By way of illustration of these facilitator challenges, consider this experience from one of the companies participating in the Leadership GPS program: The fourth and last company intervention had the ambition to revisit and evaluate the managers' paradox navigation in their individually chosen project, both in terms of their consequences in practice, and in terms of clarifying the experiences and general learnings. In this session, managers were asked to present what they had done since the last time we met, while two researcher consultants and the rest of the managers participating from that company would ask questions and comment on what they heard. Throughout the process leading up to this session, we had generally experienced the participants from this company as eager, engaged, and capable of adopting a paradoxical mindset being accepting of tension and energized by paradox. To our surprise, the last session revealed to us a range of actions that did not resonate the reflexivity otherwise demonstrated. A case in point would be Manager M working with the paradoxical pulls involved in pursuing an inclusive and exclusive talent management simultaneously presenting her chosen course of paradox navigation with the rest of the group (three managerial colleagues and two facilitators):

> Manager M: *"For all, ahem . . . We can still have some conversation about that [the competing demands of inclusive, respectively exclusive approach to talent management], but I am not going to do it precisely the way I thought about it then."*

> Managerial colleague J reacting: *"Okay, but . . .?"*

> Managerial colleague S reacting: *"Last time, we talked about you exploring the ties of your challenge to some of our strategic initiatives. So, you have decided not to do that after all, it seems?"*

> Manager M: *"In fact, it is my boss who told me to do something about it, and in this way, it is easy to do something about it."*

> Facilitator 1, trying to reconnect the chosen action with the paradox tools used in previous sessions: *"So, if you revisit your Paradox Quadrant from session 2 [Chapter 5 of this book, Ed.], what are the disadvantages that you are taking on in making this decision?"*

> Manager M: *"Uh . . . I am kind of jeopardizing that balance now . . ."*

Going from paradox understanding, naming, and diagnosing individual paradoxes this did not seem to transfer into paradoxical action. Following the equilibrium model of Smith and Lewis, Manager M along with a couple of the other managers had adopted a *resolution* approach, aiming to "solve" their paradox in the here and now, rather than to keep with the continuous reflexive work attached to the equally relevant acceptance strategy. Manager M had circumvented the paradox navigation process by making her own manager make an either–or choice for her, instead of her pursuing a both–and course of action.

The question is then, is this wrong? This may be a prudent choice for Manager M, who has now made her problem go away – and she will at least be in a defendable, legitimate position to encounter potential side-effects of that decision with other stakeholders (in her case the employees). Also, this may be a natural consequence: As soon as you zoom in on the everyday decision making involved in paradoxical leadership, then classical problem solving is a necessary part of the action repertoire. In a tape-recorded facilitator debriefing following this intervention (January 9, 2019) facilitators 1 of 2 reflected:

> Facilitator 1: *"I wonder: Is it possible to run around seeing everything as paradoxes all the time? Is there anything we are excluded from talking about when we talk about paradoxes all the time? What are the limitations of that? Presumably, there must be some limitation."*

> Facilitator 2 responding: *"Yes, I mean – where does it stop? Sometimes, they [participating managers, eds.] must be allowed to just solve a problem involved in their challenge. And sometimes that is just choosing option A, not A and B, and that is just fine. In the short run, they just chose A. There was no paradox 'acceptance' or 'dynamic equilibrium'. They just took a side and accepted the side-effects that came with that choice. Perhaps it is the time frame that distinguishes problem solving from paradox navigation?"*

Although it is not self-evident that a paradoxical solution is always preferable to an either–or trade-off solution (Fairhurst, 2019; Berti and e Cunha, 2022), the tension Manager M chose to work with is likely to resurface or just emerge in a different form – but perhaps not locally in Manager M's day-to-day leadership. Manager M's solution will now become somebody else's paradox in that the side-effects are going to be felt elsewhere in the organization. If all lower-level managers send their paradoxes up through hierarchy, upper-level management will be overwhelmed, and the organization is unlikely to be able to act in an agile manner.

We have no data that allow us to evaluate if indeed a paradoxical action path would be preferable or not in the case of Manager M. But, from a paradox learning perspective we believe it is important to distinguish between the choice of a non-paradoxical course of action as the result of careful deliberation, and a choice made because managers were unable or unwilling to pursue a paradoxical course of action. Our data points to the fact that *if* pursuit of paradoxical action is a (learning or leadership development) objective, some managers need ample support to stay on track. Indeed, we speculate that some managers resorted to their traditional routine decision and sensemaking style because the program offered too little in-between intervention support and we advise others to carefully consider coaching, mentoring, or other forms of consultation along the way to help paradox navigators stay on track (Nielsen, Mogensen, and Henriksen, 2022). As we shall discuss next, it is not only the design of interventions that are relevant for facilitators to consider, however, but also the facilitators themselves.

Threshold #5: Staying with the paradox

> Finally, a personal practice concern. In practice (not in theory) I am very uncomfortable
> with big tensions. In other words, in practice, I do not have a 'paradox mindset'
> (Miron-Spektor et al., 2018). Oops!
> (Paradox scholar, Professor Jean Bartunek, 2021, fifth paragraph)

In Chapter 1, we have raised the issue that paradox navigation may be an energizer to some and a stressor for others. As illustrated by the quote and our experiences this does not only hold true for managerial paradox navigators, but also for paradox scholars and facilitators. Just as we have emphasized in the cases of managerial paradox navigation in Part II, we have chosen to share both successes and failures. It therefore seems only fair that we address facilitators' paradox support work in the same way. Indeed, throughout the Leadership GPS program as well as later research projects it took extensive effort of facilitators to stay committed to a paradox lens throughout the program.

As you would expect from a research project, it was a learning journey for participants and facilitators alike. Particularly in the phases of the Leadership GPS program when paradoxical thinking was to be translated into acting paradoxically on the participants' chosen leadership challenges, facilitators were challenged. A paradox facilitator reflects on this part of the journey in a debriefing session: "It was so frustrating to me because I thought: Where are the paradoxes? Where are they [participating managers, Ed.) going with this? What are they on about? I did not have anything that allowed me to keep them on track. I thought: What are we to do?" We take comfort in the fact that other highly experienced paradox facilitators can also at times feel overwhelmed. As one of the founding mothers of organizational paradox theory, Marianne Lewis, reflects:

> Paradox is everywhere, making it an exceptionally powerful and challenging concept to apply.
> I've always felt it was "slippery". I've found that when I am "in the zone", deeply focused on para-
> dox work, I can feel like I am at the cusp of something almost spiritual. And moments later, I can
> lose the thread – it becomes too all-encompassing, and I can no longer follow the paradox from
> the everyday. But maybe that is because it is both – powerful and normal. (Marianne Lewis cited
> in Bednarek et al., 2021)

The take-away is that the work of a paradox facilitator is rewarding and challenging. All facilitators in the Leadership GPS program were – in addition to their research competencies – experienced facilitators and consultants yet had not previously engaged in paradox facilitation to the extent foreseen in the research project. We suggest that an underexplored source for reductionist tendencies leading to problem solving instead of paradox navigation in practice-based interventions on leadership paradox may be the instructors, not the participants. It is a limitation of our studies into paradox facilitation that we do not have data to capture the trainer effect, and we call for – and are engaged in conducting – more research and knowledge sharing in this area. Authors' field notes from the Leadership GPS project as well as subsequent paradox interventions point to the fact that being a facilitator duo is helpful, particularly seeing as many facilitators may themselves need help to counter classical "problem-solving behavior". It stands to reason that if instructors are not comfortable with and knowledgeable about organizational and leadership paradox, the risk is that you end up solving problems instead of navigating paradoxes. As discussed earlier that may not be a problem, yet counterproductive if the learning goal you are pursuing is to stay with the paradox.

In our experience, these considerations also hold true for paradox peers. Research literature suggests that peers and relevant others in a paradox navigator's network can assist paradox navigators in coping with paradox (Keller, Wong and Liou, 2020; Deeds Pamphile, 2022). Certainly, as we have demonstrated in Chapter 10, describing paradox navigation as a team effort, relevant others in and outside the paradox navigator's organization can have a significant (positive or negative) impact on the individual paradox navigator's ability to handle paradox. In the Leadership GPS program, a central tenet of the action learning intervention design was that managers would work on their individual paradoxes in action learning groups within their own organization as well as network and share knowledge with other managers across all the 11 participating companies and 55 managers. Yet, sharing knowledge with other paradox navigators and learning together was not as effective as we would have thought taking our cues from the action learning literature (Revans, 1982; Pedler, 2008).

Participating managers had a quite narrow conceptualization of the peers that it would be relevant for them to share knowledge with. Managers wanted to share knowledge with others working on the same paradox (the content of the paradox) and saw less value in interacting with peers working on other paradoxes – in their own company or in one of the other companies participating in the Leadership GPS project. Only in the later phases of the program participants saw value-added in sharing knowledge about the process of navigating paradoxes with others working on paradoxes different from their own. Also, it was challenging to have inexperienced paradox navigators help others in developing paradox navigation capability in action learning groups or the larger network of participating companies. Often, other managerial participants would resort to giving problem-solving advice presented as vague, general statements that were far from a paradoxical understanding of the challenge at hand. It is not our intention to point fingers at anybody – any shortcomings of the participants would reflect our failings as facilitators. Yet, it *is* our intention to show that facilitating and assisting others' paradox work is a challenge and a skill where only a select few might be naturals; the rest of us will need extensive training and practice. Therefore, we strongly encourage facilitator readers to follow the advice suggested by the HR manager road map for facilitating others' paradox navigation presented previously in this chapter: Start with yourself!

Facilitator paradox readiness

At the end of Chapter 1, p. 27, we encouraged paradox navigators to consider the three Cs of paradox work – Change, Curiosity, Challenge – before embarking on the Paradox Pathway. Now, we encourage facilitator readers to walk the pathway themselves – so at this point you may want to go back and start from Chapter 1 exploring *your* individual paradox as a facilitator.

Also, we encourage you to consider a reformulation of the three Cs outlining the preconditions for facilitating others' paradox work (Figure 12.2).

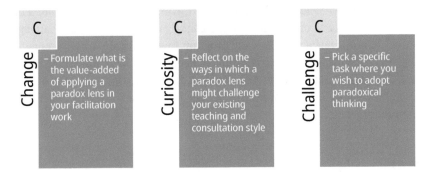

Figure 12.2: The three Cs of paradox facilitator readiness for helping others.

The figure outlines three areas where facilitators are encouraged to reflect on their own competencies and comfort zones:

Change. There must be something that you want to change, something that you want to do differently. Particularly, you may need to adjust leadership training tools that you usually use. For instance, how would this affect a personnel review template? How would you facilitate strategy implementation from a paradox point of view? And how would you explain to learners/participants why the messier view of reality inherent in paradoxical thinking is worthwhile and more beneficial than a more traditional Strengths, Weaknesses, Opportunities, and Threats (SWOT)-analysis or contingency approach?

Curiosity. You need to be curious and ready to step outside your comfort zone – or at least be interested in mapping your comfort zone and reflecting on what the current limits do or do not do for you. As you can tell from this chapter, the role of a paradox facilitator is itself paradoxical. You may need to share your challenges with the participants whose paradoxes you seek to help to navigate, yet then you will have to relinquish an expert role for that of a helpful fellow paradox navigator.

Challenge. Working with paradoxes makes the most sense if you find a specific, individual challenge that you can work on. For instance, dosing the right amount of complexity throughout a learning program, balancing amplification of complexity and reduction of complexity may be a specific facilitator challenge independent of the specific paradox you need to assist others in navigating. Facilitators are encouraged – as everybody else – to choose a paradox and properly dwell on that one, until you feel that you have a rich, nuanced view of the competing demands you are facing that is thoroughly grounded in your task, stakeholders, and organizational setting. (You can consider using the 3D Cube Model introduced in Chapter 7.)

As a facilitator, you might feel discouraged after having read this chapter, yet we also hope that you may feel better equipped to face the challenges of facilitating others' paradox work. Being a paradox facilitator is challenging, yet also a potential success criterion for successful paradox work. Managers, co-workers, or other stakeholders that you wish to introduce to or include in paradox navigation need generous support to stay on track. Even if our action learning program involved many fora for knowledge sharing and learning, it would have probably been beneficial to have even more one-to-one follow-ups along the way. As such, paradox facilitation is a challenging role, yet also an essential factor in producing productive interactions with leadership paradox in practice.

References

Bartunek, J. (2021). *Jean Bartunek – reflexive interview.*, August 16, 2021. Accessed December 24, 2022.

Bednarek, R., e Cunha, M. P., Schad, J., and Smith, W. K. (Eds.). (2021). *Interdisciplinary Dialogues on Organizational Paradox: Learning from Belief and Science.* Bingley, UK: Emerald Group Publishing.

Berti, M., & Pina e Cunha, M. (2022). Paradox, dialectics or trade-offs? A double loop model of paradox. *Journal of Management Studies*, published ahead of print, December 10, 2022, https://doi.org/10.1111/joms.12899.

Bévort, F., Henriksen, T. D., Hjalager, A-M., Nielsen, R. K., Holt Larsen, H., and Vikkelsø, S. (2018). *Ledelsesdilemmaer: Strejftog gennem faglitteraturen.* Frederiksberg, DK: Copenhagen Business School.

Brunsson, N. (1993). Ideas and actions: Justification and hypocrisy as alternatives to control. *Accounting, Organizations and Society*, 18(6), 489–506.

Cheal, J. (2012). *Solving Impossible Problems: Working through Tensions and Paradox in Business.* Carmarthen, UK: Crown House Publishing.

Cunha, M. P. E., and Putnam, L. L. (2019). Paradox theory and the paradox of success. *Strategic Organization*, 17(1), 95–106.

Fairhurst, G. T. (2019). Reflections: Return paradox to the wild? Paradox interventions and their implications. *Journal of Change Management*, 19(1), 6–22.

Gaim, M. (2018). On the emergence and management of paradoxical tensions: The case of architectural firms. *European Management Journal*, 36(4), 497–518.

Huq, J. L., Reay, T., and Chreim, S. (2017). Protecting the paradox of interprofessional collaboration. *Organization Studies*, 38(3–4), 513–538.

Johansen, J. H. (2018). *Paradox Management: Contradictions and Tensions in Complex Organizations.* Cham, SCH: Springer.

Knight, E., and Paroutis, S. (2017). Expanding the paradox–pedagogy links: Paradox as a threshold concept in management education. In W. K. Smith, M. W. Lewis, P. Jarzabkowski and A. Langley (Eds.), *The Oxford Handbook of Organizational Paradox.* Oxford: Oxford University Press, pp. 529–546.

Lewis, M. W., and Dehler, G. E. (2000). Learning through paradox: A pedagogical strategy for exploring contradictions and complexity. *Journal of Management Education*, 24(6), 708–725.

Lüscher, L. S., and Lewis, M. W. (2008). Organizational change and managerial sensemaking: Working through paradox. *Academy of Management Journal*, 51(2), 221–240.

Mogensen, M., Nielsen, R. K., Henriksen, T. D., Bévort, F., and Vikkelsø, S. (2018). *Working with Paradox as Entity and Process – Projecting and Eliciting Paradoxes in Managerial Practice through an Action Learning Programme*. Paper accepted for the European Group of Organization Studies Annual Colloquium, Tallin, Track 06 – Taken by surprise: Expanding our understanding of paradoxes and contradictions in organizational life.

Nielsen, R. K., Bartunek, J., Smith, W., Greco, A., Hansen, M. P, Lyndgaard, D. B., Omeife, N., Pradies, C., and Keller, J. (2021). *Interacting Productively with Paradox Theory in Practice – Education, Interventions & Dissemination*. Professional Development Workshop accepted for the Academy of Management Annual Meeting, 2021.

Nielsen, R. K., Cheal, J., and Pradies, C. (2021). Fostering paradox resonance: Exploring leaders' communication of paradoxes during crisis. *Journal of Management Inquiry*, 30(2), 157–159.

Nielsen, R. K., Mogensen, M., Bévort, F., Henriksen, T. D., Hjalager, A. M., and Lyndgaard, D. B. (2019). *Ledelses GPS til en ny tid – Håndtering af ledelsesparadokser og dilemmaer i praksis*. Copenhagen, DK: Copenhagen Business School, University of Southern Denmark, Aalborg University & Network of Corporate Academies.

Nielsen, R. K., Mogensen, M., and Henriksen, T. D. (2022). *Leveraging Complexity in (Educational) Practice. Exploring the Dynamics of Tame and Wild Paradoxes in an Action Learning Program*. Paper presented at PREP (Paradox Research Education Practice) conference, March 16 –18, 2022.

Pedler, M. (2008). *Action learning for managers*. Aldershot and Burlington, UK: Gower Publishing Limited.

Pradies, C., Carmine, S., Cheal, J., e Cunha, M. P., Gaim, M., Keegan, A., Miron-Spektor, E., Nielsen, R. K., Pouthier, V., Sharma, G., Sparr, J., Vince, R., and Keller, J. (2021). The lived experience of paradox: How individuals navigate tensions during the pandemic crisis. *Journal of Management Inquiry*, 30(2), 154–167.

Revans, R. W. (1982). What is action learning? *Journal of Management Development*, 1(3), 64–75.

Schein, E. H. (2009). *Helping. How to Offer, Give, and Receive Help. Understanding Effective Dynamics in One-to-One, Group, and Organizational Relationships*. San Francisco, LA: Berrett-Koehler Publishers.

Sleesman, D. J. (2019). Pushing through the tension while stuck in the mud: Paradox mindset and escalation of commitment. *Organizational Behavior and Human Decision Processes*, 155, 83–96.

Spaapen, J., and Van Drooge, L. (2011). Introducing "productive interactions" in social impact assessment. *Research Evaluation*, 20(3), 211–218.

Chapter 13
Concluding the never-ending story of paradox navigation

Leadership in times characterized by uncertainty and change is an ongoing endeavor to navigate sustained and irresolvable tension and contradiction – leadership paradoxes. The point of departure of this book is that one of the most significant management challenges in modern companies and organizations is dealing with unavoidable, complex paradoxes in organization and management. We have been working from a definition of paradoxes as "[c]ontradictory yet interrelated elements – elements that seem logical in isolation but absurd and irrational when appearing simultaneously" (Lewis, 2000, p. 760) that "persist over time" (Smith and Lewis, 2011, p. 382). In this final chapter, we shall provide a recap of what we believe are essential take-aways from the previous 12 chapters as well as share some concluding, hopeful reflections about the challenging, yet rewarding leadership discipline of paradox navigation.

Leadership of paradox is the art of balancing competing, opposing demands. Instead of either–or decision making, leadership can be understood as a both–and balancing act. For instance: Acting sustainably as an individual or corporation is not a question of privileging environmental, social, *or* economic concerns; it is about addressing environmental, social, *and* economic concerns. During the COVID-19 crisis, it was not a question for leaders to choose *either* financial health *or* public health; it was a balancing act between *both* financial health *and* public health at the same time. Organizations continuously must strike a balance between *both* stability *and* change; managers need to engage in operational, administrative concerns in the here-and-now *as well as* innovate and develop products, people, and processes for the longer run. In the first part of the book, we have presented 10 fields of paradoxical tensions in leadership that we have experienced as particularly helpful and relevant starting points for working with leadership paradox in practice. In addition to the examples just mentioned, we have pointed to paradoxical tensions such as the competing demands between local and global concerns in internationally operating companies, between inclusive and exclusive approaches to dealing with talent management, between physical presence and virtual presence in the workplace. Our suggested fields of paradoxical fields are by no means exhaustive, but this is a place to start. We hope that our readers will use these examples to get to paradox work and as a springboard for working with other paradoxes in their everyday leadership. In our experience you cannot only think or contemplate paradox; you need to pick a specific challenge and work your way through it.

https://doi.org/10.1515/9783110788877-015

Get to (paradox) work!

> You can't fix a paradox. Don't try to make it go away,
> learn to live with it and embrace it.
> (Claudy Jules, PhD, seminar at Sørup Herregaard, Denmark, June 2014)

Ability to understand contradictions and appreciate the tensions involved in paradox is a necessary starting point for paradox work, but it is not enough. Paradoxical thinking must be transformed into paradoxical action in practice. It is a central idea in this book that we not only "tell" paradox, but also "show" paradox in practice. In our experience, ability to think about paradox and complexity is a long way from transferring this world view to actual practice. This transfer is a critical point for paradox theory as it is for much other research and thinking about leadership. We aim to help the readers not only cross the threshold from "classical management theory" to "paradox theory-informed VUCA leadership thinking", but also to bridge the gap from *thinking* paradox to *acting on/navigating/working through* paradox in practice with others.

To that end, the book contains 15 tools (such as self-test, exercises, check lists, models, and visualizations) that are developed for practical use by managers and other paradox navigators from the intervention techniques used in our data collection and intervention process. Also, we share more than 20 case stories of the challenges and potentials of real managers' work with their individual paradoxes in practice derived from the qualitative data analysis in the Leadership GPS project and paradox interventions in other companies and organizations after the conclusion of the GPS research project. Together these led to the outline of a Paradox Pathway and 25 GPS coordinates, learning points to consider while working through five phases of paradox navigation.

It has been our point of departure that research insights about organizational and leadership paradoxes present a frame of understanding that matches the complexity and ambiguity of contemporary organizational life (Smith and Lewis, 2011; Schad et al., 2016). Consequently, we based our insights not only on extant research literature on organizational and leadership paradox, but also on our concluded and ongoing research projects into leadership paradox work in practice based on a theoretically informed understanding of paradox, yet with a clear (research) ambition of putting this understanding to practical use. Throughout the book we have (attempted to) walk the tightrope of staying true to paradox research while at the same time placing a premium on practical actionability. In this respect, our challenge as authors has been the same as for all other paradox navigators: If you simplify too much, by softening the edges, you deflate the concept, in effect, discharging the batteries of the metaphorical "paradox energizer bunny" introduced in Chapter 1. If complexity levels are too high, paradox navigators might be perplexed, overwhelmed with complexity, and left with a feeling of powerlessness and paralysis.

As you would imagine, navigating this knowledge-sharing paradox is work-in-progress that we will never resolve, and we recognize this as a central life-time challenge as paradox scholars and facilitators. We are humbled, as well as inspired by the difficulty and importance of this task, and we have deliberately sought to share not only success stories of paradox navigation, but also the not-so-successful, difficult, or frustrating experiences of working through paradox. This holds true of our own experiences as paradox navigators and facilitators of others' paradox navigation, such as we have openly shared in Chapter 12, but it also describes the 20 cases of managerial paradox navigation shared in Part II based on the work of the courageous 55 managers participating in the Leadership GPS project. It also holds true for the managers, HR professionals, and consultants participating in some of the additional research projects from which we have shared insights, particularly in Part III. We cannot and will not claim "best practice", but we do believe that it is possible to learn from practice, perhaps particularly from different practice (for better and for worse) that in time may inspire your next practice.

If only we had all the information . . .

> If you are not confused, you are not paying attention!
> (Kim Cameron, Academy of Management Annual Meeting, San Antonio, 2011)

We have at times encountered the view that paradoxes in leadership are a consequence of the fact that there are conditions that we do not understand or do not have full information about. That is, we cannot adequately perceive the challenge and are therefore relegated to understanding it as a paradox. In these times, analysis of Big Data promises us the opportunity to eavesdrop on everyday life and its hitherto hidden connections, enabling us to see commonalities by collecting and processing large amounts of information – information that we are either not used to having available or that we cannot normally overlook. With artificial intelligence and machine learning, we are faced with the prospect that we can put ourselves beyond our own cognitive limitations and perhaps begin to understand contexts and trade-offs that we did not realize before. If these promises are fulfilled, there may be immediately incompatible quantities in the future, that is, paradoxes, which we, with a better basis for decision making at hand, may see as dilemmas or problems. An increased amount of information will allow us to prioritize ourselves out of a difficult situation or simply give us the opportunity to side-step the problem. We may find that when we look at it all from above, there are seemingly incompatible conditions that may not be so incompatible after all.

(More) information and a solid basis for decision making are undoubtedly desirable for all managers. However, if we pursue this line of thinking, it will most likely be the case that with more information we will also spot new dilemmas and paradoxes. These may be complicated relationships that we have so far been spared because we have not previously noticed how various phenomena were interrelated and interacted with one another. At the same time, "more information" (or "better information") is not necessarily synonymous with "full information". There must still be someone who selects and assembles "small data" into "Big Data", and there should at least be someone who understands and can explain what our intelligent machines have "figured out" for us.

The point is that paradox leadership is relevant competence *because* new knowledge leads to new opportunities *and* paradoxes arising. Just as you have completed one change initiative, changes in the environment will lead you to reconsider your balancing point – due to financial crisis, evolving climate crisis, war, migration crisis, or public health crisis, or perhaps a more organization-specific crisis evolving as your corporation finds itself the centre of attention in a social media "shit-storm" or having to respond to sudden competitor threats.

Vicious and virtuous circles of paradox navigation

> Tensions are neither good nor bad; they can drive creativity and sustainability or lead to defensiveness and destruction. Their impact depends on how we respond.
> (Paradox scholar, Professor Wendy Smith, LinkedIn post, July 7, 2022)

The underlying assumption of the book is that there is no position that is right or wrong per definition when it comes to leadership – no predesignated best practice or sweet spot. The core premise is that there are opposite push and pulls that need to be navigated. For example, one should not be deciding whether to be vulnerable or not as a leader. Rather one should learn to be both vulnerable and authoritarian at the same time and learn to live with opposite pulls. The point about paradoxes, then, is not necessarily to try to find a compromise or a golden mean between two points or otherwise attempt to identify a new common third way, meant to make the causes of the problem go away or dissolve (Smith et al., 2017). This is one of the aspects that distinguishes paradox thinking and leadership from classical managerial thinking and from the way many managers are used to making decisions. Paradoxes are not problems that can be solved; they are navigated on an ongoing basis. Seeing as paradoxes are persistent, closure is not an option, making navigation of paradox a never-ending story of chasing the end of the rainbow At the same time, that makes paradoxes an inexhaustible source of renewable friction energy, where opposing demands and perspectives can enrich each other for better, more sustainable decisions and ideas. Different perspectives and interests represented in the paradox may, however, also crash and collide. Conflict is an inevitable part of paradoxical leadership, and the challenge is then to make conflict and collision into constructive controversies rather than paralyzing disagreement and quarrel – or to simply deny their existence.

Not every organization or individual are able to strike this delicate balancing act involved in paradox navigation. Smith and Lewis (2011) refer to managerial responses to organizational paradoxes as potentially producing either "virtuous" or "vicious" circles. While virtuous circles allow for managers and organizations to prosper and learn from organizational paradoxes, vicious circles, on the contrary, are defined by defensive patterns, which may show to be effective managerial responses in the here and now but will prevent the organization from performing and surviving in the long run. The developmental path of either vicious or virtuous circles of paradox leadership is dependent on the type of responses chosen by individual managers, but not least on the resources available on an individual and organizational level. Being able to act in situations of tensions and paradox demands for individuals to be both cognitively and emotionally capable and it calls for organizational capabilities such as have been our focus in Part III – structures, processes, routines, and cultures collectively supporting individuals in dealing with the tensions of ongoing shifts and changes.

Much too often neither individuals nor organizations can deal with the tensions and paradoxes of organizing and leading. Both individuals and organizations often turn to their usual routines of translating and simplifying management into a series of either–or choices or deny the existence of choice and tension altogether. Throughout the cases in Part II and particularly in the chapters of Part III we have directed the attention to the fact that individual paradox navigation does not happen in a vacuum – it may not always be successful. We have described paradox navigation as a team sport – a co-creative endeavor where communication and collaboration with internal and external stakeholders impacts the individual paradox navigator's available action repertoire and room to maneuver. Sometimes the synergies and impact are positive, at other times negative.

So, the individual paradox navigator is important yet embedded in a context, situation, and stakeholder set-up. Consequently, while paradox navigation can be seen as an individual competency, we suggest that paradox navigation can also meaningfully be seen as an organizational capability. "An organization capability refers to an organizational ability to perform a coordinated task, utilizing organizational resources, for the purpose of achieving particular results" (Helfat, 2017, p. 1). As our cases of paradox navigation have demonstrated – leadership codes, organizational culture, organizational design, leadership development, supporting actors, and professional helpers as well as governance structures are all example of initiatives at the organizational level that may assist organizational actors in navigating paradox. In a VUCA-world (Bennett and Lemoine, 2014), the competitiveness of companies not only includes the development of new products and services. It also includes organizational patterns and forms of collaborating, organizing, and sensemaking. In effect, paradoxical leadership as a collective endeavor can be seen as a form of management innovation (Birkinshaw, Hamel, and Mol, 2008). By management innovation what is meant here is "everything that fundamentally changes the way in which management work is carried out or significantly adjusts familiar forms of organization, and which thereby promotes organizational goals" (Hamel and Breen, 2007, p. 19). Paradox navigation capability can be a source of leadership innovation – at the individual and organizational level – that allows organizations to act on grand challenges and "wicked problems" (McMillan and Overall, 2016), experiment and learn in an environment of need for fast failure and ongoing change.

Leading, longing, and dancing with paradox

> Wicked problems aren't 'wicked' as in bad, naughty, misbehaving . . . . Seems to me that the only reason why they're called 'wicked' is that there's a perception – or expectation, perhaps – that they somehow 'should' be 'tame', predictable, controllable, certain, like all of those other nice, easy, solvable problems that stay solved once we've solved them. You know, the ones that behave? Like they ought to?
> (Business anarchist and confusionist Tom Graves, 2014, seventh paragraph)

For the individual leader, paradoxes can change character over time, or new paradoxes can become salient. Even the most paradoxically minded individuals will find themselves bewildered at times. An article (Lê and Pradies, 2022) investigating French President Macron's corona communication provides a telling example of the way the president – who is known for his insistence on both–and thinking – needed to improvise, regroup, and rethink on an ongoing basis. Even if you are paradoxically minded, you may not be paradox-savvy (Waldman and Bowen, 2016) when a new paradox arises, or the underlying tensions of an existing paradox are in movement.

Changing initiatives and changing circumstances will require that you start from scratch. Or more accurately, if you start with the expectation that you can "fix" a paradoxical situation once and for all, then it will be to start over again. If you accept paradoxes as persistent, interconnected, and characterized by opposing demands that must be addressed simultaneously, then tensions and challenges are natural and to be expected. Changes and shifts are not (per se) the same as "game over". Adjustments and tensions are integral to the leadership role. On the one hand, it can feel like quite a mess, where you never draw a line in the sand or get closure, while on the other, it also represents a resource and a great deal of freedom and empowerment to act. The presence of paradoxes is not necessarily a sign that something has gone wrong, or that something is wrong. Paradoxes are integral parts of the leadership role and task. Paradox leadership thus becomes a way to tackle challenges that matches the complexity that many leaders experience in their changing everyday lives.

As it has emerged in the pages of this book, paradox leadership is a never-ending task. Indeed, many key challenges in leadership are paradoxical, characterized by interrelated but opposing considerations that must be continually and constantly weighed, balanced, and navigated, without arriving at a definitive solution. This may seem a somewhat discouraging morale. Unfortunately, leaders are not like the troubled Greek hero Heracles, who had to perform 12 seemingly impossible tasks, but in the end managed the job and was successful. The role of the leader navigating paradox may seem more like another figure from Greek mythology, Sisyphus. For his disrespect to Zeus, he was condemned to eternal punishment, eternally pushing a heavy rock to the top of a steep hill, where it would always roll down again. Although this legend may seem depressing, we suggest taking heart in the French philosopher Camus's essay on the existential learnings to be detracted from the Greek myth. This essay concludes on Sisyphus's never-ending work that "[t]he struggle itself toward the heights is enough to fill a man's heart. One must imagine Sisyphus happy" (Camus, 1942, p. 47, authors' translation). Taking comfort in the fact that paradox navigation is an ongoing struggle can be liberating, emancipating managers from unrealistic ideas about control, leaving them humbled by the profoundness of the task and mindful of their responsibility. We have often experienced a relief in the managers when they understand the idea of leadership paradox. Typically, they have past experiences of problems that they have been trying to solve, only to have them resurface over and over regardless of the different ways they had tried to solve them, and suddenly they understand that this is because they have tried to deal with a paradox as if it were a problem.

Longing for closure of problems that stay solved and rocks that do not roll downhill is natural; it is more manageable, easier to explain and control, but in the case of paradox also a dream. If your longing for closure is fulfilled, you have probably reduced a paradox to a problem, which is a short-term strategy, and your paradox is likely to reappear. Accepting and finding comfort in the longing is the only sustainable way ahead, in the following exemplified by Oliver Burkeman, author of *4000 Thousand Weeks. Time Management for Mortals* (2021), reflecting on his own ongoing longing for a world in which balancing work and life was not an issue:

> The longing does not disappear. I still catch myself longing for endless personal capacity even if I know that it is an illusion. But I no longer have the urge to treat that as a problem to solve, only to become frustrated when I find out that it is not possible. Because it is impossible to reach that stage that we long for. And it is simply a pity to spend your life trying to solve a problem that logically cannot be solved (Cited in Bernsen, 2022, last paragraph, authors' translation)

Your paradox cannot and will not disappear. But take courage; the longing for closure can be an engine, supplying energy to paradox navigation. Paradox scholars Lewis & Smith (2022) encourages us to explore ways of finding comfort with paradox and longing, and we like to think about paradox leadership as tango-dancing about which it is said that tango is the longing for that which never happened and never could happen. So, longing is not a problem – it can be seen as part of the excitement and meaningfulness of dancing. The energy, joy, and potentiality of paradox may lie precisely in the longing for what is never going to happen, as you prepare to lose what you have never had. If you remain in the longing, without choosing sides, you are mindful, on your toes and out on the floor, navigating the paradox.

References

Bennett, N., and Lemoine, J. (2014). What VUCA really means for you. *Harvard Business Review*, 92(1/2), https://hbr.org/2014/01/what-vuca-really-means-for-you

Bernsen, M. (2022). Døden som time manager. *Weekendavisen*, June 2 p. 27.

Birkinshaw, J., Hamel, G., and Mol, M. J. (2008). Management innovation. *Academy of Management Review*, 33(4), 825–845.

Camus, A. (1942). Le Mythe de Sisyphe. https://archive.org/details/le_mythe_de_sisyphe/page/n53/mode/2up, published online May 22, 2017, accessed October 7, 2022.

Graves, T. (2014). Not so wicked. *Tetradian Weblog*, May 9, http://weblog.tetradian.com/2014/05/09/not-so-wicked/, accessed July 2, 2022.

Hamel, G., and Breen, B. (2007). *The Future of Management*. Oxford, MA and Harvard: Business School Press.

Helfat, C. E. (2017). Stylized facts regarding the evolution of organizational resources and capabilities. In C. E. Helfat (Ed.), *The SMS Blackwell Handbook of Organizational Capabilities. Emergence, Development, and Change*. Oxford: Blackwell Publishing, pp. 1–11.

Lê, P., and Pradies, C. (2022). Sailing through the storm: Improvising paradox navigation during a pandemic. *Management Learning*, Online ahead of print, June 3, 2022, 13505076221096570.

Lewis, M. W. (2000). Exploring paradox: Toward a more comprehensive guide. *Academy of Management Review*, 25(4), 760–776.

Lewis, M. W., and Smith, W. K. (2022). Reflections on the 2021 Decade Award: Navigating paradox is paradoxical. *Academy of Management Review*. https://doi.org/10.5465/amr.2022.0251

McMillan, C., and Overall, J. (2016). Wicked problems: Turning strategic management upside down. *Journal of Business Strategy*, 37(1), 34–43.

Schad, J., Lewis, M. W., Raisch, S., & Smith, W. K. (2016). Paradox research in management science: Looking back to move forward. *Academy of Management Annals*, 10(1), 5–64.

Smith, W. K., Jarzabkowski, P., Lewis, M. W., & Langley, A. (Eds.). (2017). *The Oxford handbook of organizational paradox*. Oxford, UK: Oxford University Press.

Smith, W. K., & Lewis, M. W. (2011). Toward a theory of paradox: A dynamic equilibrium model of organizing. *Academy of management Review*, 36(2), 381–403.

Waldman, D. A., and Bowen, D. E. (2016). Learning to be a paradox-savvy leader. *Academy of Management Perspectives*, 30(3), 316–327.

Bibliography

Andersen, I., Bakka, J.F. and Larsen, H.H. (1990). *Ledelsesudvikling i Undervisningsministeriet*. Copenhagen, DK: Nyt fra Samfundsvidenskaberne.

Andersen, T. (1987). The reflecting team: Dialogue and meta-dialogue in clinical work. *Family process, 26*(4), 415–428.

Andersen, T. (1991). *The reflecting team: Dialogues and dialogues about the dialogues*. New York, NY: WW Norton & Co.

Andriopoulos, C., and Lewis, M. W. (2009). Exploitation-exploration tensions and organizational ambidexterity: Managing paradoxes of innovation. *Organization Science*, 20(4), 696–717.

Argyris, C. (1990). *Overcoming Organizational Defenses: Facilitating Organizational Learning*. Boston, MA: Allyn & Bacon.

Aurik, J. C. (2018). Why automation, not augmentation is needed in leadership, weforum.org, January 19, World Economic Forum, https://www.weforum.org/agenda/2018/01/the-case-for-automating-leadership/

Backhaus, L., Reuber, A., Vogel, D., and Vogel, R. (2022). Giving sense about paradoxes: Paradoxical leadership in the public sector. *Public Management Review*, 24(9), 1478–1498.

Bartlett, C. A., and Ghoshal, S. (1987). Managing across borders: New strategic requirements. *Sloan Management Review*, 28(4), 7–17.

Bartlett, C. A., and Ghoshal, S. (1990). Matrix management: Not a structure, a frame of mind. *Harvard Business Review*, 68(4), 138–145.

Bartunek, J. (2021). *Jean Bartunek – reflexive interview.*, August 16, 2021. Accessed December 24, 2022.

Bednarek, R., Paroutis, S., and Sillince, J. (2017). Transcendence through rhetorical practices: Responding to paradox in the science sector. *Organization Studies*, 38(1), 77–101.

Bednarek, R., e Cunha, M. P., Schad, J., and Smith, W. K. (Eds.). (2021). *Interdisciplinary Dialogues on Organizational Paradox: Learning from Belief and Science*. Bingley, UK: Emerald Group Publishing.

Beech, N., Burns, H., de Caestecker, L., MacIntosh, R., & MacLean, D. (2004). Paradox as invitation to act in problematic change situations. *Human relations*, 57(10), 1313–1332.

Benbenisty, Y., and Luria, G. (2021). A time to act and a time for restraint: Everyday sensegiving in the context of paradox. *Journal of Organizational Behavior*, 42(8), 1005–1022.

Bennett, N., & Lemoine, J. (2014). What VUCA really means for you. *Harvard Business Review, 92* (1/2), https://hbr.org/2014/01/what-vuca-really-means-for-you, accessed December 24, 2022.

Benkert, J. (2021). Reframing business sustainability decision-making with value-focused thinking. *Journal of Business Ethics*, 174(2), 441–456.

Bennis, W. G., and Townsend, R. (1989). *On Becoming a Leader* (Vol. 36). Reading, MA: Addison-Wesley.

Bennis, W. (2007). The challenges of leadership in the modern world: Introduction to the special issue. *American Psychologist*, 62, 2–9.

Bergström, O., Styhre, A., and Thilander, P. (2014). Paradoxifying organizational change: Cynicism and resistance in the Swedish Armed Forces. *Journal of Change Management*, 14(3), 384–404.

Bernsen, M. (2022). Døden som time manager. *Weekendavisen*, June 2, 27–28.

Berti, M., and Simpson, A. V. (2021). The dark side of organizational paradoxes: The dynamics of disempowerment. *Academy of Management Review*, 46(2), 252–274.

Berti, M., and Pina e Cunha, M. (2022). Paradox, dialectics or trade-offs? A double loop model of paradox. *Journal of Management Studies*, published ahead of print, December 10, 2022, https://doi.org/10.1111/joms.12899.

Bévort, F., Henriksen, T. D., Hjalager, A-M., Nielsen, R. K., Holt Larsen, H. and Vikkelsø (2018). *Ledelsesdilemmaer: Strejftog gennem faglitteraturen*. Frederiksberg, DK: Copenhagen Business School.

Birkinshaw, J., Hamel, G., and Mol, M. J. (2008). Management innovation. *Academy of Management Review*, 33(4), 825–845.

https://doi.org/10.1515/9783110788877-016

Boström, M., Andersson, E., Berg, M., Gustafsson, K., Gustavsson, E., Hysing, E., . . . and Öhman, J. (2018). Conditions for transformative learning for sustainable development: A theoretical review and approach. *Sustainability*, 10(12), 4479.

Bourton, S., Lavoie, J., and Vogel, T. (2018). Leading with inner agility. *McKinsey Quarterly*, March 29, McKinsey.com, https://www.mckinsey.com/business-functions/organization/our-insights/leading-with-inner-agility, accessed October 16, 2022.

Broundal, M. (2016). *One company, multifaceted governance. Balancing the local customer interface and global processes in the VELUX Group*. Unpublished teaching case, September 8, 2016. Hørsholm, Denmark: The VELUX Group.

Brunsson, N. (1993). Ideas and actions: Justification and hypocrisy as alternatives to control. *Accounting, Organizations and Society*, 18(6), 489–506.

Cameron, W. B. (1963). *Informal sociology: A casual introduction to sociological thinking* (Vol. 21), 13. New York, NY: Random House.

Cameron, K. S., and Quinn, R. E. (2011). *Diagnosing and Changing Organizational Culture: Based on the Competing Values Framework*. Hoboken, NJ: John Wiley and Sons.

Cameron, K. S., Quinn, R. E., DeGraff, J., and Thakor, A. V. (2014, 2022). *Competing Values Leadership*. Cheltenham, MA: Edward Elgar Publishing.

Camus, A. (1942). Le Mythe de Sisyphe. https://archive.org/details/le_mythe_de_sisyphe/page/n53/mode/2up, published online May 22, 2017, accessed October 7, 2022.

Cappellaro, G., Compagni, A., and Vaara, E. (2021). Maintaining strategic ambiguity for protection: Struggles over opacity, equivocality, and absurdity around the Sicilian Mafia. *Academy of Management Journal*, 64(1), 1–37.

Centre for Future Studies (2016). *Trendanalyse*. Copenhagen, DK: Danish Industry Foundation.

Cheal, J. (2013). Exploring the perceptions of efficacy of an NLP related intervention: a linguistic analysis of the 'Dilemma Integration Technique'. *Current Research in NLP*, Vol.3, 21–33.

Cheal, J. (2020). *Solving Impossible Problems 2nd Ed.: Working through tensions & managing paradox in business*, Crowborough, UK: GWiz Publishing.

Christensen, L. T., Morsing, M., and Thyssen, O. (2013). CSR as aspirational talk. *Organization*, 20(3), 372–393.

Christensen, L. T., Morsing, M., and Thyssen, O. (2015). The polyphony of values and the value of polyphony. *CHRISTENSEN, Lars Thøger, The Polyphony of Values and the Value of Polyphony, ESSACHESS – Journal for Communication Studies*, 8 (1), 15, 9–25.

Christensen, L. T., Morsing, M., and Thyssen, O. (2020). Timely hypocrisy? Hypocrisy temporalities in CSR communication. *Journal of Business Research*, 114, 327–335.

Clegg, S. R., Da Cunha, J. V., and e Cunha, M. P. (2002). Management paradoxes: A relational view. *Human Relations*, 55(5), 483–503.

Cunha, M. P. E., and Putnam, L. L. (2019). Paradox theory and the paradox of success. *Strategic Organization*, 17(1), 95–106.

Cunha, M. P. E., Simpson, A. V., Clegg, S. R., and Rego, A. (2019). Speak! Paradoxical effects of a managerial culture of "speaking up". *British Journal of Management*, 30(4), 829–846.

Cunha, M. P. E., Simpson, A. V., Rego, A., and Clegg, S. (2022). Non-naïve organizational positivity through a generative paradox pedagogy. *Management Learning*, 53(1), 15–32.

Daft, R. L., and Lengel, R. H. (1986). Organizational information requirements, media richness and structural design. *Management Science*, 32(5), 554–571.

Dalkey, N., and Helmer, O. (1963). An experimental application of the Delphi method to the use of experts. *Management Science*, 9(3), 458–467.

Danish Industry Foundation. 2016. *INSPIRE16: Ide- og Udfordringskatalog*. Copenhagen, DK: Industriens Fond.

Deeds Pamphile, V. (2022). Paradox peers: A relational approach to navigating a business–society paradox. *Academy of Management Journal*, 65(4), 1274–1302.

De Waal, A., Weaver, M., Day, T., and van der Heijden, B. (2019). Silo-busting: Overcoming the greatest threat to organizational performance. *Sustainability*, 11(23), 6860.

D'Souza, D. E., Sigdyal, P., and Struckell, E. (2017). Relative ambidexterity: A measure and a versatile framework. *Academy of Management Perspectives*, 31(2), 124–136.

Eisenberg, E. M. (1984). Ambiguity as strategy in organizational communication. *Communication Monographs*, 51(3), 227–242.

Fairhurst, G. T., and Connaughton, S. L. (2014). Leadership communication. In L. L. Putnam and D. K. Mumby (Eds.), *The SAGE Handbook of Organizational Communication: Advances in Theory, Research, and Method*, 401–423. Thousand Oaks, CA: Sage Publications.

Fairhurst, G. T., Oliver, N., and Waldman, D. A. (2019, July). Paradox and uncertainty. In *Academy of Management Proceedings* (Vol. 2019, No. 1). Briarcliff Manor, NY 10510: Academy of Management, 11398.

Fairhurst, G. T. (2019). Reflections: Return paradox to the wild? Paradox interventions and their implications. *Journal of Change Management*, 19(1), 6–22.

Gabrielsen, J., and Christiansen, T. J. (2010). *The Power of Speech*. Copenhagen, DK: Hans Reitzels Forlag.

Gaim, M. (2018). On the emergence and management of paradoxical tensions: The case of architectural firms. *European Management Journal*, 36(4), 497–518.

Gaim, M., Clegg, S., & Cunha, M. P. E. (2021). Managing impressions rather than emissions: Volkswagen and the false mastery of paradox. *Organization Studies*, *42*(6), 949–970.

Galbraith, J. R. (1971). Matrix organization designs. How to combine functional and project forms. *Business Horizons*, 14(1), 29–40.

Gao, J., and Bansal, P. (2013). Instrumental and integrative logics in business sustainability. *Journal of Business Ethics*, 112(2), 241–255.

Gioia, D. A., and Chittipeddi, K. (1991). Sensemaking and sensegiving in strategic change initiation. *Strategic Management Journal*, 12(6), 433–448.

Grant, D., and Wolfram Cox, J. (2017). Using a discourse lens to explore tensions and contradictions in organizational theory and change: A conversation with Linda Putnam. *Journal of Change Management*, 17(3), 189–202.

Graves, T. (2014). Not so wicked. *Tetradian Weblog*, May 9, http://weblog.tetradian.com/2014/05/09/not-so-wicked/, accessed July 2, 2022.

Greenwood, D. J., & Levin, M. (1998). *Introduction to action research: Social research for social change.* Thousand Oaks, CA: Sage.

Grote, G.; Sparr, J. L.; Smith, W. K.; Fairhurst, G. T.; Oliver, N., and Waldman, D. A. (2019). Paradox and Uncertainty, *Academy of Management Proceedings*, 1 Aug 2019, https://doi.org/10.5465/AMBPP.2019.11398symposium.

Hahn, T., Jarzabkowski, P., and Knight, E. (2019). Sub-theme 09: [SWG] Change for good? Organizational paradoxes and unintended consequences of transforming modern societies, Egos.org, https://www.egos.org/jart/prj3/egos/main.jart?rel=de&reserve-mode=active&content-id=1564449184268&subtheme_id=1542700474982, accessed October 14, 2022.

Hahn, T., Figge, F., Pinkse, J., and Preuss, L. (2018). A paradox perspective on corporate sustainability: Descriptive, instrumental, and normative aspects. *Journal of Business Ethics*, 148(2), 235–248.

Hamel, G., and Breen, B. (2007). *The Future of Management*. Oxford, MA and Harvard: Business School Press.

Hansen, M.P. (2013). How to lead complex situations. *Military Studies Magazine. Contemporary conflicts*, 1 (1), 1–6. Copenhagen, DK: The Royal Danish Defence College.

Hatch, M. J., and Cunliffe, A. L. (2006). *Modern, Symbolic, and Postmodern Perspectives*. Oxford: Oxford University Press.

Helfat, C. E. (2017). Stylized facts regarding the evolution of organizational resources and capabilities. In C. E. Helfat (Ed.), *The SMS Blackwell Handbook of Organizational Capabilities. Emergence, Development, and Change*. Oxford: Blackwell Publishing, 1–11.

Henriksen, T. D., Nielsen, R. K., Vikkelsø, S., Bévort, F., and Mogensen, M. (2021). A paradox rarely comes alone a quantitative approach to investigating knotted leadership paradoxes in SMEs. *Scandinavian Journal of Management*, 37(1), 101135.

Henriksen, T. D., Vikkelsø, S., Nielsen, R. K., and Bévort, F. (2021). *From Managers' Practical Problems to Complex Understandings: Three Approaches for Understanding the Development of Management Problems*. Paper accepted for the European Group of Organization Studies 2020 Annual Colloquium, Paradox track.

Hjalager, A. M. (2018). Indefra-ud kontra udefra-ind. Åbne og lukkede videnflows. In R. K. Nielsen, A. M. Hjalager, H. H. Larsen, F. Bévort, T. D. Henriksen and S. Vikkelsø, *Ledelsesdilemmaer – og kunsten at navigere i moderne ledelse*. Copenhagen, DK: Djøf Publishing, 43–54.

Holsting, V. S., and Damkjer, A. (2020). *Militært Chefvirke: At skabe handlekraft i komplekse situationer*. Copenhagen, DK: Samfundslitteratur.

Hughes, C. P. (2019). A paradox perspective on sustainable human resource management. In S. Mariappanadar (Ed.), *Sustainable Human Resource Management. Strategies, Practices and Challenges*. London: Macmillan International Higher Education, 59–77.

Huq, J. L., Reay, T., and Chreim, S. (2017). Protecting the paradox of interprofessional collaboration. *Organization Studies*, 38(3–4), 513–538.

Jacobsen, A. J., Nielsen, R. K., and Eskjær, M. (2019). *Kortlægning af barrierer og muligheder om bæredygtighed*. Copenhagen, DK: Aalborg University and Copenhagen Hospitality College.

Jarzabkowski, P., Lê, J. K., and Van de Ven, A. H. (2013). Responding to competing strategic demands: How organizing, belonging, and performing paradoxes coevolve. *Strategic Organization*, 11(3), 245–280. https://doi.org/10.1177/1476127013481016

Jarzabkowski, P. A., and Lê, J. K. (2017). We have to do this and that? You must be joking: Constructing and responding to paradox through humor. *Organization Studies*, 38(3–4), 433–462.

Jarzabkowski, P., Bednarek, R., Chalkias, K., and Cacciatori, E. (2021). Enabling rapid financial response to disasters: Knotting and reknotting multiple paradoxes in interorganizational systems. *Academy of Management Journal*, published online ahead of print. https://doi.org/10.5465/amj.2019.0745

Jay, J., Soderstrom, S., and Grant, G. (2017). Navigating the paradox of sustainability. In W. K. Smith, M. W. Lewis, P. Jarzabkowski, and A. Langley (Eds.), *The Oxford Handbook of Organizational Paradox*. Oxford: Oxford University Press, 357–372.

Johansen, J. H. (2018). *Paradox Management: Contradictions and Tensions in Complex Organizations*. Cham, SCH: Springer.

Johnsen, E. (2006). Paradoksledelse. *Danish Journal of Management & Business*, 69(4), 245–246.

Johnsen, E. (1984). Ledelseslærens rødder. *Danish Journal of Management and Business*, 48(1), 65–84.

Johnson, B. (2014, 1992). *Polarity Management: Identifying and Managing Unsolvable Problems*. Amhearst, MA: HRD Press.

Johnson, B. (2014). Reflections: A perspective on paradox and its application to modern management. *The Journal of Applied Behavioral Science*, 50(2), 206–212.

Johnson, D. W., Johnson, R. T., & Tjosvold, D. (2000). *Constructive controversy: The value of intellectual opposition*. In M. Deutsch & P. T. Coleman (Eds.), *The handbook of conflict resolution: Theory and practice* (65–85). San Francisco, CA: Jossey-Bass/Wiley.

Jules, C., and Good, D. (2014). Introduction to special issue on paradox in context: Advances in theory and practice. *The Journal of Applied Behavioral Science*, 50(2), 123–126.

Kanter, R. M. (1979). Power failure in management circuits. *Harvard Business Review*, 57, 65–75.

Kanter, R. M. (2017). Power failure in management circuits. In A. Hooper (Ed.), *Leadership Perspectives*. London, UK: Routledge, 281–290.

Keller, J., Wong, S. S., and Liou, S. (2020). How social networks facilitate collective responses to organizational paradoxes. *Human Relations*, 73(3), 401–428.

Kniffin, K. M., Detert, J. R., and Leroy, H. L. (2020). On leading and managing: Synonyms or separate (and unequal)? *Academy of Management Discoveries*, 6(4), 544–571.

Knight, E., and Paroutis, S. (2017). Expanding the paradox–pedagogy links: Paradox as a threshold concept in management education. In W. K. Smith, M. W. Lewis, P. Jarzabkowski and A. Langley (Eds.), *The Oxford Handbook of Organizational Paradox*. Oxford: Oxford University Press, 529–546.

Kuhn, K. M., and Maleki, A. (2017). Micro-entrepreneurs, dependent contractors, and instaserfs: Understanding online labor platform workforces. *Academy of Management Perspectives*, 31(3), 183–200.

Larsen, H.H. (1990). Ledelsesudvikling i Undervisningsministeriet. In H. H. Larsen, (Ed.), *Lederudvikling på jobbet – der er fremtid i erfaringer*, 159–176. Copenhagen, DK: Forlaget Valmuen.

Larsen, H.H. (1996). The Ministry of Education: Action learning based management development. In J. Storey (Ed.), *Blackwell Cases in Human Resource and Change Management*, 206–215. Oxford, UK: Blackwell.

Larsson, M., Holmberg, R., and Kempster, S. (2020). "It's the organization that is wrong": Exploring disengagement from organizations through leadership development. *Leadership*, 16(2), 141–162.

Lawrence, P. R., Kolodny, H. F., & Davis, S. M. (1977). The human side of the matrix. *Organizational Dynamics*, 6(1), 43–61.

Lawrence, P. R., and Lorsch, J. W. (1967). Differentiation and integration in complex organizations. *Administrative Science Quarterly*, 12 (1), 1–47.

Lê, P., & Pradies, C. (2022). Sailing through the storm: Improvising paradox navigation during a pandemic. *Management Learning*, published ahead of print, 13505076221096570.

Leigh Star, S. (2010). This is not a boundary object: Reflections on the origin of a concept. *Science, Technology, and Human Values*, 35(5), 601–617.

Li, X. (2021). Solving paradox by reducing expectation. *Academy of Management Review*, 46(2), 406–408.

Lewis, M. W., and Dehler, G. E. (2000). Learning through paradox: A pedagogical strategy for exploring contradictions and complexity. *Journal of Management Education*, 24(6), 708–725.

Lewis, M. W. (2000). Exploring paradox: Toward a more comprehensive guide. *Academy of Management review*, 25(4), 760–776.

Lewis, M. W., and Dehler, G. E. (2000). Learning through paradox: A pedagogical strategy for exploring contradictions and complexity. *Journal of Management Education*, 24(6), 708–725.

Lewis, M. W., Andriopoulos, C., & Smith, W. K. (2014). Paradoxical leadership to enable strategic agility. *California management review*, *56*(3), 58–77.

Lewis, M. W., and Smith, W. K. (2022). Reflections on the 2021 Decade Award: Navigating paradox is paradoxical. *Academy of Management Review*, published online ahead of print, https://doi.org/10.5465/amr.2022.0251

Lojeski, K. S., and Reilly, R. R. (2020). *The Power of Virtual Distance: A Guide to Productivity and Happiness in the Age of Remote Work*. Sussex, UK: John Wiley and Sons.

Lunenburg, F. (2013). Leadership versus Management: A key distinction – at least in theory. *Main Issues of Pedagogy and Psychology*, 3(3), 15–18.

Lindorf, M. and Lynge, J. (2010). *Effektiv talentudvikling, praksis for praktikere*. Copenhagen, DK: DEA.

Lüscher, L. S., Lewis, M., and Ingram, A. (2006). The social construction of organizational change paradoxes. *Journal of Organizational Change Management*, 19(4), 491–502.

Lüscher, L. S., and Lewis, M. W. (2008). Organizational change and managerial sensemaking: Working through paradox. *Academy of Management Journal*, 51(2), 221–240.

Lüscher, L. (2017). *Lederen mellem tvivl og handlekraft: Paradokser og personligt lederskab*. Copenhagen, DK: Dansk Psykologisk Forlag.

McMillan, C., and Overall, J. (2016). Wicked problems: Turning strategic management upside down. *Journal of Business Strategy*, 37(1), 34–43.

March, J. G. (1991) Exploration and exploitation in organizational learning. *Organization Science*, 2(1), 71–87.

Manyika, J., and Sneader, H. (2018). AI, automation, and the future of work: Ten things to solve. www.mckinsey.com, McKinsey Executive Briefing, https://www.mckinsey.com/featured-insights/future-of-work/ai-automation-and-the-future-of-work-ten-things-to-solve-for Last accessed December 22, 2022.

Manz, C. C. (1986). Self-leadership: Toward an expanded theory of self-influence processes in organizations. *Academy of Management Review*, 11(3), 585–600.

McMillan, C., and Overall, J. (2016). Wicked problems: Turning strategic management upside down. *Journal of Business Strategy*, 37(1), 34–43.

Minsky, M. (2007). *The Emotion Machine: Commonsense Thinking, Artificial Intelligence, and the Future of the Human Mind*. New York, NY: Simon and Schuster.

Miron-Spektor, E., Gino, F., & Argote, L. (2011). Paradoxical frames and creative sparks: Enhancing individual creativity through conflict and integration. *Organizational Behavior and Human Decision Processes*, *116*(2), 229–240.

Miron-Spektor, E., Ingram, A., Keller, J., Smith, W. K., and Lewis, M. W. (2018). Microfoundations of organizational paradox: The problem is how we think about the problem. *Academy of Management Journal*, 61(1), 26–45.

Mogensen, M., Nielsen, R. K., Henriksen, T. D., Bévort, F., and Vikkelsø, S. (2018). *Working with Paradox as Entity and Process – Projecting and Eliciting Paradoxes in Managerial Practice through an Action Learning Programme*. Paper accepted for the European Group of Organization Studies Annual Colloquium, Tallin, Track 06 – Taken by surprise: Expanding our understanding of paradoxes and contradictions in organizational life.

Mormann, H., and Sender, A. (2022). Breaking up order through temporal role taking: HRM professionals as jesters in navigating paradoxes. In *Academy of Management Proceedings* (Vol. 2022, No. 1). Briarcliff Manor, NY 10510: Academy of Management, 10, 352.

Nielsen, R. K, Maznevski, M., Poulfelt, F., Broundal, M., Hansen, P. G., Mortensen, E., and Bird, A. (2016). Exploring the individual-organizational global mindset nexus: An MNC-practitioner-academia dialogue. In *Academy of Management Proceedings*, (Vol. 2016). Briarcliff Manor, NY: The Academy of Management.

Nielsen, R. K. and Nielsen, J. B. (2016). *Global Leadership Practice and Development Revisited. Exploring 3 roles – discovering 7 dualities*. Global Leadership Academy – Copenhagen Business School and Danish Confederation of Industry.

Nielsen, R. K., Hjalager, A.-M., Larsen, H. H., Bévort, F., Henriksen, T. D., and Vikkelsø, S. (2018). *Ledelsesdilemmaer – og kunsten at navigere i moderne ledelse*. Copenhagen, DK: Djøf Publishing.

Nielsen, R. K., Mogensen, M., Bévort, F., Henriksen, T. D., Hjalager, A. M., and Lyndgaard, D. B. (2019). *Ledelses-GPS til en ny tid – Håndtering af ledelsesparadokser og dilemmaer i praksis*. Copenhagen Business School, University of Southern Denmark, Aalborg University and Network of Corporate Academies, https://www.industriensfond.dk/Ledelses-GPS-

Nielsen, R.K., and Hansen, M.P. (2020). *Exploring the Unintended Consequences of Managerial "Paradox Sharing" with Subordinates and Superiors. The Case of the Royal Danish Defence*. Paper accepted for European Group of Organization Studies 2020 Colloquium, Hamburg.

Nielsen, R. K., Mogensen, M., Bévort, F., Henriksen, T. D., Hjalager, A. M., and Lyndgaard, D. B. (2020). *Bådeand – værktøjer til effektiv paradoksledelse*. Copenhagen, DK: Djøf Publishing.

Nielsen, R. K., Cheal, J., & Pradies, C. (2021). Fostering Paradox Resonance: Exploring Leaders' Communication of Paradoxes during Crisis. *Journal of Management Inquiry*, *30*(2), 157–159.

Nielsen, R. K., Bartunek, J., Smith, W., Greco, A., Pingel Hansen, M., Bjerre Lyndgaard, D., Omeife, N., Pradies, C., and Keller, J. (2021). *Interacting Productively with Paradox Theory in Practice – Education, Interventions and Dissemination*. Professional Development Workshop accepted for the Academy of Management Annual Meeting.

Nielsen, R. K., Mogensen, M., and Henriksen, T. D. (2022). *Leveraging Complexity in (Educational) Practice. Exploring the Dynamics of Tame and Wild Paradoxes in an Action Learning Program*. Paper presented at PREP (Paradox Research Education Practice) conference, March 16 –18, 2022.

Nielsen, R. K. (2022). *A Sea Of(f) Balance? Facilitating Paradox Navigating between Guardrails and Stumbling Blocks in "Life below Water" Sustainabilities*. Paper accepted for the annual International Organizations Network (ION) conference, February 24 –26, 2022.

Nielsen, R. K., and Lyndgaard, D. B. (2023). Developing Global Leaders in Denmark via Academic-practitioner Collaboration: Lessons for Educators and Consultants. *Advances in Global Leadership* (Vol. 15), 255–268.

Nordhaug, O. (1998). Competence specificities in organizations: A classificatory framework. *International Studies of Management and Organization*, 28(1), 8–29.

North, M., and Coors, C. (2010). Avoiding death by dotted line. *HFM (Healthcare Financial Management)*, 64(1), 120–121.

O'Reilly III, C. A., and Tushman, M. L. (2013). Organizational ambidexterity: Past, present, and future. *Academy of Management Perspectives*, 27(4), 324–338.

Örtenblad, A. (2018). *Professionalizing Leadership: Debating Education, Certification and Practice*. Cham, SCH: Springer.

Örtenblad, A., Hong, J. and Snell. R. (2016) Good leadership: A mirage in the desert? *Human Resource Development International*, 19, 349–357.

Pearce, C. L., Conger, J. A., and Locke, E. A. (2008). Shared leadership theory. *The Leadership Quarterly*, 19(5), 622–628.

Pedler, M. (2008). *Action learning for managers*. Aldershot and Burlington, *UK: Gower Publishing Limited*.

Phan, P., Wright, M., and Lee, S. H. (2017). Of robots, artificial intelligence, and work. *Academy of Management Perspectives*, 31(4), 253–255.

Poulfelt, F. (1997). Professionel Ledelse? *Danish Journal of Management*, 61, 85–95.

Pradies, C., Tunarosa, A., Lewis, M. W., and Courtois, J. (2021). From vicious to virtuous paradox dynamics: The social-symbolic work of supporting actors. *Organization Studies*, 42(8), 1241–1263.

Pradies, C., Carmine, S., Cheal, J., e Cunha, M. P., Gaim, M., Keegan, A., Miron-Spektor, E., Nielsen, R. K., Pouthier, V., Sharma, G., Sparr, J., Vince, R., and Keller, J. (2021). The lived experience of paradox: How individuals navigate tensions during the pandemic crisis. *Journal of Management Inquiry*, 30(2), 154–167.

Problem (n.d.). https://tinyurl.com/bp6bnzpe, Google Dictionary, accessed October 7, 2022.

Putnam, L. L., Fairhurst, G. T., & Banghart, S. (2016). Contradictions, dialectics, and paradoxes in organizations: A constitutive approach. *Academy of Management Annals*, 10(1), 65–171.

Quinn, R. E. and Nujella, M. (2017). Foreword: Paradox in organizational theory. In W. K. Smith, M. W. Lewis, P. Jarzabkowski, and A. Langley (Eds.), The *Oxford Handbook of Organizational Paradox*, Oxford: Oxford University Press, v–viii.

Quinn, R. E., and Cameron, K. S. (1988). *Paradox and Transformation: Toward a Theory of Change in Organization and Management*. New York, NY: Ballinger Publishing Co/Harper and Row Publishers.

Raisch, S., and Krakowski, S. (2021). Artificial intelligence and management: The automation–augmentation paradox. *Academy of Management Review*, 46(1), 192–210.

Ren, S., and Jackson, S. E. (2020). HRM institutional entrepreneurship for sustainable business organizations. *Human Resource Management Review*, 30(3), 100691.

Rennison, B. W. (2014). Ledelse. In S. Vikkelsøe and P. Kjær, *Klassisk og Moderne Organisationsteori*, Copenhagen, DK: Hans Reitzel, 613–640.

Rennison, B. (2017). Polyfon ledelse. Fra kakofonisk krydspres til kreativ polyfoni. *Lederliv*, March 16, http://www.lederliv.dk/artikel/polyfon-ledelse, accessed October 1, 2022.

Revans, R. W. (1982). What is action learning? *Journal of Management Development*, 1(3), 64–75.

Revans, R. W. (1998). *The ABC of Action Learning: Empowering Managers to Act and to Learn from Action.* London: Lemos and Crane.

Robert, K., and Ola, L. (2021). Reflexive sensegiving: An open-ended process of influencing the sensemaking of others during organizational change. *European Management Journal*, 39(4), 476–486.

Rothman, N. B., and Wiesenfeld, B. M. (2007). The social consequences of expressing emotional ambivalence in groups and teams. *Affect and Groups: Research on Managing Groups and Teams*, (10), 275–308.

Sharma, G., and Good, D. (2013). The work of middle managers: Sensemaking and sensegiving for creating positive social change. *The Journal of Applied Behavioral Science*, 49(1), 95–122.

Schad, J., Lewis, M. W., Raisch, S., and Smith, W. K. (2016). Paradox research in management science: Looking back to move forward. *The Academy of Management Annals*, 10(1), 5–64.

Schad, J., and Smith, W. K. (2019). Addressing grand challenges' paradoxes: Leadership skills to manage inconsistencies. *Journal of Leadership Studies*, 12(4), 55–59. https://doi.org/10.1002/jls.21609

Schein, E. H. (2009). *Helping. How to Offer, Give, and Receive Help. Understanding Effective Dynamics in One-to-One, Group, and Organizational Relationships.* San Francisco, LA: Berrett-Koehler Publishers.

Schneider, A., Bullinger, B., & Brandl, J. (2021). Resourcing Under Tensions: How frontline employees create resources to balance paradoxical tensions. *Organization Studies*, 42(8), 1291–1317.

Sheep, M. L., Fairhurst, G. T., & Khazanchi, S. (2017). Knots in the discourse of innovation: Investigating multiple tensions in a reacquired spin-off. *Organization Studies*, 38(3–4), 463–488.

Sleesman, D. J. (2019). Pushing through the tension while stuck in the mud: Paradox mindset and escalation of commitment. *Organizational Behavior and Human Decision Processes*, 155, 83–96.

Smith, W. K., and Lewis, M. W. (2011). Toward a theory of paradox: A dynamic equilibrium model of organizing. *Academy of Management Review*, 36(2), 381–403.

Smith, W. K., and Lewis, M. W. (2012). Leadership skills for managing paradoxes. *Industrial and Organizational Psychology*, 5(2), 227–231.

Smith, W. K. (2014). Dynamic decision making: A model of senior leaders managing strategic paradoxes. *Academy of Management Journal*, 57(6), 1592–1623.

Smith, W. K., Lewis, M. W., Jarzabkowski, P., and Langley, A. (2017a). Introduction. The paradoxes of paradox. In W. K. Smith, M. W. Lewis, P. Jarzabkowski, and A. Langley (Eds.), *The Oxford Handbook of Organizational Paradox*, Oxford: Oxford University Press, 1–24.

Smith, W. K., Lewis, M. W., Jarzabkowski, P., and Langley, A. (Eds.). (2017b). *The Oxford Handbook of Organizational Paradox.* Oxford: Oxford University Press.

Smith, W. K.; Erez, M., Jarvenpaa, S., Lewis, M. W., & Tracey, P. (2017). Adding complexity to theories of paradox, tensions, and dualities of innovation and change: Introduction to organization studies special issue on paradox, tensions, and dualities of innovation and change. *Organization Studies*, 38(3–4), 303–317.

Smith, W. K., & Besharov, M. L. (2019). Bowing before dual gods: How structured flexibility sustains organizational hybridity. *Administrative Science Quarterly*, 64(1), 1–44.

Smith, W. & Lewis, M. (2022). *Both/And Thinking: Embracing Creative Tensions to Solve Your Toughest Problems.* Brighton, MA: Harvard Business Review Press.

Spaapen, J., and Van Drooge, L. (2011). Introducing "productive interactions" in social impact assessment. *Research Evaluation*, 20(3), 211–218.

Sparr, J. L. (2018). Paradoxes in organizational change: The crucial role of leaders' sensegiving. *Journal of Change Management*, 18(2), 162–180.

Sparr, J. L., van Knippenberg, D., and Kearney, E. (2022). Paradoxical leadership as sensegiving: Stimulating change-readiness and change-oriented performance. *Leadership and Organization Development Journal*, 43 (2), 225–237.

Starik, M., and Kanashiro, P. (2013). Toward a theory of sustainability management: Uncovering and integrating the nearly obvious. *Organization and Environment*, 26(1), 7–30.

Sterling, S. (2010). *Sustainability Education: Perspectives and Practice across Higher Education*. London, UK: Taylor and Francis.

Sterling, S., and Gray-Donald, J. (2007). Special issue on sustainability and education: Towards a culture of critical commitment. *International Journal of Innovation and Sustainable Development*, 2(3–4), 241–248.

Stewart, G. L., Courtright, S. H., and Manz, C. C. (2011). Self-leadership: A multilevel review. *Journal of Management*, 37(1), 185–222.

Sundaramurthy, C., & Lewis, M. (2003). Control and collaboration: Paradoxes of governance. *Academy of management review*, 28(3), 397–415.

Sveningsson, S., and Larsson, M. (2006). Fantasies of leadership: Identity work. *Leadership*, 2(2), 203–224.

Taylor, F. W. (2004). *Scientific management*. London, UK: Routledge.

The Municipality of Billund (2020). *Leder- og medarbejdergrundlag*. Billund, DK: The Municipality of Billund.

The Municipality of Fredensborg (2021). *Bæredygtigt lederskab – fælles for Fredensborg*. Ledelsesgrundlag 2021. Fredensborg, DK: The Municipality of Fredensborg.

The Prime Minister's Office (2020). Pressemøde om COVID-19 den 11. marts 2020, https://www.stm.dk/presse/pressemoedearkiv/pressemoede-om-covid-19-den-11-marts-2020/, accessed October 7, 2022.

The Royal Danish Defence Academy (2008). *Forsvarets Ledelsesgrundlag*. Copenhagen, DK: The Royal Danish Defence Academy.

Tuckman, B. W. (2001). Developmental sequence in small groups. *Group Facilitation*, 3(3), 66–81.

Van Dierendonck, D. (2011). Servant Leadership: A Review and Synthesis. *Journal of Management*, 37(4), 1228–1261.

Van Poeck, K., Goeminne, G., and Vandenabeele, J. (2016). Revisiting the democratic paradox of environmental and sustainability education: Sustainability issues as matters of concern. *Environmental Education Research*, 22(6), 806–826.

Waldman, D. A., and Bowen, D. E. (2016). Learning to be a paradox-savvy leader. *Academy of Management Perspectives*, 30(3), 316–327.

World Commission on Environment and Development (1987). *Report of the World Commission on Environment and Development: Our Common Future*. United Nations through Oxford: Oxford University Press.

Zhang, Y., Waldman, D. A., Han, Y. L., and Li, X. B. (2015). Paradoxical leader behaviors in people management: Antecedents and consequences. *Academy of Management Journal*, 58(2), 538–566.

List of cases

https://doi.org/10.1515/9783110788877-017

List of tools

https://doi.org/10.1515/9783110788877-018

List of figures

https://doi.org/10.1515/9783110788877-019

About the authors

Rikke Kristine Nielsen, PhD is Associate Professor at the Department of Communication & Psychology at Aalborg University. She completed her PhD at the Doctoral School of Management & Organization Studies at Copenhagen Business School and Innovations Fund Denmark's Industrial PhD program, following an entrepreneurial corporate career in HR and leadership development. Her main research areas are organizational and leadership paradox, global leadership as well as academia-practitioner co-creation. Nielsen has written and contributed to several books on leadership paradox and global leadership as well as published in journals such as *Journal of Management Inquiries, Scandinavian Journal of Management* and *Advances in Global Leadership*. Nielsen is an active research disseminator, speaker, and consultant in private, public, and civil society organizations, as well as an engaged scholar co-producing research with managers and HR professionals in practice.

Frans Bévort, PhD, is Associate Professor at the Department of Organization, Copenhagen Business School. His main research focusses on HRM, professions and management. A special research interest is the tensions between management as a professional discipline and other disciplines. His work is informed by institutional theory and symbolic interactionism. He has written and contributed to several books on HRM and management as well as published in journals like *Journal of Professions and Organizations, German Journal of Human Resource Research*, and *Scandinavian Journal of Management*. His other research interests are: comparative HRM (Cranet), paradox management, critical HRM studies, HRM and AI and HRM as a professional discipline.

Thomas Duus Henriksen, PhD, is Associate Professor at the Department of Communication and Psychology at Aalborg University, Copenhagen, Denmark. As a business psychologist he is preoccupied with the human impact of organizational processes. He completed his PhD at the Doctoral School of Organizational Learning at Learning Lab Denmark, Aarhus University and subsequently an EBA at the Royal School of Engineering. His main research interests are in the intersections between learning theory and technology, addressing areas like virtual human resource development, hybrid work forms, hybrid management, and learning games for organizational development, while using paradox theory and French philosophy to address the complexity of such processes.

Anne-Mette Hjalager is a Professor at the Department for Entrepreneurship and Relationship Management at University of Southern Denmark. She works with innovation, entrepreneurial processes, and management – particularly, but not only, in the tourism sector. She has published extensively in the fields mentioned, and her present focus is on the boundary shifts between public and private sectors, and the related spatial and relationship transformations. She is involved in international research endeavors under EU programs.

https://doi.org/10.1515/9783110788877-020

Danielle Bjerre Lyndgaard holds a Master of Science in Economics and Business Administration (MSc(Econ.)) from Copenhagen Business School (CBS) and a Master of Management Development (MMD) also from CBS. Lyndgaard is Director at the Confederation of Danish Industry, Department of Global Talent & Mobility, where she is responsible for all aspects of (global) leadership and HR processes related to global talent and mobility. She is currently engaged in academia-practitioner research collaboration focusing on the paradoxes in global leadership and her research interests focus on global leadership development as well as the individual and organizational paradoxes and complexity in global collaboration.

About the series editor

Bernd Vogel is a Professor in Leadership and Founding Director of the Henley Centre for Leadership at Henley Business School, UK.

Bernd has more than 20 years of global experience in research, educating, speaking, and consulting with outstanding companies, business schools and universities. He supports organisations and people in life-long learning journeys that transform lives, organisations, and society. He bridges academia with practice and is an executive coach.

His expertise is in leadership and leadership development; future of work and leadership; strategic leadership to mobilise and sustain healthy energy and performance; developing leadership and followership capability; healthy and performing senior management teams; change, transformation and culture; leadership development architectures.

Bernd features regularly in media. He publishes in top-tier global academic journals and has written and edited several books, case studies and industry reports.

Throughout his career Bernd has had academic roles at the Leibniz University Hannover, Germany, and University of St. Gallen, Switzerland. He has held global visiting positions at Claremont Graduate University, USA; IESE Business School, Spain; and Marshall School of Business, USC, USA.

https://doi.org/10.1515/9783110788877-021

Index

https://doi.org/10.1515/9783110788877-022